AF531339

MODERN DEVELOPMENT OF ENVIRONMENT AND AGRICULTURE

MODERN DEVELOPMENT OF ENVIRONMENT AND AGRICULTURE

Edited by

Dr. Govind Prasad
M.A., Ph.D., D.Litt. FAMSE
Associate Professor
Rana Pratap P.G. College
Sultanpur, (U.P.) (India)
(Writers & Editor of Numerous Books)

&

Dr. Anupam Pandey
Diploma (i) Tourism, (ii) Creative Writing
M.A. (Geography) Ph.D. (Geomorphology)
Dr. R.M.L. Awadh University
Faizabad, (U.P.) (India)
(Writers & Editor of Numerous Books)

DISCOVERY PUBLISHING HOUSE PVT. LTD.
NEW DELHI-110 002

Published by:
Tilak Wasan
DISCOVERY PUBLISHING HOUSE PVT. LTD.
4383/4B, Ansari Road, Darya Ganj
New Delhi-110 002 (India)
Phone : +91-11-23279245, 43596064-65
Fax : +91-11-23253475
E-mail : parul.wasan@gmail.com
discoverypublishinghouse@gmail.com
web : www.discoverypublishinggroup.com

***First Edition:* 2012**

ISBN: 978-93-5056-107-2

Modern Development of Environment and Agriculture

© 2012, Editors

All rights reserved. No part of this publication should be reproduced, stored in a retrieval system, or transmitted in any form or by any means: electronic, mechanical, photocopying, recording or otherwise, without the prior written permission of the author and the publisher.

This book has been published in good faith that the material provided by authors is original. Every effort is made to ensure accuracy of material, but the publisher and printer will not be held responsible for any inadvertent error(s). In case of any dispute, all legal matters are to be settled under Delhi jurisdiction only.

Printed at:
Shree Balaji Art Press
Delhi

Preface

Development is a process of providing existence and promoting and powering the improvement for all around the global earth through the chronicles of history. Any break of a time either it is little or worldwide may cause stagnation in progressive and successive growth of civilization. Personality upliftment and upgradation in nature is an outcome of modernization and change ornamented with eco-materials, eco-energy and eco-stage. 'Ecology' is defined as the totality or pattern of relation between organisms and its environment. 'Eco-system' is an organic system composed of an organic community of flora and fauna viewed under environment or habitat. 'Habitat' may be expressed as 'Happy Home' for living organisms while all surroundings of a designated ecosystem is thought to be as environment. 'Environment' is an inseparable whole constituted and converted by interacting system of physico-bio and culture elements day by day. Thus, the measurement of post and present scenario of ecological glamour is necessary to trace out the future prospects of environmental outlook.

Eco-culture as well as human civilization is undoubtedly a gift of 'Earth, Water, Five, Sky (Atmosphere) and Air (KSHITI, JAL, PAWAK, GAGAN, SAMIRA)'. The A to Z globe and its environs is basically governed by these five life supporting attributes. The mother earth in her lovely lap has nutrited the global life system providing essential food and energy. The three primary needs of existing generation like

'Food, clothes and Shelter' (Happy Home) are based upon primary producers cropped out on the surface of the earth. Earth produces primary food for every consumers before their birth. The plant kingdom is an example of eco-agriculture. To fulfil the primary needs of consumers agricultural advancement must be focussed on fertile global screen. It may be only possible by man's-environmental interrelationships. Thus, the study of environment as an universal regime and development of agriculture as a primary base of life is too much essential for fascinating eco-generation and human's imagination.

Thinking about the above precidence and performance of environment and agriculture, the present book entitled 'Modern Development of Environment and Agriculture' is edited in two parts—A and B. Part-A is related to 'Modern Development of Environment' and comprises 11 chapters (Chapter 1 to 11). Part-B is well arranged of researches on 'Modern Development of Agriculture' embracing 08 chapters (Chapter 12 to 19) systematically. Thus, the present volume incorporates total 19 chapters. The existing subject matter is fashioned by suitable tables maps and references reated in the last separately.

First of all, we express our heartiest gratitude and thanks to all pioneer scholars who have contributed the original research papers for this volume. We are also thankful to all academicians who have created an excellent atmosphere for editing the book on current topic.

In the view of publishing this book credits go to Mr. Tilak Wasan and Mr. Parul Wasan, Directors of Discovery Publishing House Pvt. Ltd., Daryaganj, New Delhi for their holistic work.

We hope that the volume will be useful for students, researchers, teachers and academicians of concerning subject. The comments about the book will be treated praiseworthy.

Editors

Contents

List of Contributors

1. **Dr. Anupam Pandey,** Writer and Editor of Various type of books in Social Sciences and Humanities, Devkali, C.S.M. Nagar, U.P.
2. **Dr. Gitanjali,** Writer of books of Comerce Subject, Reserve Police Lines, Sitapur, U.P.
3. **Dr. Govind Prasad,** Associate Professor, Department of Geography, Rana Pratap P.G. College, Sultanpur, U.P.
4. **Dr. Kanhaiya Lal Gupta,** Lecturer in Geography, Bapu Smarak Intermediate College, Dargah, Mau Bhanjan.
5. **Dr. Shardendu Kislaya,** Education Instructer, Indian Army.
6. **Mr. Aditya Narain Pandey,** Devkali, C.S.M. Nagar, U.P.
7. **Mr. Kaushalesh Pandey,** Loknathpur, Sultanpur, U.P.
8. **Mr. Mahendra Kumar,** Research Scholar, Geography, Dr. Ram Manohar Lohia Awadh University, Faizabad, U.P.
9. **Mr. Mohammad Ashfaq,** Research Scholar, Geography, Dr. Ram Manohar Lohia Awadh University, Faizabad, U.P.
10. **Mr. Mohammad Izhar,** Assistant Teacher, Shivdaspur, Amaniganj, Faizabad, U.P.
11. **Mr. Pramod Kumar Yadav,** Department of Post-graduate Studies in Geography, Rana Pratap P.G. College, Sultanpur, U.P.

12. **Mr. Santosh Kumar Singh,** Research Scholar, Dr. Ram Manohar Lohia Awadh University, Faizabad, U.P.
13. **Mr. Shailesh Kumar,** Department of Postgraduate Studies in Geography, Rana Pratap P.G. College, Sultanpur, U.P.
14. **Mrs. Amita Pandey,** Barhaiapur, C.S.M. Nagar, U.P.
15. **Mrs. Madhavi Gupta,** Assistant Teacher, Maharana Pratap College, Etawah, U.P.
16. **Mrs. Vibha Rani Pandey,** Devkali, C.S.M. Nagar, U.P.
17. **Miss. Chhaya Pandey**, Faculty of B.Ed., Maneeshi Mahila Vidyalaya Gauriganj, C.S.M. Nagar, U.P.
18. **Miss. Saroj Kumari,** Research Scholar, Economics, U.P.R.T. Open University, Allahabad, U.P.
19. **Miss. Surabhi,** Faculty of B.Ed., City College of Management, Chinhat, Lucknow.

PART-A

MODERN DEVELOPMENT OF ENVIRONMENT

CHAPTER

1

Landscape Ecology and Environmental Illustration

Govind Prasad and Mohd. Ashfaq

Introduction

The present theme of landscape illustration is based on geo-physical and socio-economical study of Betul plateau, M.P. India. The effort is ornamented with etymology, topò, climo, floral, faunal, drainage, Agro, educational, trade, industry, culture, attractions and demographic features which in turn have fascinated the country concerned in a new designated geo-environmental mosaic. The facts and findings are elaborated with appropriate cartographical techniques.

Glimpse of the Region

Betul is one of the southern district of Madhya Pradesh India. It is totally located on Satpura plateau. Covering the entire width of Satpura range, it is delimited between Narma valley in the north and Barar plain in the south. The region is extended between 21°, 04′ north latitude to 22°, 24′ north latitude and 77°, 04′ east longitude to 78°, 33′ east longitude. The district is bounded by Hoshangabad district, M.P. in the north, Amaravati district, Maharashtra in the south, Chhindawara district, M.P. in the east and Hoshangabad, East Nimar and Amaravati districts in the west respectively. From east to west and north to south the length of the region is about 161 kms and 106 kms. It covers the total geographical area of 10043 km^2 having population of 13,95,175 as per 2001 census. The region forms the southern most part of the Bhopal division.

Etymology

Betul derives its name from the small town of Betul Bazar about 5 km. south of the present city which was the district headquarters. In 1822 the District Headquarters was shifted to the present place which was a village called 'BADMUR' at that time. The lateral meaning of Betul is 'Without (be) cotton (tool). It was the border of the cotton growing area. The district contains the most developed town Amla, which is a tahsil too while others are less developed. It is a town sorrounded by hills on all sides and was used by the British for exportation of coal and that's why they established a railway station in the early 1910s. Presently it is serving as connecting junction for railways. Betul is famous for Teak (Tectona Grandis) conservator of forests. There is a famous temple of Lord Balaji in Betul Bazar.

Topo-Features

The mean elevation above the sea is about 2000 ft (600 mts). The country is essentially a highland tract, divided naturally into three distinct portions, differing in their superficial aspects, the pedological characteristics and their geological formation. The northern part of the plateau forms an irregular plain of the sandstone formation. It is a well-wooded tract, in many places stretching out in charming glades like an english park, but it has a very sparse population and little cultivated background. In the extreme north a line of hills rises abruptly out of the great plain of the Narmada valley. The central tract alone possesses a rich soil, well drained by the Machana river and Sapnadam, almost entirely cultivated and studded with villages. To the south lies a rolling plateau of basaltic formation (with the sacred town of Multai and the springs of the Tapti river at its highest point) extending over the whole of the southern face of the district, and finally merging into the wild and broken line of the Ghats, which lead down to the plains. This tract consists of a succession of stony ridges of trap rock, enclosing valleys or basins of fertile soil to which cultivation is for the most part confined except where the shallow soil on the tops of the hills has been turned to account.

Climo-Features

Climate of Betul is fairly healthy. Its heights above the plains and the neighbourhood of extensive forests moderate the heat and render the temperature pleasant throughout the greater part of the year. During the cold season the thermometer at night falls below the freezing point. Little or no hot wind is felt before the end of April and even then it ceases after sunset. The nights in the hot season are comparatively cool and pleasant. During the monsoon the climate is very damp and at times even cold and raw, thick clouds and most enveloping the sky for many days together. The average annual rainfall is 100 cm.

Floral and Faunal Features

Betul district to rich in forests and biodiversity. The main timber species of Betul forest is teak. Many miscellaneous types of trees such as Haldu, Saja, Dhaoda etc. are also found in abundance. Many medicinal plants are also registered in the forest areas of Betul. Large amounts of commercially important minor forest produce such as Tendu leaves, Chiranji, Harra, Amla are also collected from the forests of the region. Asia's biggest wood depart is nominated in Betul. The forest area of Betul is divided in northern and southern part and generally forest area is covered with teak and bamboo forest, mixed forest, salai forest or by separately Bamboo forest. Another major trees of the forested area are Landia, Tinsa, Mahua, Kalam Kari and Jamun. Siharu, Marorfali, Dhanvai, Birhul Khareta, Lantana, Mahul, Palas Bet etc. are the major herbs founded in the region.

According to district gazetter the forest area is inhabited by Sher, Chita, Sanbhar, Chital, Neelgai, Kala hiran, Chinkara, Bhashmirig, Chaushinga Hiran, Jangali suar, Reechh, Vaison and Jangali kutta. Monkeys are common each other. Birds like Titar, Kukkut, Bater, Larika, Kapot, Battakh, Snaip, Mor, Tota and fishes like Labeo bata, L. bogot, L. boga, B. Sarana, Barbus ticto Barbus stigma, C. Reba, Rasbora, Mastacemlic lus armatus wallgo attu, M. singhal, Ophicephalus, Catla-Catla, Labeo Rohia, cirrhina mirgala, Labeo Calbosu and B. toa are the other faunal categories of the region.

Drainage Features

The major river flowing in the area are the Ganjal river which is the tributary stream of Tapti River. Morand and Tawa are the other major streams making confluence with Narmada River. The Tapti river originates from Multai of Betul district, Mutai's sanskrit name 'Multapi' means 'Origin of Tapi or the Tapti River.' Tapti is the biggest river of Western India. It originates from Yaom high hills in the north of Multai. Tawa drains in the north-east flank of the region and originates from Chhindwara district. Vardha river drains from the southern slopes of Dahadhana Peaks (811 m) located about 11 km north east of Multai. The district drainage pattern is basically controlled by (1) Narmada River System (2) Tapti River System and (3) Godavari River System. The water of northern and central part moves towards Narmada river in the north through Tawa, Machana, Morand and Bhogi drainage basins of the region. The water flowing in the western and southern central part generally entered in the Tapti river who moves towards western direction. The small drainage systems like Purna, Maru and Vardha are located in the south. Maru and Vardha meets in Godawari drainage system while Purna makes confluence with Tapti river in Khandesh. Bail river flows between north-eastern Satpura range and central ridges of plateau. It flows towards east in the anti direction of river Tawa in the north and river Tapti in the south.

Agricultural Features

Betul is a one of the tribal populated districts of Madhya Pradesh. The region falls under Satpura Plateau. In view of agricultural climatic system, the region exposes itself as Jawar and Wheat crop zone. According to **Table 1.1** and **Fig. 1.1** the total geographical area of the district is 1028.0 thousand hectares out of which 415.8 thousand hectares land is under cultivation. 388.8 thousand hectares (73.58%) land is used under Kharif and 139.6 thousand hectares (26.42%) land is harvested under Rabi Crops. With respect to total cropped area of 528.4 thousand hectares the forest, uncultivated, fodder and barer areas of the region have been tabulated as 405.2, 42.4, 26.4 and 25.3 thousand hectares respectively.

The district consist of nearly 1.76 lakh agricultural families out of which 46 per cent belong to SC/ST category. Average agricultural land 2.90 thousand hectares is under propritership. Irrigation area from all sources is 97.7 thousand hectares and irrigation percentage is 23 in the district.

Table 1.1 : Land Classification

Sl.No.	Type	Area in Thousand Hectares	
1.	Forest Area	405.2	
2.	Uncuitivated Area	42.4	
3.	Fodder Area	26.7	
4.	Barer Area	25.3	
5.	Crop Area	415.8	528.4
6.	Double Crop Area	112.6	
	(*a*) Kharif Crop Area	388.8	528.4
	(*b*) Rabi Crop Area	139.6	
	Total Crop Area	**528.4**	
	Total Area	**1028.0**	

Source: Betul District Report, 2010.

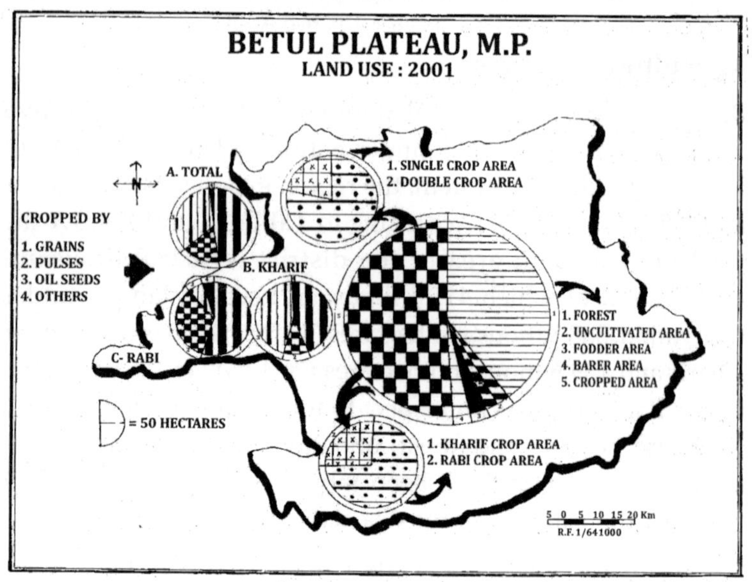

Fig. 1.1.

According to **Table 1.2** and **Fig. 1.2** it is illustrated that the region registers 48.86% foodgrains 43.07% oil seeds, 15.67% pulses and 1.40% other crop production. Thus foodgrains are dominating in agriculture. During the Kharif and Rabi crops separately total food grains, total oil seeds, pulses and other crops percentage are depicted as 44.11 and 62.11, 44.24 and 5.73, 11.34 and 27.74 and 0.31 and 4.44 respectively. As far as the source of irrigation in agriculture wells, electrical pumps, diesel pumps, hand pumps medium irrigation projects, small irrigation projects, stop dems and sprinkler sets are found in numbers like 49387, 26584, 5535, 2182, 4,86,341 and 2357 in the assessment year of 2010. The area needs a classical scientific change in agriculture in place of tribal agriculture which may take time because planning processes are very slow in progress. The land-use capacity of the region is given in figure.

Table 1.2 : Crop Area

Crop	Kharif		Rabi		Total	
	Area in 000 Hect.	Percen-tage	Area in 000 Hect.	Percen-tage	Area in 000	Percen-tage
Foodgrains	171.5	44.11	86.7	62.11	258.2	48.86
Pulses	44.1	11.34	38.7	27.72	82.8	15.67
Oil seeds	172.0	44.24	8.0	5.73	180.0	34.07
Others	1.2	0.31	6.2	4.44	7.4	1.40
Total	**388.8**	**100.00**	**139.6**	**100.00**	**528.4**	**100.00**

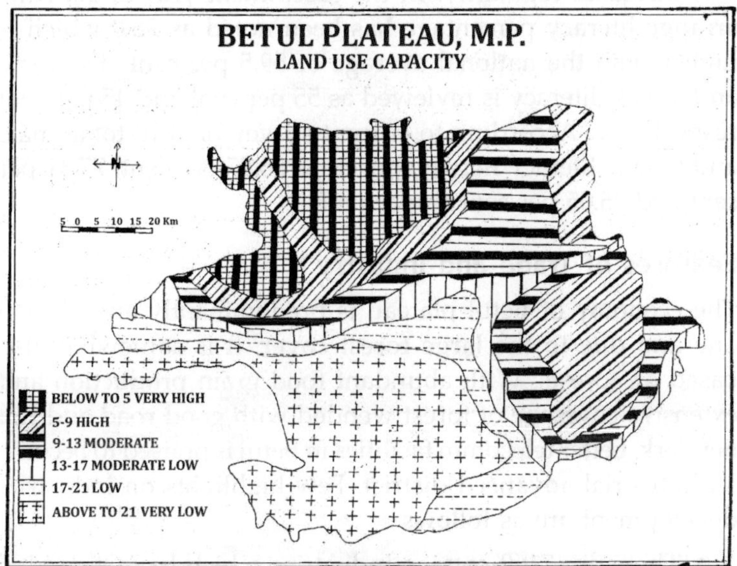

Fig. 1.2.

Educational Features

Educationally the plateau region is less developed. Governmental non-governmental educational institutions registered in the district like primary schools, high schools, middle schools, higher secondary schools, Ashram Shalas and government colleges have enrolled the number of students as 1568,59,336 50,03 and 08 respectively. Government and private colleges are found 12 in number wherein 05 colleges are located at Betul and 01 each is established at Amia, Multai, Bhainsdehi, Athnair, Sarani and Sonagati Betul. Sarani has registered another one college recently. There are two polititic colleges located in Betul.

During the census years of 1951 and 1961 total, rural and urban literacy percentage have been calculated as 10.7 and 16.6, 8.7 and 13.7 and 37.30 and 47.7 respectively. The literacy rate increases regularily. In the assessment year of 2001 the arrange literacy percentage has been noted as 76.0 which is higher than the national average of 59.5 per cent. The male and female literacy is reviewed as 55 per cent and 45 per cent respectively. According to current survey of 2010 total, male and female literacy may be traced as 66.87 per cent, 77.31 per cent and 56.05 per cent respectively.

Features of Trade and Industry

The economy of Betul plateau is predominantly an agrarian one and due to the large forest cover, it is somewhat also based on forests. With abundant food grain production and extensive coverage of forest wended with good road and rail network, better telecomm facilities in Betul is praised to become an industrial advanced district. Few highlights on industrial development are as follows :

- There are 7160 cottage industries which have provided employment to 17682 people and have a total investment over 1235.65 lakhs.
- There are 33 small scale industries (SSI) which have given employment to 667 people and have total investment over 819.99 lakhs. Out of 33 SSI's 08 are agro-based, 13 are medical based, 01 is forest based and 11 are others.
- There are 5 large and medium scale units which have engaged employment to 999 people and have total

investment over 1681.37 lakhs. The details of large and medium scale units are given in **Table 1.3**.

Table 1.3 : List of Large and Medium Scale Industrial Units

Sl.No.	Name and Address	Total Investment (in lakhs)
1.	M/S Betul Oils and Flours Ltd. Kosmi Industrial Area-Betul	130.12
2.	M/S Madhyavarta Ex-Oil Ltd. Kosmi Industrial Area-Betul	595.00
3.	M/S Adhishwar Oil and Fats Ltd. Chouthia, Multai, Betul	348.73
4.	M/S Betul Tyre and Tube Industry Pvt. Ltd. Sohagpur, Betul	302.25
5.	M/S Wearwell Tyre and Tube Industries Panka, Amia, Betul	305.27

Inspite of the above industries Kosmi Industrial Area-Betul, Bhaggu Dhana Industrial Area-Betul and Gramin Karmashala-Multai separately cover the area of 226.47, 10.74 and 3.00 acres respectively. The industrial goods produced in this area largely moves through road transport. Few industries mainly large and medium industries use rail networks for transporting their finishing products. Exporting units mainly tyre industry use water ways which are exported to U.S.A., U.K., Middle East and African countries.

Culture and Attrative Features

The northern part of the plateau is totally cultured with Bundelkhani language and socio-economic framework. The southern flank is predominated by Marathi language and Maharashtrian culture. The remaining parts of the district is inhabited by tribal population mainly dominated by Gonds and Korkus. They worshipped Bada Mahadeo. Their rituals are mostly of sacrificial nature. They have no cure of education and still believe in superstitions. They generally use natural herbs for the healthcare. There are some institutions for classifical music and music directors from the research point of view. An archeological museum and collection of statues and sculptures has been noted as a historical interests. All over the region are scattered monuments and relics of historical interests such as Khedia which was the seat of the Gond Dynasty was back in the 13th century. Multai Tahsil exhibits some caves at Ashirghad and Bhawarghad as the hiding place of the Pindaries.

There is an old Shiva temple built of carved stones at Bhainsdehi. The roof of the temple had been collapsed and only some beautifully carved pillars are seen as a remnants. There are old temples of Hindus and Jains located at Kazili and Kanigiya villages about 7 km away from Amla. Some Jain temples are also visualized at Muklagiri. The area is famous for the apprising of the tribals against the British rule. Banjaridal a village in Betul tahsil is well known for the martyr Vishnur Singh Gond. The district participated in the growth of freedom movement too much so that not less than 50 volunteers to part in the conference of Congress at Nagpur.

Demographic Features

The total geographical areas of the district of 10043 sq. km. registers 1395175 population according to census year of 2001. Thus the density of population exists as 138 persons per sq. km. The male and female contribution of population is demarkated as 50.89 (709956) and 49.11 per cent (685219) respectively. Rural and urban population is counted as 1136056 and 259119 which in turn shows 81.43 per cent and 18.57 per cent in respect of rural and urban areas. Thus the region is dominated by rural inhabitants. About 50 per cent population of the total population belong to Scheduled Caste (10.58% and 147604) and Scheduled Tribes (39.42% and 549907). The total scheduled tribes population consists 50.15 per cent (275793) male and 49.85 per cent (274114) females respectively. Similarly the total scheduled caste population occurs 51.35 per cent male (57589) and 49.65 per cent (71815) female population. Thus the ratio between male and female population is more or less equal in number and percentage. The population growth rate between the two succeeding decades is found as 18-20 per cent.

Figure 1.3, 1.4 and **1.5** separately show the rural and urban population of the region by multiple dof method, Stil Gen Bauers Method and Sten De Geers Method respectively. The urban population is depicted at Sarani, Betul and Amla Nagar Palika and Multai, Betul Bazar and Bhainsdehi Nagar panchayats headquarters only. As for as the population growth of the region the negative attitudes in rural (-1.55%) and urban (-7.01%) population is noted during the decade of 1921. From 1901 to 2001 the rural population growth rate ranges between 0.48 per cent (1951) to 36.02 per cent (1911) while the urban population deviates between 17.80 per cent (1931) to 50.55 per cent (1951) respectively.

The continuous growth of population have caused too much problems of essential needs as well as the higher requirements of the society. The tribal population of the region is innocent about family planning processes.

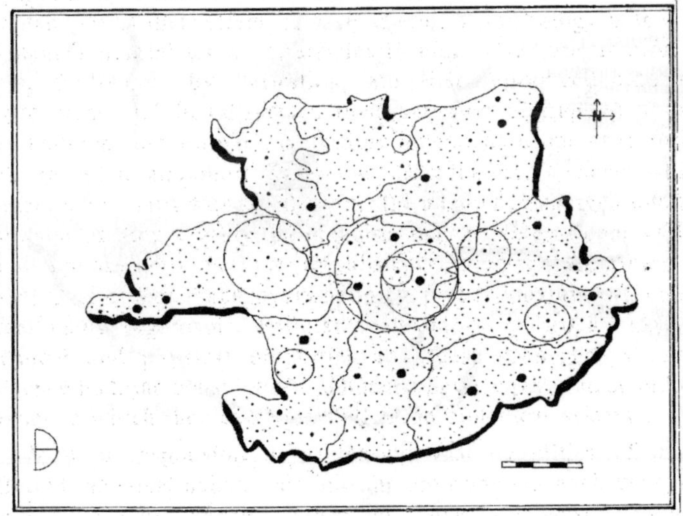

Fig. 1.3.

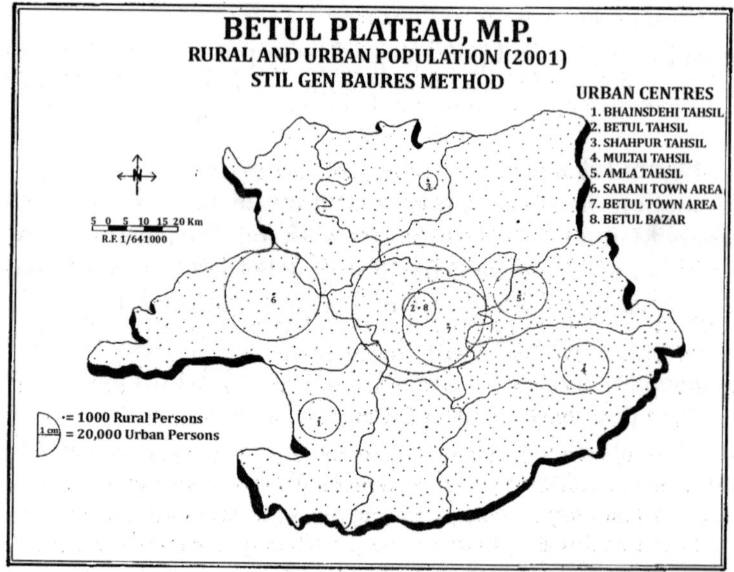
BETUL PLATEAU, M.P.
RURAL AND URBAN POPULATION (2001)
STIL GEN BAURES METHOD
URBAN CENTRES
1. BHAINSDEHI TAHSIL
2. BETUL TAHSIL
3. SHAHPUR TAHSIL
4. MULTAI TAHSIL
5. AMLA TAHSIL
6. SARANI TOWN AREA
7. BETUL TOWN AREA
8. BETUL BAZAR
5 0 5 10 15 20 Km
R.F. 1/641000
·= 1000 Rural Persons
1 cm = 20,000 Urban Persons

Fig. 1.4.

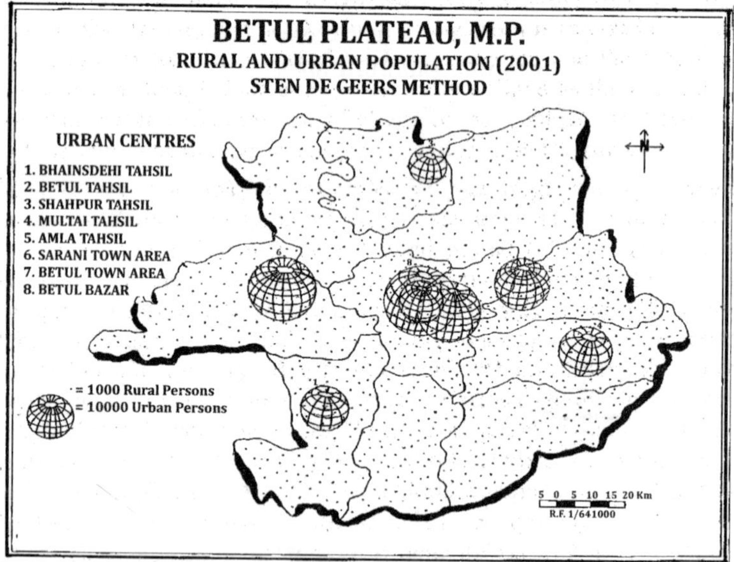
BETUL PLATEAU, M.P.
RURAL AND URBAN POPULATION (2001)
STEN DE GEERS METHOD
URBAN CENTRES
1. BHAINSDEHI TAHSIL
2. BETUL TAHSIL
3. SHAHPUR TAHSIL
4. MULTAI TAHSIL
5. AMLA TAHSIL
6. SARANI TOWN AREA
7. BETUL TOWN AREA
8. BETUL BAZAR
·= 1000 Rural Persons
= 10000 Urban Persons
5 0 5 10 15 20 Km
R.F. 1/641000

Fig. 1.5.

Conclusion

On the basis of the overall discussion, it may be illustrated that the region is dominated by rural population in the lap of uneven plateau country. The tribal in habitation incorporates an unique socio-economic structure which demands some special kinds of development above to standard of common living. Everything of developing process is stagnant and in traditional forms so that a new light of sustainable development in all aspects of activities is most desirable. The landscape features existing in the area are more or less in previous form where they are untouched by human civilization but remarkable change is noticed everywhere with the growing crop of urbanisation, land use and agro-culture is until backward but new efforts of scientific handling flowered by governmental and non-governmental planning processes have delighted a candle of developing hopes. The region is suitable for regional development and planning. It is also attractive in trekker's point of view.

REFERENCES

1. Betul District—Wikipedia, the Free Encyclopea.
2. District Statistical Handbook 2001, Betul District M.P.
3. District Census Handbook, 2001, Betul District M.P.
4. Srivastava, P.N. 1990 : Betul District Gazetter Deptt. of Culture, M.P. Bhopal.

CHAPTER

2

Dynamics of Geo-Ecological Processes and Paradigms

Govind Prasad and Surabhi

Introduction

The study of "geo-ecological process and geo-spatial paradigm" have the greater importance in view of modern geography specially in eco-logical as well as environmental studies. The geo-ecological processes are the function of consecutive change of conditions and development stages within the time span of global phenomenon. The processes follow the cyclic stages and each cycle constitutes a chronosystem. The process may be grouped as territorial structural (*e.g.* differentiation, concentration absorption, agglomeration etc.) in nature. Each process has a definite force or set of forces necessary for it to go on.

Geo-spatial paradigm is thought to be as inter disciplinary methodology in the latest object of geo-environmental research. It incorporates the inter connections between geoversum and universum. Prominent Scientists like Kuhn, Haggett, Chorley, Grigoryev, Saushkin, Gerasimov, Ishmuratov, Hombolt, Vernadsky, Berg, Kalesnik etc. Have recognised the ecological paradigm and believed that the basic features of paradigm not only determine the development of the necrosphere and the biosphere but also influence occasionally considerably the development of the sociosphere and the technosphere.

The present theme incorporates the conceptual chrono-structure of geo-ecological process and geo-spatial paradigm mirrored through recent literatures.

CONCEPT OF GEO-ECOLOGICAL PROCESSES

A process is a consecutive change of conditions development stages, *i.e.* the time factor is always present in this phenomenon: the difference between the states of an object (system) t_o and t_n. A description of states to, $t_1......t_n$ maybe regarded as the object's chronostructure. If development is cyclic, each cycle constitutes a 'CHRONOSYSTEM'. In cyclic process an analysis of deviations in the first cycle permits corrections in the next cycle, the process can be controlled, which justifies the use of the term 'CHRONOSYSTEM.' (A layer Enrid, 1986).

A general characteristics of all geo-ecological processes is also that they can be mapped either by the simplest method in the form of a series of maps representing various process of different time-periods or by means of special devices on one map.

The study of process is between the descriptive and genetic approach to the environment. The geomorphic laws and the studies of process were first enunciated by Hutton in 1985. It was beautifully restated by play-fair in 1802 and popularized by Lyell in the numerous editions of his 'principles of Geology' explaning the concept that—

"The same physical process and laws that operate today operated through geologic time, although not necessarily always with the same intensity as now."

Hutton advocated that—

"The present is the key to the past."

He applied this principle very rigidly and postulated that geologic processes operated through out geologic time with the same intensity as now. But the concept of Hutton is not possible in nature because numerous examples could be seated to show that the intensity of various geologic process has varied through geologic time, but there is no reason to believe that streams did not cut valleys in the past as they do now.

The importance of processes clearly exist by Davis 'Trio', structure, process and stage, where he stated that—

"Land form is a function of structure process and stage."

The concept of Davis is validated till now. It can be examined that the geologic structure plays dominant role in the evolution of landforms as a chief controlling factor. One can also examined a different types of relief features and a multidimensional land form assemblage over the surface of the earth because geomorphic processes operate at different rates.

In the study of fundamental concepts of geomorphology, Thornbury, W.D. (1954) postulated that—

"Geomorphic processes leave their distinctive imprint upon landforms and each geomorphic process develops its own characteristic assemblage of land forms."

The observation of Thornbury is found correct in the field analysis. Landforms have their individual distinguishing features depending upon the geomorphic process responsible for their development. It is observed that the different erosional agents acting upon the earth's surface produced on orderly sequence of land-forms. Ecological landscapes are the products of a group of the processes. The present day multicyclic landforms are caused by the interractions of a complex set of a geo-spatial processes (Jayaswal, S.N.P. and Prasad, G. 1989).

The basic geo-spatial process is thought to be the continual change in the geographical position of phenomena and their displacement in geographical space. Such process is also called as the 'location' process or simply 'diffusion'. The dynamic term 'diffusion' and be through uniform, dispersed compact, equivalent etc.

Diffusion is linked in content with displacement of objects and phenomena from one geographical point to another, *i.e.* change of place. Moreover, structural or functional changes must necessarily occur both in 'exit' places and in 'entrance' places. As a rule, displacements or relocations are irreversible at least in the period of observation (Alayev, Enrid 1986.)

The concept 'link' includes the act of displacement. It involves an exchange of link carriers like energy, matter, information etc.

Kinds of Geo-Ecological Processes

A part from the above basic geo-spatial processes, geographers, as researchers, in other disciplines, studying

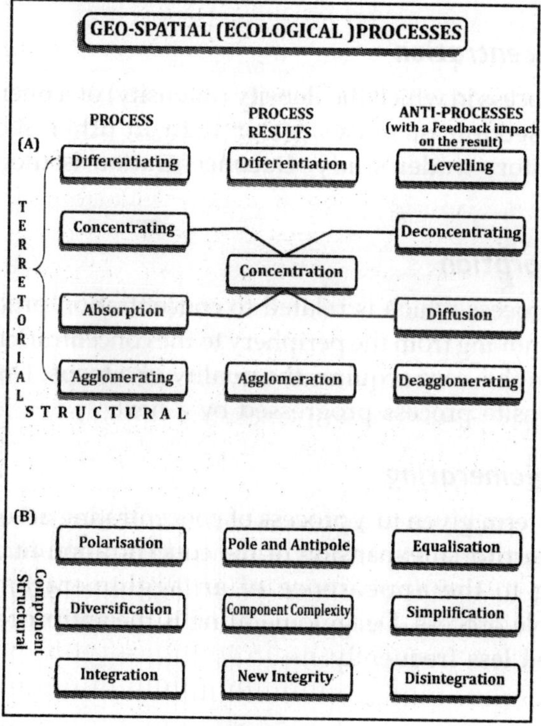

Fig. 2.1.

geographical space have also studied two kinds of structures for example territorial structural and components structural. Thus, almost all the geographical phenomena or objects may be divided into two large classes territorial structural and component structural. The geo-ecological processes are also grouped on the basis of the above two structures and cartographically shown in **Figure 2.1**.

Territorial—Structural Processes

(a) Differentiation

It is a process in which the territorial structure of a geographical formation becomes more complex and its fragmentation increases. Mosaic structure is also a term which is used to define landscape where levelling is the opposite process.

(b) Concentration

It is a process in which the density (intensity) of a phenomenon in one section increases faster than in other sections of the territory under study. Deconcentration is the opposite process.

(c) Absorption

It is a process which is related to concentration produced by objects moving from the periphery to the concentration nucleus which in this case acquires the quality of a focus. Diffusion is the opposite process progressed by a next.

(d) Agglomerating

It is the term given to a process of concentrating accompanied by the territorial expansion of the concentration nucleus and leading to the appearence of an agglomeration. It is a reversible process. Deagglomerating is the antiprocess and is observed less frequently.

(e) Polarisation

It is a term used to those processes which incorporate the salient features of both territorial-structural and component-structural process. It is thought as development .in which phenomena typical of one volume (component) are frequently closed to opposite phenomena marked in another or other components. It may be absolute and relative. In absolute form development of comparable sections varies in various directions while in relative conditions it is found in one direction. Equalisation is the anticoncept of polarisation process. It is apparent that territorial-structural processes illustrate one or several nests like monocentric or polycentric in nature.

Component-Structural Processes

The component-structural processes may be grouped by the following terms:

(a) ***Divercification:*** It is a special term used for complexifying a geographical formation's component structure. Simlification is the anticoncept.

(b) ***Intergration:*** It is a term used for increasing the closeness of links between geographical formations, often accompanied by a growing number of comman features. Disintegration is used as the anticoncept.

Figure 2.1. illustrates the inter connections between the concepts and terms as discussed above. Each process has a definite force or a set of forces necessary for it to go on, usually these forces are called factors *i.e.* polarisation factor, regionalisation factor etc. Factors, chains of casuse and effect links and conditions regulating the quantitative characteristics of a process constitute in their totally the mechanism of the process.

GEO-SPATIAL PARADIGM AS INTERDISCIPLINARY METHODOLOGY

Conceptual Approach to Development of Methodology

Geographical knowledge is thought to be as the parental base of all science. The conceptual outlook which is mirrored through the heart of the discipline is extraordinary having multidimensional characteristics. The subject has been reached that stage of development when an acute need has arisen to develop one theoretical basis out of separate prepositions and concepts to link together the object, subject, method and aim of research fully conforming to the present level of knowledge.

The process of the subjects theoretisation will be stepped up if the characteristic features of the object method and language of that science are specified.

Geo-spatial paradigm is now termed as interdisciplinary methodology in the latest object of environmental research. It incorporates the interconnections between geoversum and universum. Several scientific attempts were repeatedly made to develop a complete non-contradictory theoretical basis for modern geography. Prominent scientists like Kuhn T., Haggett, P. and Chorley R. (Model Paradigm), Harvey, D. (systems Paradigm), Bunge, W.

(Theoretical Paradigm or Geography), Girgoryev, A.A. (Geographical form of Movement), Saushkin, Y.G. (Mathematical Geography), Gerasimov, I.P. (Constructive Paradigm or Geography) and Ishmuratov, B.M. (Terrotoria-lisation of society's life or Sociological paradigm) have recognised the concept of ecological paradigm and believed that the basic features of paradigm not only determine the development of the necrosphere and the biosphere but also influence occasionally considerably the development of the sociosphere and the technosphere. Thomos Kuhn in his book "Structure of Scientific Revolution" introduces first time concept of paradigm. Richard Chorley (1967) has also recognised the conceptual matrix of paradigm in his book 'Models of Geography'.

Thought concerning to every discipline, generally based on the philosophy, theory and methodology. These elements are separately connected with objective, base and logic together make the explanation. In a long term thought is closely concerned with explanation. Kuhn, T. has termed this interactions as 'conceptual matrix' (**Figure 2.2**). On the basis of the conceptual matrix, the paradigm may be explained. Mishra, H.N. (1990) believed that the matrix who provides any type of thought to be developed is paradigm. The existing thought of conceptual matrix contains numerous theories, models, structures and so many objects combined together in a superficial form. Thus it may be concluded that all the theories, models structures logic and so many objects which combined together make superficial explanation of a new concept is paradigm.

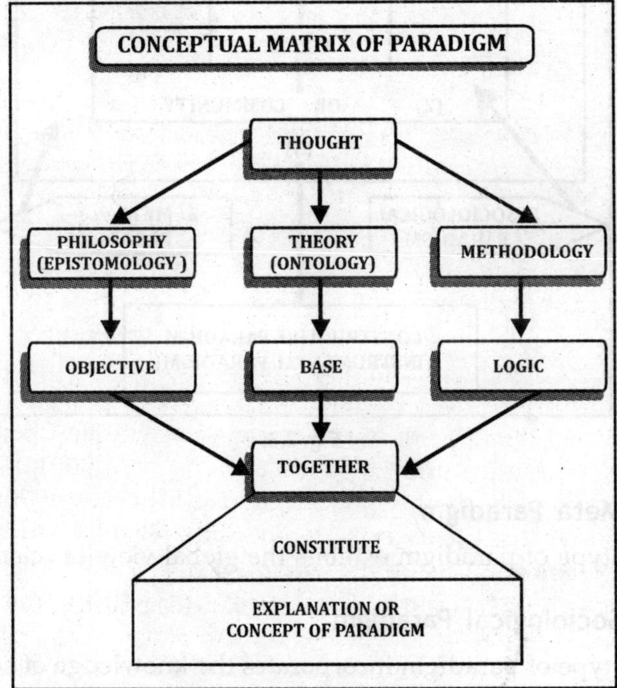

Fig. 2.2.

Following the concept of Richard Chorley (1967) the ecological paradigm deserves the following characteristics (**Figure 2.3**):

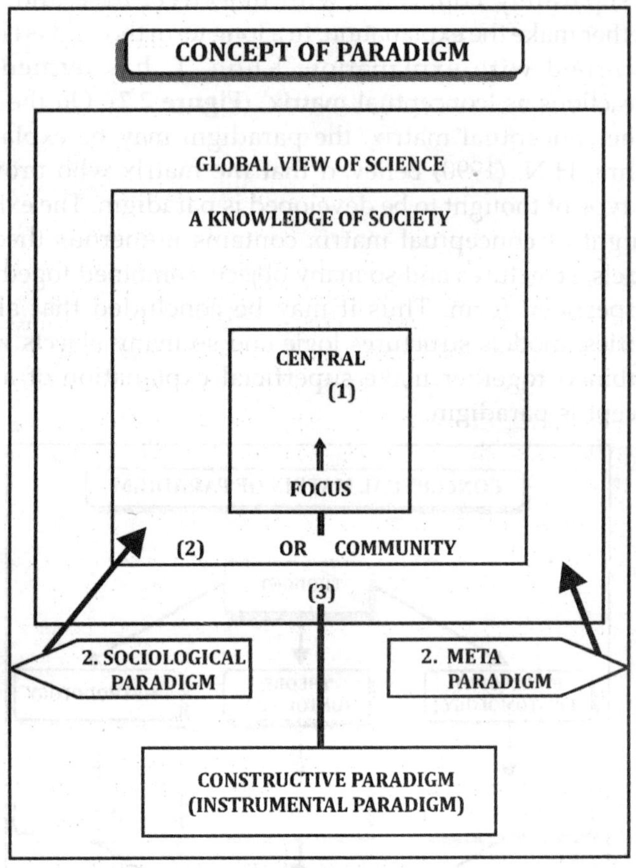

Fig. 2.3.

(a) Meta Paradigm

This type of paradigm exhibits the global view of science.

(b) Sociological Paradigm

This type of paradigm incorporates the knowledge of society or community.

(c) Constructive Paradigm

This type of paradigm is known as "Instrumental paradigm which can be obtained through the deep knowledge of the book. It is the central focus as shown in Fig. 2.3.

In "Geographical Paradigm" thought is discussed through Epistomology, Ontology and Methodology (Fig. 2.2.) Epistomology is the philosophy having certain objective and basic framework. As far as the geographical knowledge is concerned, the historical view of up-to-date thought (geographical thinking from ancient period till now) illustrates two types of paradigm:

(a) Traditional Paradigms

This type of paradigm appears before the Second World War in every thinking of geographical explanation. It is basically based on philosophical concept. The geographical philosophy of ancient world shows the concept of traditional paradigm.

(b) Contemporary Paradigm

This paradigm exists after the Second World War. It is basically correlated with theories and methodologies of the disciplines. Traditional paradigm is classified as indicated.

(Ai) Explorative Paradigm

It is known as paradigm of exploration operated in geography until the beginning of 20th century. The major objective of this paradigm is to know more and about the world wide differences, culture and soon.

(Aii) Environmental Paradigm

It was developed by German philosophers in the beginning of 20th century. This paradigm incorporates the study of situations and its dominant role on biotic and abiotic elements.

(Aiii) Regional Paradigm (Regionalism)

It is based on environmentalism, possiblism and explorations related to geographical study until the Second World War. Hartshorne started a supreme idea and super theory of regionalism at that time. Regionalism teaches the theory of uniqueness in which it is stated that people must be divided and analyse and city-region relationship must be explained. Shephord was the economist and proved himself as a geographer. He criticised the regionalism theory appeared in 'Perspective of nature of Geography'.

(Aiv) Spatial System Paradigm

After the Second World War positivist philosophy promoted by Viena group of philosophers which illustrate the concept of spatial system.

(B) Contemporary Paradigm

Contemporary paradigm depends upon theory or ontology of the disciplines and incorporates some major quantitative techniques. This is the reason why the above paradigm is termed as theoretic-quantitative paradigm. It was thought very imporant until 1960 when many logic cameout, quantitative movement incorporating factor analysis started and the subject as a whole converted in mathematical form. Thus the era of that time was fashioned with quantitative paradigm.

Apart from the above contemporary quantitative paradigm, the important paradigm which are constructed have been given in the following manner—

(i) ***Behavoral Paradigm:*** The basic philosophy of behavoral paradigm is phenomenalogical or idealistic in nature. It includes the study of human mind over the surface of this planet earth. This paradigm is also termed as subjective qualitative paradigm.

(ii) ***Model Paradigm:*** Model paradigm is introduced by Kuhn, T., Haggett, P. and Chorley R. It belongs to mathematical and geometrical structure.

(iii) ***System Paradigm:*** It is also related to applied mathematical structure where the geographical knowledge is discussed through different approaches. Geomorphic analysis, cause and effect analysis etc, are more or less such type of paradigm.

(iv) ***Structural Paradigm:*** This paradigm appeared in 1970 when very impressive concept of structuralism is focussed in geographical study all over the world. Anthropology and linguistic is the base of structural paradigm. Structural paradigm is classified in three groups:

(*a*) Physical world - Realistic Paradigm

(*b*) A world of Ideas - Idealistic Paradigm

(*c*) Mental world - Mental Paradigm (Existed in mind)

Structuralism philosophy exhibits three stage of development like:

(a) ***Stage of Super structural paradigm:*** In this stage, the super or top structuralism of society or natural phenomena is existed.

(b) ***Stage of Inermediate structural paradigm:*** In this stage, the cause and effect of super-structuralism is generated for example infrastructure etc.

(c) ***Stage of Deep structural paradigm':*** Deep structuralism shows the parental base of the case and effect.

(v) ***Applied Paradigm:*** In modern researches and any type of the geographical study, the application has been thought as the major task. The developmental processes and forthcoming should be more fruitful for society and nature in all respect to applied sense. The project must be applied in nature and the benefits may be in multidimensions.

Conceptual Paradigm vs. Geo Spatial Paradigm

Conceptual paradigm means the paradigm which incorporates the chronicles of Historical development in a systematic order. The development should be studied with respect to any discipline whether it is related to science or humanities and social sciences. The distinctions of the research chronology will highlight the nature of conceptual paradigms. Thus all the paradigm which are discussed earlier are the result of systematic chronology of geographical researches and may be termed as a whole the example of conceptual paradigms.

Prominent scientists like Hombolt A., Dokuchayev V.V., Vernadsky V.I. Berg L.S., Grigoryev A.A., Kalesnik, S.V., Neef, E. and other have studied and revealed the characteristics features of physical landscapes of the earth. They have termed the study which is further titled as 'Geoversum'. The geoversum should be regarded as the ultimate, *i.e.* maximal, object of geography. It has the multitude of parameters, characteristics and features. Among numeromus features, geoversum contains nine notable features, for which the scientists not only determine in view of necrosphere and the biosphere but all the system of sociophere and the technosphere. Thus the study of geoversum incorporating nine notable features, basic principles and specific language together make the concept of geo-spatial paradigm. Although all the discussions as made earlier have been related to geoversum (geo-spatial study) but the orientation of paradigms thrown upon the human activities, their thinking, observations and timely changes of their geographical concept. So, it may be strongly stated that these paradigms are conceptual paradigms made for researches accomplished by thinkers over geoversum. The present geo-spatial paradigms are closely confined with the physical framework and regime of the earth specially in the case of the notable features. The principles and specific language are the mode of paradigm.

Major Features of Geoversum

The geo-spatial paradigm incorporates nine major features of geoversum which are discussed in the following manner:

(a) ***Unity:*** It is a term applied for interconnection and interaction between all the components of the landscape mantle and complete exclusion of independent objects and phenomena.

(b) ***Zonality:*** It is a law governed change in the energy potential from the equator to the poles, determined by the angle of incidence of the sun's radiant energy on the spherical surface of the earth.

(c) ***Cyclicity:*** It is the periodical changing of the energy potential of the different parts of the earth's surface as the result of the planet's rotation round its axis and round the sun. Cyclicity is one of the most general laws of development of the geographical mantle and its components.

(d) ***Gyroscopic Effect:*** Gyroscopic effect in any body moving parallel to the surface of the earth as a result of the addition of the given body's movement and the relation of the planet.

(e) ***Centrosymmetry of the Geosphere:*** It is due to the central symmetry of gravitation. This results in a vertical anistropy of geospace and its horizontal isotropy. The five above mentioned features taken in isolation, out of touch with others. The next four features are important for the development of life and Human society.

(f) ***Limitedness:*** It is simply the absence of infinite geographical space abstracting ourselves from the inter connections between the geoversum and the universum, cosmic and elluric forces and also from such of its properties as the ability to accumulate energy. We can also termed the geoversum as a whole a closed system.

(g) ***Substance Polymorphism:*** To be more precise it is the existence in the landscape mantle of physical chemical and other conditions contributing to the emergence of various forms and structure of substance which donot occur in the nearly regions of the cosmos, this phenomena is increasingly being used by man to create new materials unknown to nature.

(h) ***Geo-spatial Polymorphism:*** Geo-spatial polymorphism defines a variety of forms of combination of phenomena at different points of the earth's surface, uneven distribution of phenomena and bodies over that surface. It is closely connected with processes of the differentiation of the earth's surface. Geography's ultimate object of research is structural from whatever stand point we analyse it.

(i) ***Regionality:*** It reflects the structure of the landscape mantle and the oecumene *i.e.* division of geographical space into regions. It is also a strong objective factor opposing the geosphere's entropy, while regions of the basic objects of research specific to geography.

Basic Principles of Geospatial Paradigm

Baransky (1956) has identified the four basic principles (**Figure 2.4**) of approach to objects of geographical thinking and research. In the research of modern geography 'triune' approach including 'territorially', 'Integrity' and 'conceteness' is found very essential. However today this approach should apparently be supplemented by other feature 'globality' *i.e.* the necessity of correlating local, regional, national, continental, zonal and the particular problems to their world (global) background. The need of the principle of globality in the geographical method in due to the following empirically justifiable fact all the modern so-called global problems initially arise not on a globlal but at lower geographical levels-regional, local.

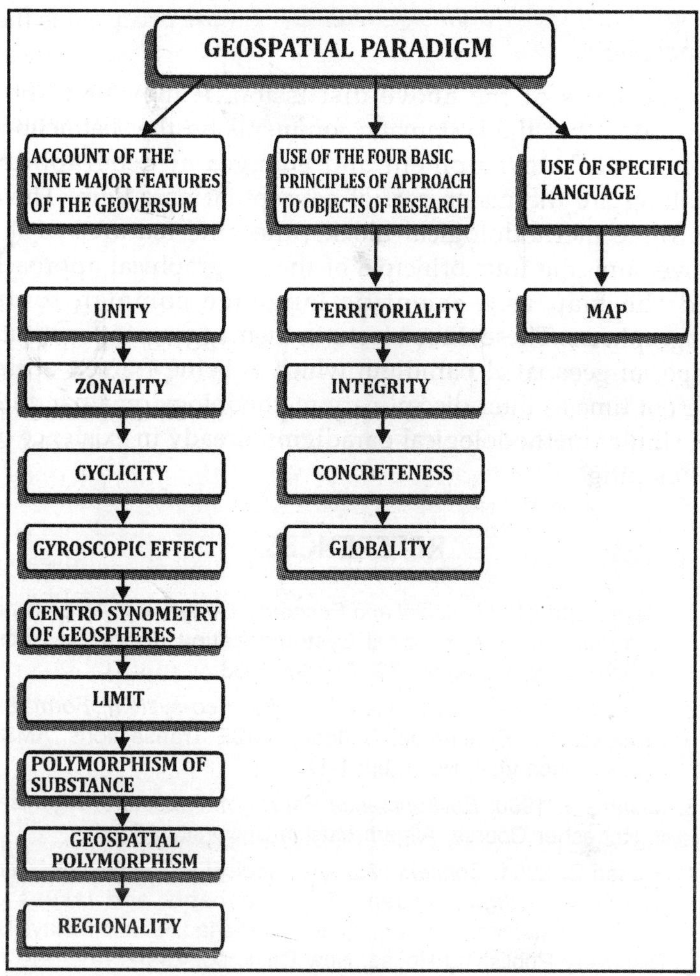

Fig. 2.4.

Specific Language of Geospatial Paradigm

Baransky stated that map and cartography should be singled out first and for most basic language of geography and geospatial paradigm. He explainined that the map is the alpha and omega of geography; the initial and final element of geographical research.

Conclusion

On the basis of the above discussion, it may be finally concluded that the systematic comments on the distinctions of historical development and changes of geographical thinking are the major part of conceptual paradigm. There are three methodological blocks: the nine features of the geoversum, the four principle of the geographical approach and the map as a scientific language comman to all geographrers. These three blocks in their aggregate constitute a special geospatial paradigm which is being framed at the present time as inter disciplinary methodology on a par with the similar methodological paradigms already in existence or developing.

REFERENCES

1. Alayen Enrid,1986: *Social and Economic Geography*. An Essay in Conceptual Terminological Systematisation, Progress Pabs. Moscow (Eng Trans) pp. 72, 74 and 78-83.
2. Jayaswal S.N.P. and Prasad G. 1989: *Eco-system, Form and Processes*. A Conceptual Outlook, AMSE Transactions, AMSE Press France VI, 4, No. 1, pp. 1-17.
3. Mishra, H. 1990: *Environmental Paradigm*: A Lecture Organised in Refresher Course, Aligarh Muslim University Aligarh.
4. Prasad G. 2004: *Concept of Geo-ecological Processes and Geo-spatial Paradigm*, Appeared in '*Concepts and Issues of Environmental Management*, Edited by Prasad, G. and Kislaya S., Discovery Publishing House, New Delhi, pp. 23-37.
5. Thornbury, W.D. 1954: *Principles of Geomorphology*, John Wiley and Sons, Inc. New York.

CHAPTER

3

Concept of Eco-system, Form and Processes

Introduction

The present attempt illustrates the summary account of environment, eco-system, geo-form, process and eco-management schemes through the up-to-date knowledge of literatures. The concept of environment ecology and eco-system is defined with several modes. Morphological forms and processes have been studied and their relationship are also taken into consideration.

Concept of Environment, Ecology and Eco-Balance

Environment has been defined as the sum total of all conditions and influences that affect the development and life of organisms. This is a comprehensive definition as it stresses its totality and every living organism, from the lowest to the highest including human being, has its own environment. In a wide term, it includes every action, reaction, interrelationship, response factors, orientation and reorientations of mass, energy modifications and transformations in a number of ways that set a balance among them at least for some time, the said balance being adjusted and readjusted by the forces of dynamism: natural or cultural. The earth surface presents an ever-changing 'geocomplex' which comprises the physiosystem *i.e.* The cycle of abiotic components of the landscape with their dynamic relationship and also the biotic complexes (better known as biocenosis) working on the said land scape. The nature of the action under eco-circumference is termed as 'holocoenosis'. It pertains to those factor of the structure and function of natural systems which exist as a vast complex and therefore donot act separately and independently. This principle lies, at the core of ecological thinking (Jayaswal, S.N.P. and Prasad G., 1989). Environment is an inseparable whole and is constituted by the interacting system of physical, biological and cultural elements (**Fig. 3.1**) which are interlinked individually as well as collectively in myriad ways. Physical elements (space, landforms, water bodies, climate, soils, rocks and minerals) determine the variable character of human habitat, its opportunities as well as limitations. Biological elements (Plants, animals, micro-organisms and man) constitute the biosphere. Cullural elements

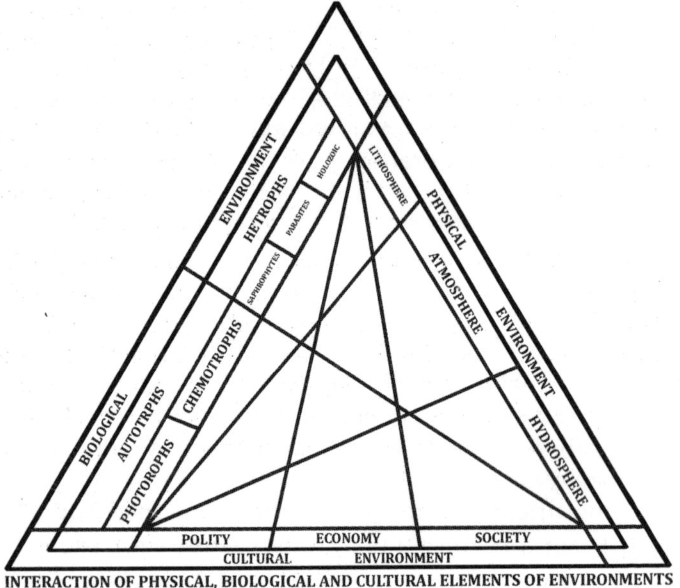

INTERACTION OF PHYSICAL, BIOLOGICAL AND CULTURAL ELEMENTS OF ENVIRONMENTS

Fig. 3.1.

(economic, social and political) are essentially man made features which go into the making of cultural milieu (Singh, S. and Dubey, A. 1983). Thus, it may be expressed that all surroundings of a designated ecosystem in environment.

The word 'Environment' may be explained as—

ENVIRONMENT = E+N+V+I+R+O+N+M+E+N+T
where

E =	Entity of Abiotic and biotic world
	Encroachment of Bio-geo-chemical system
	Evolution and essence of Biota
	Enclave of material and energy system
	Education of eco-definition, eco-decoration and eco-restoration
	Elucidation of the chapter of ecological history
	Employment of rules and regulations circumference

N =	Native land of Biomass
	Nest of Plants and Animals
	Nutrition of Biological Community
	Navigation of Matter and Energy System
	Notation and Notification of Most Wanted and Unwanted Eco-system
	Nursing of bio-eco-diversity

V =	Views of vivid Biota
	Vacuum for biological genesis
	Vale of abiotic and biotic relationships
	Validity of life generating security system
	Value of system analysis
	Van of Biome
	Variety of natural phenomena
	Vase of vast eco-community
	Vallut of vegetal cover
	Vehicle of energy circulation
	Vanue of live, love and loyality
	Village of values
	Volume of bio-books
	Voice of process, Form and stage
	Vision of making happy habitat for living world

I =
Island of happy home of biological world
Ins and Out of geo-eco-chemical society
Inhabitation of bio-distribution, bio-composition and bio-diversity
Introduction of eco-circumference
Identification of matter, energy circulation
Illustration of set of surroundings
Imagination of eco-thoughts, eco-change and eco-balance
Immigration of live, love and life system
Impression of act and fact from earth to heaven
Imprint of natural phenomena
Inauguration of wonderful world
Influence of atmospheric circumference
Initiation of morning and evening, day and might, life and death
Issue of eco-items

R =
Rating, routing and rationing of biosystem
Race from earth to space
Rack of Abio-bio structure
Rapport between physical biological community
Reasoning of nature
Recital of system systemisation
Recognition of eco-excellence
Realm of homely happenings
Region of regularity, regulations and interrelations
Remembrance of use, views and eco-news
Report of renowned reasonings
Resort of plants, animals and human life

O =
Opening corridor for living worlds
Outlook of the face of the earth
Output of eco-activities
Out appearance of eco-culture
Occurrence of natural system
Offer of God
Oxygen for humanity
Order of eco-administration
Outcome of structure, process and stage

N =

Nutrition of biological community
Navigation of matter and energy system
Notation and notification of most wanted and unwanted eco-elements
Nursing of bio-eco-diversity
Narration of cyclic system

M =

Means of life system
Management of worldwide eco-balance
Maintenance of bio-geo-chemical cycle
Maker of system neat and clean
Maker of system evergreen
Maker of system A to Z teen
Maker of system having nice scene
Money of living world
Materials of earth making structure
Market of living, non-living world
Momentum of life generating system

E = As defined previously

N = As defined previously

T =

Truth of system generation
Trust of biological agglomeration
Teacher of cause of laws
Thought of local and global sphere
Tunning of water, air, fire, atmosphere and earth
Trend of growth, cycle and recycle
Techniques of eco-management
Tracing of system of past, present and future
Track of moving/rotating earth
Tent of natural system
Terrace of eco-turning points and events
Territory of life and life generating system
Theory of life cycle
Tone of all around eco-character

The Webster's Dictionary has aptly defined ecology as "the totality or pattern of relation between organisms and their environment. The word ecology is derived from the

Greek word oikos" meaning 'home' or place to live. Literally ecology is the study of organisms 'at home' and is defined as the study of the relation of organisms or groups of organisms to their environment. Following to Odum E.P. (1971) modern ecology can be considered in terms of the concept of 'level of organistion' visualized as a sort of biological spectrum as depicted in **Fig. 3.2.** Community, population organism, organ, cell and gene are widely used terms for several major biotic level illustrated in the hierarchical arrangement from large to small in **Fig. 3.2.** Interaction with the physical environment (energy and matter) at each level produces characteristic of functional systems. Thus the circumference of ecology and environment is most common.

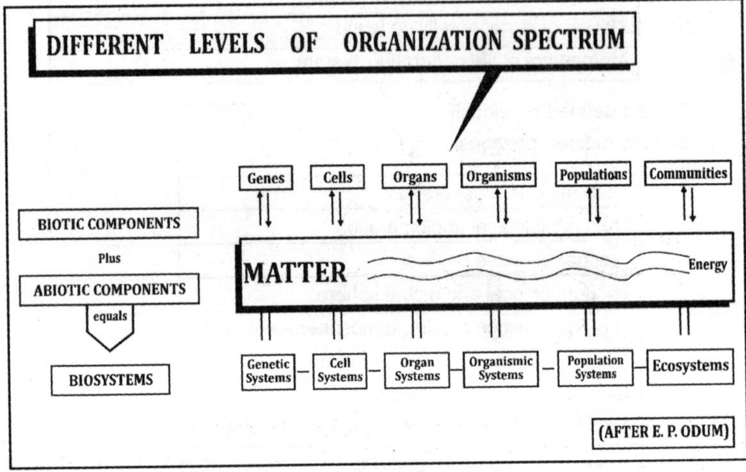

Fig. 3.2.

Generally ecology has been used to measure inter relationship of various organisms with their changing environments. This term is first used by Ernst Haechal in 1966.The scientific terms "geoecology" "synecology, and biocenosis" have taken birth in eco-circumference. The term 'Geoecology' also known as 'Landscape Ecology' was coined by Carl Troll in 1939 to refer to qualitative and quantitative interactions between different components of the geocomplex.

The application of ecology to the functional aspect of biotic communities is the field of 'Synecology'. The self regulating and self sustaining community of plants and animals has come sort of stable equilibrium with the environment which is known as 'Biocenosis'.

The concept of eco-balance is directly related to man's transformatory action in the geosphere *i.e.* extension of noosphere (the reasoning zone) through man's activity. The other sub-zones in different perspectives may be called as sociosphere and technosphere which respectively promote humanized and technocratic (Cultural) eco-society. In the beginning of scientific development a new branch called 'Habitat Ecology' has also been postulated with respect to comprehend 'Habital Science'.

CONCEPT OF ECO-SYSTEM, FORM AND PROCESSES

Eco-system is an ecologic system composed of an organic community (Biotic complex) of plants and animals (Biome) viewed within it physical environment or habitat. It is essential to some what more technical term for 'a segment of nature' and the result of interaction between biological, geochemical and geophysical system. It is often used in 'Ecology' for the physical background.The study of an 'e' provides a methodogical basis for complex synthesis between organisms and their environment.

'Eco-system' was the term enunciated by 'Tansley' to express "integrating system comprising living things and non-living environment (Tansley A.G.1935)". Stoddart D.L. (1965) has developed it as the fundamental organising concept of geography because "Firstly", it is monistic, it brings together environment, man and the plant and animal worlds within a single framework, within which the interaction between the components can be analysed....... Secondly, ecosystems are structures in a more or less orderly, rational and comprehensible way. The essential fact here, for geography, is that once structures are recognised they may be investigated and studied. Thirdly, Eco-systems function, they involve continuous throughout of matter and energy. Fourthly, the ecosystem is a type of general system and possesses the attributes of general system. In general system terms the ecosystem in an open system tending towards a steady-state under the laws of open system thermodynamic. Eco-system is an integrated system in nature which may be studied as an independent entity, *e.g.* A rolling log in the Forest, a cral atoll, *a* continent or the earth with all its biota. Eco-system ecology deals with plant and animal communities in term of total eco-system. From a structural stand point four constituents of eco-system can be recognised (**Fig. 3.3.**). **Fig. 3.3.** denotes, (i) abiotic substances, basic elements and compounds of the

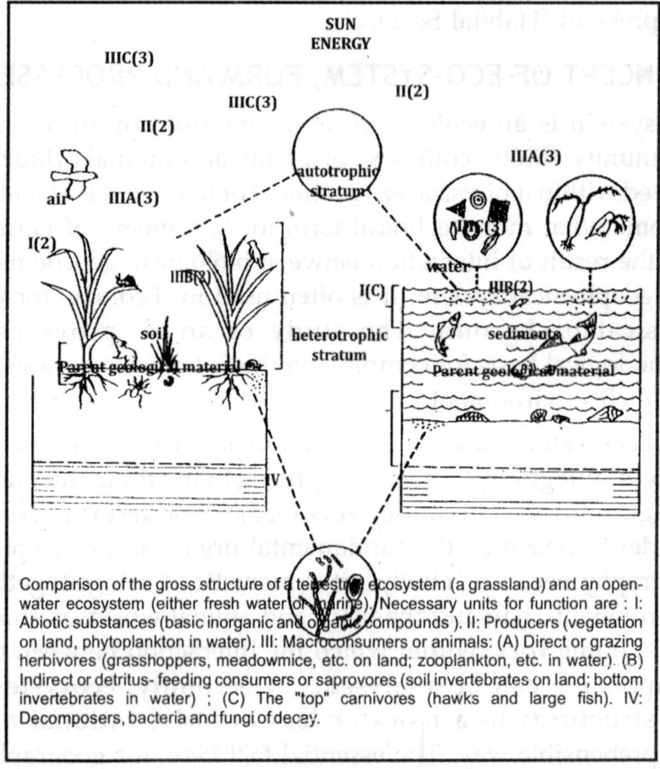

Comparison of the gross structure of a terrestrial ecosystem (a grassland) and an open-water ecosystem (either fresh water or marine). Necessary units for function are : I: Abiotic substances (basic inorganic and organic compounds). II: Producers (vegetation on land, phytoplankton in water). III: Macroconsumers or animals: (A) Direct or grazing herbivores (grasshoppers, meadowmice, etc. on land; zooplankton, etc. in water). (B) Indirect or detritus- feeding consumers or saprovores (soil invertebrates on land; bottom invertebrates in water) ; (C) The "top" carnivores (hawks and large fish). IV: Decomposers, bacteria and fungi of decay.

Fig. 3.3.

environment. (ii) producers, the autotrophic organisms, largely the green plants; (iii) the large consumers, chiefly animals that ingest other organisms a particulate organic matter; (iv) the decomposers or micro consumers (also called saprobes or saprophytes) heterotrophic organisms, chiefly the bacteria and fungi that break down the complex compounds of dead protoplasm, absorb some of the decomposition products and release simple substances usable by the producers.

The clearer perception of ecosystem can be obtained by **Fig. 3.4. Fig. 3.4.** is a combination of energy and nutrients (part of

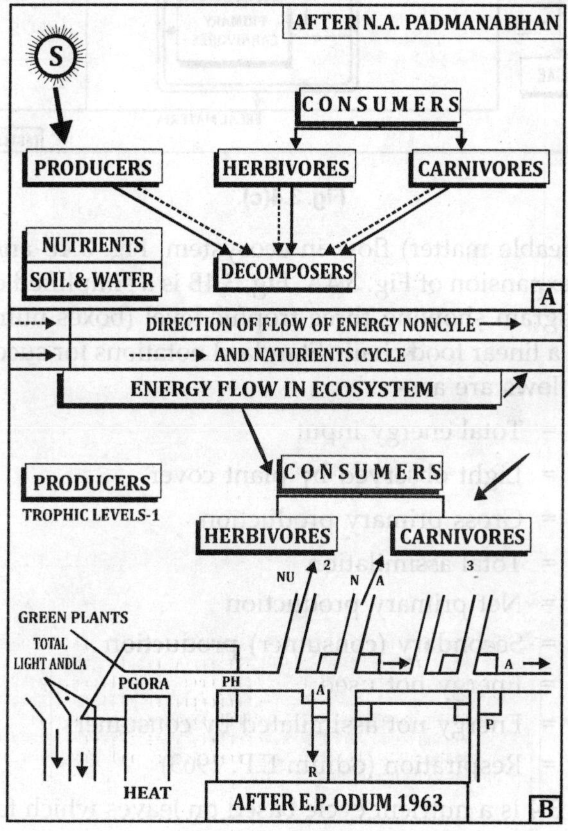

Fig. 3.4 (a) and (b).

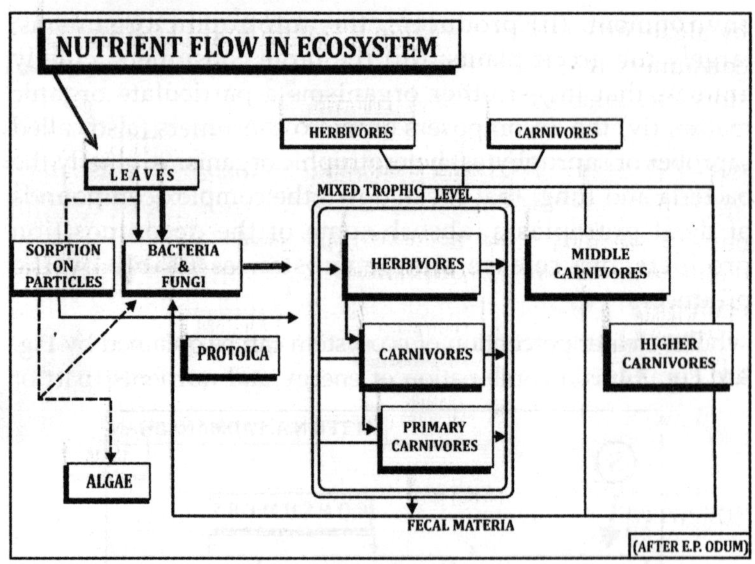

Fig. 3.4(c).

exchangeable matter) flow in ecosystem. Fig. 3.4B and 3.4C are the expansion of Fig. 3.4A. Fig. 3.4B is a simplified energy flow diagram showing three trophic level (boxes numbered 1,2,3) in a linear food chain. Standard notations for successive energy flows are as—

1 = Total energy input

LA = Light observed by plant cover

PG = Gross primary production

A = Total assimilation

PN = Net primary production

P = Secondary (consumer) production

NU = Energy not used

NA = Energy not assimilated by consumers

R = Respiration (odium E.P. 1963)

Fig. 3.4 is a nutrient cycle based on leaves which fall into shallow esturine water. Leaf fragments acted on by colonised by algae are eaten and reeaten a key group of small detritus consumers which in the main food for game fish, haerom, stork etc. (odum E.P. 1956).

Park C.C. (1980) advocated that the Eco-system stresses the unity of all parts of the environment, including both biotic and abiotic elements, it facilitates measurement and comparison of the components of different types of equalibrium and non-equalibrium states; and it highlight basic ecological principles which should be carefully evaluated when guidelines of ecological management and exploitation are completed.

Law one	:	Every thing is connected to every thing else.
Law two	:	Every thing must go some where .
Law three	:	Nature knows best.
Law four	:	There's no such thing as a free lunch (some body, some where must foot the bill).

The structure of an eco-system needs to be considered from various angles recognising the interplay of structure and function. In the study of any aspect of the physical environment there is a distinction between form and process. Following to young A (1972), form applies to what is there, the morphology at a given moment in time ; process to what is happening, the agents active in causing form to change. In soil science, form refers to the existing characteristics of soils, the Soil type present in an area, their distribution, profile morphology, mineralogical composition and also non-visible properties such as reaction, young advocates that process applies to such phenomena as hydrolysis, oxidation reduction, mechanical eluviation and the leaching of exchangeable cations, agents that have given the soil its form and are currently modifying it. In plant ecology, the vegetation communities present, their floristic composition and physiognomic structure, constitute form, photosynthesis transpiration and the various mechanisms of growth and reproduction are among the process.

In the case of slopes, form can be clearly recognised by the shape of the ground surface, young further describes that form sensu lato' is not confined to the surface, but include the thickness and composition of the regolith. Process refers to agents such as soil creep, surface wash and the processes of weathering. The environmental conditions exist as the elements of form. Both form and process have appeared in the past. The succession of past form, leading to that of the present, constitutes some new ones. For the past with respect to process, no recognised comprehensive term exits. The general problem of relating form to process at the present and in the past is as follows.

The present form and process can be surveyed but it technically it is difficult task because of their extreme slowness. Evidence of past processes is derived mainly from deposited material but the interpretation of such evidence is frequently uncertain. The past morphological history denoting forms is very difficult to judge. It can be reconstructed the complexity of processes, the spatial diversity of the environment conditions and their Variation in time are among the understanding of the reactions between, form and their evolution.

PROCESS—FORM CHRONOLOGY AND ECO-MANAGEMENT SCHEMES

The study of form and process is between the descriptive and genetic approaches to the environment. The geomorphic laws and the Studies of processes were first enunciated by Hutton in 1785. It was beautifully restated by Blayfair in 1802 and popularized by Lyell in the numerous editions of his 'Principles of Geology' explaining the concept that the same physical processes and laws that operate today operated through out geologic time, although not necessarily always with the same intensity as now. "Button advocated that present is the key to the past". He applied this principle very rigidly and postulated that ecologic processes operated throughout geologic time with the same intensity as now. But the concept of Hutton is not possible in nature because numerous examples could be seated to show that the intensity of various geologic processes has varied through geologic time, but there is no reason to believe that streams did not cut valleys in the past as they do now.

The importance of form and processes can be well recognised by Davis 'Trio' structure, process and stage. In his 'Geographical cycle' he stated that Landform is a function of structure, process and stage. The concept of Davis is validated till now. It can be examined that the geologic structure plays dominant role in the evolution of landforms as a chief controlling factor.

In the study of fundamental concepts of geomorphology Thornbury, W.D (1954) postulated that geomorphic processes leave their distinctive imprint upon landforms and each geomorphic process develops its own characteristic assemblage of landforms. The observation of Thornbury is found correct in the field of analyses. Landforms have their individual distinguishing features depending upon the geomorphic process responsibly for their development. Landscapes are the products of a group of processes. It is observed that the different erosional agents acting upon the earth's surface produced an orderly sequence of landforms. The present day multicyclic landforms are caused by the action of complex set of geomorphic processes.

Eco-degradation is a major problem arising before the existing civilization of the earth surface. It is a matter of great satisfaction that India took note of all these integrated environmental problems and this concern was the first time articulated in the Fourth Five-year Plan 1969-74. The plan drew our attention to the environmental issues in these words. It is an obligation of each generation to maintain the productive capacity of land, water, air and wild life in a manner which leaves its successors some choice in the creation of a healthy environment...........planning for harmonious development recognizes this unity of man and nature. Such planning is possible only on the basis of comprehensive appraisal of environmental issues particularly economic and ecological. There are instances in which timely specialized advice on environmental aspects could have helped in project design and in averting subsequent adverse effects on environment, leading to loss of invested resources. It is necessary, therefore, to introduce the environment aspect into our planning and development. The Sixth Five Year Plan (1980-1985) attracted great importance to the protection of environment initiating the integrity of our natural resources and soil water forests, wild life etc. The seventh Five Year Plan was operated in the right direction of all development of environment. The Ganga Authority for cleaning the water of the Ganges and the surrounding slums has been established.

The fundamental issues of eco-development has been meritoriously getting reflections in various national and international conferences such as those of Finland (1971), Stockholm (1972) and Vancouvur (1976) convened under the auspices of the United Nations. The stockholm conference (June 1972) on human Environmental pollution problems by a scientific advisory committee of United Nations.

The National committee on Environmental Planning (NCEP) reconstituted in April 1981 has done valuable work in a number of areas related to eco-development planning. The Government of India constituted a High Power committee under the chairmanship of the deputy chairman of the Planning Commission Shri N.D. Tiwari. It was submitted to the Prime Minister in September 1980 and had identified the following major areas of environmental concern:

(i) Environmental pollution
(ii) Mismanagement of land and water resources
(iii) Depletion of natural resources consciously and in ignorance
(iv) Poor condition of human settlements
(v) Need for environmental awareness and education.

The committee suggested some of the important legislative measures concerning with biosphere reserves, protection of grazing lands, protection of endangered species, toxic substances control act, scientific land use, prevention of noise pollution and the prevention of denudation of forests. The National Environmental Advisory committee as also constituted in 1983 for high lighting environmental issues and giving advice on remedial, action. A new integrated Department called Department of Environmental, Forest and Wildlife in the Ministry of Environment and Forests came into being in 1985. The allocation of work to the new department includes National Land-use and Wasteland Development council. National Wasteland Development Board, Central Ganga Authority (CGA) set up in February 1985 in the Department of Environment. The GGA over seas the implement action of the Ganga Action plan. Several actions like pollution control, land resource management, conservation of natural living resources environmental awareness programmes, environmental impact assessment and monitoring and environmental information are set in motion to preserve the environment.

There is a specific reference in our constitution about environment in the state policy. The following duties have been laid down for the state and the citizen.

Article 48A: (42nd Amendment 1976):

"The state shall endeavour to protect and improve the environment and to safeguard the forests and wildlife of the country."

Article 51A among other things states:-

"It shall be the duty of every citizen of India -(9) to protect and improve the natural environment including forests, lakes, rivers and wildlife and to have compassion for living creatures."

There are over 400 central and state legislations which may be relevant to varying extent to environmental protection.

Our laws relating to environmental problems are scattered over different statute books. In recent years our Parliament has enacted the following legislation to save the environment from being polluted.

(i) The water (Prevention and control of pollution) Act 1974.

(ii) The water (Prevention and control of pollution) Cess Act 1977.

(iii) The Air (Prevention and control of pollution) Act 1981.

(iv) The Wild life (Protection) Act 1972.

(v) The Forest (Conservation) Act 1980.

(vi) The Environment (Protection) Act 1986.

(vii) Bioshphejre Reserves.

(viii) Revison of Mines and Minerals (Regulation and development) Act 1957.

(ix) Hazardous Substances Management.

(x) Resource Recovery, Recycling and Reuse.

(xi) Indian legislation for effective implementation of convention on International Trade in Endangered species and Wild Fauna and Flora (Cites).

(xii) Marine Resources Conservation (including over-fishing, estuaries, mangroves, control of Pollution in coastal waters and EEZ etc).

REFERENCES

1. Jayaswal, S.N.P. and Prasad G. 1989: *Eco-System, Form and Processes.* A Conceptual Outlook, AMSE Transaction, AMSE Press France, Vol. 4, N.I, pp. 1-17.
2. Odum, E.P. 1971: *Fundamentals of Ecology*, W.S. Sunders company.
3. Park, C.C. 1980: Ecology and Environmental Management: A Geographical Perspective pp. 109-110, 195-196.
4. Singh S. and Dubey A., 1983: Environmental Management some

new Dimension, Appeared in Environmental Management, Edited by Singh L.R. *et. al* . The Alld.Geog. Society, 1st ed. pp. 82-86.

5. Stoddart, D.L. 1950: Geography and Ecological Approach, the Ecosystem as a Geographical Principle and Method, Geography, vol. 50, pp. 242-257.
6. Surabhi and Madhavi, 2007 : Eco-system, Form and Process: A Conceptual Framework, Appeared in 'Concepts and Issues of Environmental Management' Edited by Prasad, G. and Kislay S., Discovery Publishing House, New Delhi, pp. 1-12.
7. Tansley, A.G. 1935: The Use and Abuse of Vegetational Concepts and Term Ecology, vol. 6, pp. 282-307.
8. Thornbury, W.D. 1954: Principles of Geomorphology Johan Wiley and Sons, Inc. Newyork.
9. Young, A. 1972: Slope: Logman Group Limited London.

CHAPTER

4

Fluvial Environment and Fluvio-Erosional Ecology

Kanhaiyalal Gupta and Pramod Kumar Yadav

Introduction

The present study deals with the study of erosional ecology of fluvial process operating the existing terrain at global perspective. The review of the attempt denotes the chronohistory of the pioneer works already done by worldwide scientists and their excellant views regarding the intensity and magnitude of fluvio-erosional typology, and techniques and those controlling fluvio-erosional determinants which have fashioned the whole system.

Fluvial Processes at A Glance

It is more than a century since Gilbert carried out of his famous investigation of the geology of the Henry Mountains. His chapter on 'Land sculpture' contained in the report of the United States Geographical Survey of the Rocky Mountain Region (1980) is a landmark in the investigation of fluvial processes because it was the first and for a long time one of the last attempts to combine the principles of, fluvial mechanics with those of fluvial morphology. Engineers followed their pragmatic paths while geomorphologists dallied with description and classification (Schumm, 1972). His work is a treasury of ideas and problems, and although his discussion of sediment transport and open-channel hydraulics is qualitative, Gilbert showed in this report how land form studies might have developed by an integration of the engineering and geomorphological approaches.

The study of the river Klaralven in Sweden made by Sunbotgs (1956) was the notable exception wherein the author was only partially successful in achieving explanation of form in terms of processes. With the brust of researches done by Acker's and Charlton's (1970) on meanders and by Calendar (1969) on channel patterns in relation to dynamics, the hydraulists have paid only relatively modest attention to geomorphological problems. In a true sense Geologists and Sedimentologists have found difficulties in marrying together sedimentation, morphology and fluid mechanics.

Methodology appears as the major cause of this difficulty. The hydraulic engineers have adopted practical experiments and field surveys and some theoretical works. In the case of analysing the behaviour of flow, particles in the flow and the conditions on the boundaries of the channel the researchers have sought deterministic or probabilistic mathematical models. The work of Ven Techow (1959) and Paudkivi (1967) were notable in this field. In the light of observation of geomorphological processes specially fluvial processes, the drainage basin study (river morphology) has been largely treated as empirical. In this case, the approaches are exemplified by the observation of temporal and spatial variations in channel characteristic or the description of the fluvial processes. In the early 1960s the debate between Mackin and Leopòld and Langbein in Albritton's book the 'Fabric of geology' (1963) revealed the deep-rooted cause of this difference of process. The rational explanation advocated by Mackin about the variation in channel slope and the study of Maddock (1970) about the behaviour of alluvial channels having changing patterns of width, depth, velocity and slope are the important attempts of this field.

The geomorphologists, view of the river is further conditioned by time and space scales over which he operates. Geomorphologists have operated to a considerable extent in recent years in small river channels where as hydraulic models have concentrated on large rivers and estuaries. Geomorphologists have been less prepared to accept propositions based on steady-state operations of channel systems and have emphasized the complexities induced by change. Schumm has done most in recognizing the inherent instanbility of channels. The popularity of hydraulic geometry, which is the investigation of statistical regularities in river forms, can be largely attributable to the apparently uniform character of the observed river responses in width, depth and velocity to temporal and spatial variations in discharge (Thorne 1978).

Most possibly the reason for the failure of geomorphologists to persue deterministic explanation of channel morphology has been the relatively unsuccessful attempt to obtain an adequate model for sadiment transport.

The situation was such in 1972 that young was still able to highlight that making in use the major equations currently adopted by practising engineers, a wide variety of results could be obtained, many of which compared poorly with the observed amount or sizes of sediment observed in true channels. Thus failure is in part linked to the parametrization of the relevant models in laboratory channels that have little or no resemblance to true rivers. Bagnold (1966) stated that :

> "During the present century innumerable flume experiments have been done and a multitude of theories have been published in attempts to relate the role of sediment transport by stream of water to the strength of water flow. Nevertheless, as is clear from the literature, no agreement has yet been reached upon the flow quantity discharge, man velocity, active force or rate of energy dissipation to which transport rate should be related."

The basic problem appears that no established branch of physics has interested itself in two phase (fluid-solid) flow so the hydraulic engineer solves the problems by empirical reasoning from past experience of the like conditions. Bangold himself attempt to provide a suitable basis for such theory from general physics, and this forms the core of much current work in sedimentary and fluvial hydraulics.

A passage of time has been travelled taking about the differences between the approaches of fluvial hydraulics and fluvial geomorphology so that the well-wisher of the subject may appreciate the difficulties. The time when we have a deterministic, spatially distributed erosion-deposition model that operates over the time-scales of interest to geomorphologists is probably still a long way ahead but that should our ultimate goal.

Introduction to Fluvio-erosional Typology

Atmospheric precipitation is distributed in different ways falling over the earth's surface. Some part of atmospheric rain percolates into the ground replenishing the ground waters. Some part is moved towards the atmosphere though evaporation and yet another parts drain along the surface in a form of river. Riverine societies confirm the fluvial culture and fluvial-morpho-structure. Drainage network and network characteristics trace the morphological script of fluvio-culture on the face the earth.

The regime of exodynamic processes along with weathering, the work of surface flowing waters affects the greatest areas of the globe. The flow is sketched with a thick network of gullies and rivers. The fluvio-culture as the product of river following to Russian geomorphologists Pavlowv, A.P. "Rivers are often called water arteries, by comparison with the arteries of the human body, which carry nutrition to and wash all the human organs."

As a fluvial agent river have a long life span and therefore in his life time man can not notice any material changes in their development. A different case is that of gullies and rills of temporary streams which play the role of small natural models; they develop right before man's eyes within relatively short period of time (Shiffer, V.V. 1973).

The geological work of flowing surface waters is based on the mass of the water and its velocity. The velocity of water accelerates through gradient. The greater the mass of water and its flow velocity, the greater the work it accomplishes. River consists erosion, transport of eroded materials and its deposition. Thus, it is clear that river acts active and passive role. As an erosional agent it makes destruction by erosion and construction by sedimentation. Destruction and construction are the two major part of fluvial cycle in juvenile and senile stage of rivers, respectively.

The river consists the following works—

(i) Sheet erosion

(ii) Denudation

(iii) Transportation of the sheet erosion and denudation products

(iv) Deposition of the transported product (accumulation).

The nature of erosion differs according to water mass and its velocity. According to Davisian normal cycle of erosion, the associated land forms come to existence by structure, process and stage.

Flovio-Erosional Techniques

As a fluvial agent rivers play a tremendous role in the life of mankind. It was along rivers that clustered the most ancient human habitations and it was with them that history of the culture of the most ancient peoples is bound.

The importance of rivers is tremendous because they are the main source of water supply, the principal source of water used for irrigation, convenient and cheap source of transportation; a source of cheap and abundant power, a source of fish, natural boundaries. The work of river is performed in four different ways which act together in many areas. Weathering assists the erosive work of rivers by weakening the rocks and rendering them more liable to removal by the rivers serve as tools for the erosion of the sides and flow of the channel these four erosional techniques are as—

(i) ***Solution or Corrosion***: Flowing water dissolves quantities of soluble materials cotained in the rocks of the valley.

(ii) ***Hydraulic Action***: This consists in the power of flowing water to sweep away or wash away loose particles of rocks.

(iii) ***Corrosion or Abrasion***: The pebbles and boulders of hard rock and the sand transported by a stream serve as a powerfull tools for the mechanical wearing of the valley. The pebbles and boulders scrape soft rocks and hard rocks while sand carried along the floor has a slow wearing acton. The above process is known as corrosion.

(iv) ***Attrition***: Attrition is the mechanical wear and tear suffered by the rock materials carried by a river by mutual collision and friction with the hard rocky floor of the valley. The products of the attrition are more easily removed than the larger fragments. The finer particles are carried in suspension while the heavier fragments are rolled along the floor.

Determinants of Fluvial Processes

The character of every river is determined by three principal features:

(i) The quantity of water carried by them

(ii) The level of water

(iii) Flow velocity.

All these do not remain constant but change from season to season and from year to year. The pattern of these changes is called regime of a water.

The work of river erosion and transport requires energy. The energy of the river is provided by the velocity and volume of water. Velocity depends upon :

(i) The gredient or- steepness of valley. The steeper the slope the greater is the velocity.

(ii) The shape of the valley or the form of the channel. Velocity will be greater in the one channel with deep and narrow form than in the other with broad and shallow form.

(iii) The volume of water. The velocity of water increases with the increase in the volume of water and that is by during the flood period the discharge increases rapidly.

(iv) The amount of load carried by a river. If a river carries a large quantity of rock materials, part of its energy is expended in the work of transport and consequent its velocity and erosive power diminish although the materials borne but its erode its bed.

Over the mountainous country rivers have V-shaped valleys and steep gradients so that their velocities are high but in the flat plain conuntry the volume increases while the valley becomes broad and shallow and gradient becomes gentle. Here the large cross section of the valley permits greater discharge in spite of reduced velocity.

The quantity and the level of water in a river depend on the sources feeding it and on their seasonal variation from one place to another. Surface and ground waters also play a role in feeding rivers. Depending on the predominant source rivers can take melting snow waters, glaciers waters and water supply mostly from rain. The nature of water mass also determines the erosional capacity.

The period of the least amount of water in the river and its lowest level is know as low water time or low water level. The period when a river is characterized of by a sharp increase in the amount of and rise of its level as a result of melting of snow or heavy rain is called high water. The level of the water in a channel also determines the characteristics of erosional capacity.

The rate of water in a river depends on the mass of water, the gradient and the flow. In rivers the flow of water is mostly turbulent *i.e.* the rate of flow at each point of the stream is not constant either with regard to velocity or direction.

Conclusion

On the basis of the above discussion, it may be concluded that the fluvial processes are more dominant causing surface irregularities under exogeneous regime. The uplifted landmass must be undergone towards peneplain if it is turbulent and accelerated in nature.

REFERENCES

1. Bagnold, R.A.,1966: An approach to the sediment transport from general physics, U.S. Geol. Surv. Prof. Pap. 422-I-P-.37.
2. Callender, R.A. 1966: Instability and river channels., J. fluid, Mech. 36, pp. 465-480.
3. Chow, V.T. (ed.) 1964: Handbook of Applied Hydrology; a compendium of water resources technology. New York, Mcgrew hill.
4. Schumm, S.A. 1972: River morphology, Dowden Hutchinson and Ross, Stroudsburg, Pennsylvania 41-2.
5. Siffer, V.V. 1972: Physical Geology (Eng. trans.) Mir Publication, Moscow.
6. Sundborg, A. 1956: The river Klaralven, A study of Fluvial processes, Georg. Annly 38, pp. 127-316.
7. Thornes, J.B. 1978: The character and problems of contemporary theory in geomorphology, Present Problems and Future Prospects (ed. Embleton, C.) Oxford Univ. Press, pp. 14-24.

CHAPTER

5

Global Water Measurement, Treatment and Management

Shardendu Kislaya

Introduction

The present effort is closely related with the distribution of global water budget, its consumption in different ways, permissible limit of toxit and hazardous elements in water and its treatment, remedial measures for the water problems and so called management procedures and review of literature on worldwide scale. The description is conceptual and reviewed through a deep sense of knowledge of literature. Where necessary, it is attempted to expose the scientific materials by cartographic laws specially drawing cartograms and models. Pollution is one of the aspect associating negatively with water and in this respect different types of pollution and its impact is seriously scaled in the present text.

Human civilization is more or less concerned with river water to a very great extent. Men and animal kingdom depend nutritionally on vegetal sod cover which in turn require a nice balance of water of good quality. Hindu mythology deeply believes the pious and holy fresh character of river water. Now a days water consumption has become the measurement of progress of a country. Due to increasing industrialization and rapid growth of population, we are facing a suicidal threat as a result of environmental pollution. The problem of environmental pollution is not only limited in our country but the entire global community is badly affected by it. Rivers are under tremendous pressure of domestic, municipal and industrial pollution. The water we drink, the food we eat and the air we breathe are more or less contaminated by toxic substances, therefore responsibility for keeping them pollution free must be shared by all of us. Pure water is not only sufficient condition for a good water quality but it should contain a number of water-soluble components essential for human health. Rapid industrialization have caused water pollution through the discharge of effluents containing toxic substances like heavy metals, flourides and arsenic water bodies. Most of the rivers of peninsular India are being polluted day by day due to input of untreated industrial effluents, domestic water and use of rivers water for bathing, washing, immersion of idols at the time of festivals and cremation of dead bodies. Pollution of water causes a large number of diseases like dysentry, typhoid, malaria, hepatitis, yellow fever, trachoma, flue and tuberculosis. About 175 million children in rural areas of our country are devoid of safe drinking water.

Water may be found in gaseous form throughout the atmosphere, in solid and liquid form over the surface of the earth, and in soil saturated form below the ground surface. Hydrological cycle plays vital role determining the distribution of global water regime. There is unseparable relation between global water budget and hydrological cycle.

The quantitative representation of the hydrological cycle for river basins, separate regions or for the globe as a whole is called the water budget. The estimated distribution of global water budget is given in **Table 5.1**. and graphically represented by **Fig. 5.1**.

Table 5.1 : Global water Resources

Sl. No.	Condition of Water Storage	Volume of water (Km^3)	% of total global water
1.	Fresh water lakes	1,25,000	0.009
2.	Saline lakes and land locked seas	1,0,4,200	0.008
3.	Rivers	1,200	0.0001
4.	Ground water (up to 800 mts depth)	41,68,200	0.31
5.	Ground water (upto 800 mts depth)	41,68,200	0.31
6.	Soil moisture	66,700	0.005
7.	Ice Caps and glaciers	2,91,77,300	2.51
8.	Atmosphere (water vapour)	12,900	0.001
9.	Oceans	1,32,13,1000	97.20
	Grand Total	**135,91,33,7000**	**100.00**

Source: Hydrology, Prasad. G. 1998.

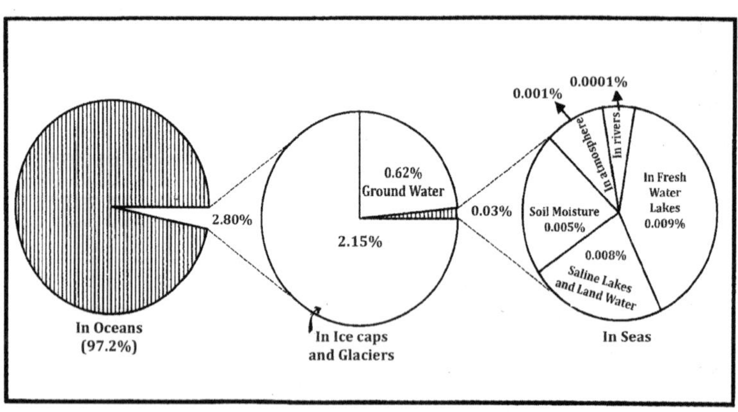

Fig. 5.1. Percentage of Total Global Water

Soviet scientist Lvovich, M.I., has estimated the total volume of water as 1454703000 km^3 under global water budget **Table 5.2**. Which is more than the estimate shown in **Table 5.1**.

Table 5.2 : Distribution of Global water Budget (After M.I., Lvovich)

Sl. No.	Condition of Water Storage	Volume of water (1000 Km^3)	% of total global water
1.	World oceans	13,70,323	93.960
2.	Ground water	60,000	4.120
3.	Active water along moving 30nes	4,000	0.270
4.	Glaciers	24,000	1.650
5.	Lakes	280[1]	0.019
6.	Soil moisture	85[2]	0.006
7.	Atmospheric water vapour	14	0.001
8.	River water	1.2	0.0001
	Grand Total	**145,4703**	**100.00**

Lvovich has also estimated the entire global surface area as 510,000,000 Km^2. Wherein about 116,800,000 Km^2, 32,100,000 Km^2, and 36100,000 Km^2 areas have been noted as exorheic continental area, endorheic continental area and oceanic area respectively. The average residence time of water in different parts is shown in **Table 5.3**.

Global water budget is badly affected by pollution. Whether developing countries can afford different measures for the control of water pollution is not crucial question but it is whether they can afford to neglect them. In absence of adequate measures for preventing water pollution, a nation would be confronted with move burden to secure adequate supplies of water for different purposes.

Table 5.3 : Average Residence Time of water

Sl. No.	Water Residential Area	Residence Time
1.	Atmosphere	10 days
2.	Terrestrial plants	
	A. Rivers	2 weeks
	B. Lakes	10 weeks
	C. Soil	2 to 50 weeks
	D.Biota	1 to 20 days
	E. Underground	1 to 10,000 years
3.	Oceans	3600 years
4.	Polar ice	15,000 years

Source: Hydrology, Prasad, G. 1998.

During the Sixth Five Year Plan (1980-85), the Government of India laid down the policy that "it is imperative that we carefully utilise our renewable resources of soil, water, plant and animal life to sustain our economic development. Over exploitation of these is reflected in soil erosion, siltation, floods and rapid destruction of our forest, floral and wild life resources. The depletions of these resources often tends to be irreversible and since the bulk of over population depends on these natural resources to meet the basic needs particularly of fuel, fodder and housing material, it has meant a deterioration in their quality of life.

In the early stages of industrialization, developing countries emphasized on suitable pollution prevention policies, they can avoid the mistakes committed by a number of developed countries in past. It is one of the essential and important job for environmental scientist to frame social and industrial structure for future.

Normal water consumption of different domestic animals is represented in **Table 5.4**.

Table 5.4 : Normal water consumption of different domestic animals

Sl.No.	Animals	Consumed water consumption per day (litres per head)
1.	Dairy Cattle	38-61
2.	Hoarser	30-46
3.	Beef cattle	27-46
4.	Pigs	11-19
5.	Sheep and Goats	04-15
6.	Turkey (per 100 birds)	0.4-0.5
7.	Chickens (per 100 birds)	0.3-0.4

Source. U.S.F. W.P.C.A. 1992.

Biosphere containing air and water sustain life on earth. The earth receive a very large input of energy daily from the Sun and maintain a steady state by giving of bulk of this energy at same rate. The earth absorb radiation mainly in the visible region but emit radiation at the same rate in the infrared region. There are various complex mechanism by means of which the earth manages to maintain heat balance with in narrow limits and there by retain optimum climatic conditions for supporting life.

Increasing agricultural and industrial outputs can also upset the earth's radiation balance by changing the albedo (fraction of sunlight reflected and scattered back to the atmosphere). Deforestation and the consequent soil erosion increase the albedo. Further more both agriculture and industry release large quantities of dust and fumes in to the atmosphere. The natural balance of Oxygen, Nitrogen, Carbon dioxide and water vapour is maintained by plants, animals and bacteria. The ever increasing smoke, CO_2, harmful effluents from factories and life destroying gases and other domestic wastes tend to upset this balance.

Some of the toxic and hazardous elements and their

permissible limit in water recommended by W.H.O. are given in **Table 5.5**.

Table 5.5: Permissible limit of the Toxic and hazardous elements in water (By WHO)

Sl.No.	Elements	Maximum Allowed limit (WHO Standard)
1.	Toxic Substances	
	A- Lead	0.05 ppm
	B- Arsenic	0.05 ppm
	C- Cadmium	0.05 ppm
	D- Chromium	0.05 ppm
2.	Components hazardous to health	
	A-Flourides	1.5 ppm
	B-Nitrates (as NO_2)	4.5 ppm
3.	Components Affecting Potability	
	A. Total Dissolved Solids	1500 ppm
	B. Iron and manganese	5,000 ppm each
	C- Copper	1.50 ppm
	D- Lime	1.50 ppm
	E- Surfactants	0.5 ppm
4.	Chemical Responsible for pollution	
	A-D.O.	4.6 ppm
	B-B.O.D.	6.00 ppm
	C-C.O.D.	10.0 ppm
	D- Total Nitrogen Exclusive Nitrate	1.00 ppm
	E- Oil And Greese	1.00 ppm

The present investigation is aimed to develop an economic and suitable method for the treatment of water and waste water. Among the techniques employed in the past for the above purpose, adsorption technique is considered as one of the advanced method. Oxygen is most abundant in lithosphere. As compared to majority of heavy metals, Oxygen is for more ubiquitous. Besides that vanadium, Manganese, Aluminium and Iron with abundances of 135,950,56300 and 82300 ppm respectively appear in the top twenty abundant elements (Tayler, 1964). Taylor reported the order of abundances of heavy metals in the lithosphere in the following manner –

Al>Fe>Mn>V>Cr>Ni>.Zn>Cu>Co>Pb>Be>Sn>Mo>Ti>Sb>Cd>Bi >Hg>Ag>Se>Te

The guide lines for levels of Toxic substances in Liver-Stock drinking water as reported by NAS (1972) is given in **Table 5.6**.

Table 5.6 : Levels of Toxic Substances in Live stock drinking water

Sl.No.	Constituent	Upper Limit (ppm)
1.	AL	5.0
2.	AS	0.2
3.	Be	0.1
4.	B	5.0
5.	Cd	0.05
6.	Cr	1.00
7.	Co	1.00
8.	Cu	0.5
9.	Nitrate+ Nitrate	100.00
10.	Se	0.05
11.	Vanadium	0.10
12.	Zn	24.00

In general, it is the overall abundance of any metal in earth crust which will reflect indirectly the amount which is extracted and utilized for human purposes. The concentration of heavy metals may be assessed in the following conditions:

1. **Geo-chemical Background:** With reference to geographical locations the national composition of soils varies with its heavy metal content. According to Nriagu (1979) about 75,000 tonnes of zinc is added in the environment per year due to soil erosion and weathering. It is also correct for the input of lead. The level present in the water bodies is affected by geological background, concentration of metals but unlikely to be of great importance as a source of heavy metals in waste water.

2. **Atmospheric Deposition:** Two types of fractions are responsible for atmospheric deposition – (i) Dry fall out and (ii) Wet Deposition.

   Dry fall out consist of matter that can be deposited into an open sample container is absence of snow or rain (Gelloway and Likens, 1976). Wet deposition includes all types of precipitation such as hail, snow and rain. The two fractions are jointly known as bulk deposition.

3. **Runoff:** Land use patterns will be a major factor in determining the concentration of heavy metals in run off. It were estimated by sonzugni *et. al.* (1980) that highest concentration of Cu, Pb and Zn in run off originated from industrial sites whereas lower concentration were associated with run off from high ways, road sides and other sources. Ranges of unit areas loading of heavy metals in run off by land use is given in **Table 5.7**.

Table 5.7 : Range of unit areas loadings of heavy metals in run-off by landuse

(Metal Loading g/Ha/Year)

Land use Types	Cu		Pb		Zn	
	Minimum	Maximum	Minimum	Maximum	Minimum	Maximum
Mixed Agriculture	02	900	02	80	05	300
RURAL						
Improved Pasture	21	38	04	15	19	172
Forest	20	30	10	30	10	30
URBAN						
General	02	210	140	500	300	1000
Restricted	30	30	60	60	20	20
Commercial	70	130	170	1100	250	430
Industrial	290	1300	2200	7000	3500	12000

Source: Environ. Sci. Technol:14(2), 149 (1980).

Through various developmental activities man has been disturbing the ecological balance thereby destroying the healthy environment for survival. Various types of water wastes released by industries automobiles and some other domestic works cause environmental degradation at a great extent.

A number of heavy metals being released from different domestic water waste are given in **Table 5.8.**

Table 5.8: Heavy metals released from different domestic water waste

Sl.No.	Sources	Heavy Metals
1	2	3
1.	Automotive Product	Al, As, Be, Co, Cr, Fe, Pb, Mo, Ti and Zn
2.	Cosmetics	Al, Be, Bi, Cd, Co, Cu, Fe, Pb, Mn, Hg, Ni, Se, Ag, Sn, Ti, V, Zn,

1	2	3
3.	Disinfectants	Hg
4.	Fuels	Be, Cu, Pb
5.	Pesticides	Al, As, Cd, Cr, Cu, Fe, Pb, Mn, Hg, Mo, Zn
6.	Inks	Al, Cu, Ti, Zn
7.	Lubricants	Be, Cr, Pb, Ni, Zn
8.	Medicine	Al, Sb, As, Bi, Co, Cu, Fe, Zn
9.	Paints	Al, As, Be, Cr, Co, Fe, Pb, Mn,Hg, Ti, Zn
10.	Photography	Al, Ag, Cr, Fe, Pb, Hg, Sn
11.	Pigments	Al, Sb, As, Be, Bi, Cd, Cr, Co, Cu, Fe, Mn, Hg, Ne, Se, Sn, Ti, Zn, Pb
12.	Powders	Al, Fe, Ag, Ti, Zn
13.	Preservatives	Fe, Pb, Zn
14.	Water Treatment	Al, Co, Fe, Mn, Zn

Source: Atkins and Howley, 1978.

Different Heavy Metals given By industries are as follows

Sl.No.	Sources	Heavy Metals
1	2	3
1.	Power Plant	Cr, etc.
2.	Ferrous Foundaries	Al, Sb, As, Bi, Cd, Cr, Co, Cu, Fe, Pb, Mn, Hg, Mo, Ni, Se, Te, and Sn
3.	Non-ferrous Plating	Al, Sb, As, Bi, Cd, Cr, Cu, Pb, Ni, Ag
4.	Cement and Glass Industries	As, Cr, Se, Te
5.	Organic and Petro-Chemicals	Al, As, Cd, Cr, Fe, Pb, Hg, Sn

1	2	3
6.	Paper Industries	Cr, Cu, Pb, Hg, Ni, etc.
7.	Textile and Leather Industries	Cr, Sb etc.
8.	Electronics	Sb, Cu, Hg, Se, Te, Sn, etc.
Source: Dean J.G. *et al* (1972)		
1.	Inorganic chemicals	Al, As, Cd, Cr, Cu, Fe, Mn, Sn,
2.	Fertilizer	Al, As, Cd, Cr, Cu, Fe, Pb, Ni
3.	Oil Refining	Al, As, Bi, Cd, Cu, Fe, Pb, Ni
4.	Textile Industries	Sb, Cr
5.	Electronics	Sb, Cu, Hg, Se, Te, Sn

Source: Dean, J.G. *et al* (1972).

Types of Pollution

Addition of any undesirable foreign material for any physical change in the environment adversely affecting the life directly or indirectly is called pollution. Different types of pollution like air, soil, radioactive, noise and water may be recognised. Among these air and water pollution are most dangerous because they occur more frequently than the rest. Air is never found clean in nature due to natural and man made pollution, Gases such as CO, SO_2, H_2S are continuously released in to the atmosphere through natural activities, volcanic activity, vegetation decay and forest fires. Besides that tiny particles of solids or liquids are distributed throughout the air by winds, volcanic explosions and other similar natural disturbances. In addition to these 'natural pollutants' there are man made pollutants like gases, mist and particulate aerosols resulting from the chemical and biological processes used by man.

The ever increasing level of pollutants in air is causing unfavourable affect on growth, metabolism and productivity of plants. Air pollutants are responsible for a number of hazards like green house effect, acid rain, depletion of ozone layer, climatic changes and a number of disorders for plants and human life. Green house effect is responsible for global warming. It may also cause the rise in sea water level. Acid rain causes extensive damage to buildings and sculptural material of marbles, lime stone, slate mortar etc. The acid rain damage leaves of trees and plants and regards the growth of forests. Air pollution is responsible to cause a number of diseases *e.g.* lachry mation, asthma, headache, suffocation etc.

Radio-active pollution is caused due to use of radio active material. Besides being carcinogenic, they may also cause physical and mental imbalance for future generation. These affect water, air, food and soil. Radio-active pollution is mainly due to cosmic rays from outer space, use of radio-nucleides like U- 238, Th- 234, C-14 Ra- 226 Xrays used in medicines, radioactive fall out resulting from nuclear weapones testing in air or on the ground, increasing use of radio-active isotope in industry, research and medicines. An additional hazard is from accidental leakage of radiation from nuclear reactors.

Soil pollution is mainly due to excessive and continuous use of fertilizer and pesticides while noise pollution causes deafness and mental disturbances.

WATER POLLUTION

The quality of water is much concerned to mankind because it is directly linked with human welfare. Water is one of the most essential requirement for living world. Water pollution causes a large number of water borne diseases. The domestic and industrial wastes cropped out from urban and rural areas are the major sources of water pollution. The factors affecting water pollution may be discussed as follows—

Domestic Discharge

Domestic discharge is also responsible for merger of heavy metals in water from residential areas. This also include automobile repairing shops and service stations. Approximately 250 mg/kg heavy metals have been found to present in human faeces (Spectra 1956). Faeces concentration of Cu is approximately, 68 Mg/Kg followed by Pb, Ni and Cd at 11,4.7 and 2.0 Mg/Kg respectively (Davis and Copper (1980). Discharge of metals to sewers in residential areas is also by bathing, brushing the teeth and washing of hair (Atkins and Hawlay, 1978). Household products such as medicines, cosmetics, polishes all contain heavy metals. Flouride and Tin (II) is a popular ingredient of toothpaste. As reported by Crosby (1987) approximately 1,000,000 Kg of tin from these sources is released per year in U.S.A. A few anti dandruff shampoos may contain upto 1.1% Selenium sulphides (Harr, 1978).

Industrial Discharge

Heavy metals have wide applicability in industries and it will also influence their appearences in waste water. Different heavy metals are discharge from different industries to add up the concentration of heavy metals in the river water for example Cr from power plant Fe and Cr from steel industries, Al, As, Cd, from fertiliser industries, Cu, Pb, Hg from paper industries and so on.

The pollution is the greatest crime of mankind against himself. Water pollution is a state of deviation from the pure condition where by its normal function and properties are affected. Any shift in the naturally dynamic equilibrium existing among the environmental segment gives rise to the state of pollution. The bad taste of water, the offensive odours from lakes, river, the unchecked growth of aquatic weeds in water bodies decrease in number of fish in fresh water, river water and in sea water, the oil and grease floating on water surfaces etc. are the chief characteristics of water pollution. These disturb the normal use of water in sense of public water supply, recreation and aesthetics, fish, other aquatic life and wild life, agriculture, Industries, etc.

Water Pollutants

Water pollutants may be broadly classified as organic pollutants, inorganic pollutants, sediments, radioactive materials and thermal pollutants.

Organic Pollutants

Organic pollutants include oxygen demanding wastes, disease causing agents, plant nutrients, sewage, synthetic organic compounds and oil, pesticides and toxic organic pollutants.

Dissolved oxygen is an essential requirement of aquatic life. The optimum D.O. in natural water is 4.6 ppm. Decrease in this D.O. value is an index of pollution mainly due to organic matter *e.g.* sewage, (Domestic and animal) , industrial wastes from food processing plants, paper mill and tanneries, wastes from slaughter house and meat packing plants, run off from agricultural land etc. All these materials undergo degradation by bacterial activity. In the presence of D.O. the net result being the deoxygenation process and quick depletion of D.O. Water is the carrier of pathogenic micro-organism and causes immense harm to public health. The water borne diseases are typhoid and paratyphoid fevers, dysentry and cholera , polio and infectious hepatitis. The responsible organisms occur in the faeces or urine of infected people and are finally discharged into a water body.

The production of synthetic organic chemicals includes fuel, plastics, fibres, solvents , detergents, paints, insecticides and pharmaceuticals. There presence in water impairs objectionable and offensive tastes odours and colours to fish and aquatic plants.

Oil pollution of the seas has increased over the years due to the increased use of oil based technology. The sources of oil pollution are oil spilt from cargo oil tankers on the seas and leakages from oil pipelines. Oil pollution reduces light transmission through surface water and hence photo synthesis by marine plants decreases D.O. in water and causes damage to water birds, coastal plants and animals. A large number of health problems have been associated with the manufacture of pesticides. About 0.1% of the total insects are harmful. Mostly agricultural pests are thought to be as carriers of human or animal diseases.

Inorganic Pollutants

Inorganic salts, mineral acids, finely divided metals or metal compounds, trace element, complexes of metal with organic in natural water and organo-metallic compounds are major inorganic pollutants. Polyphosphates in detergents are the major sources of phosphate in water serve as algal nutrients and are of much concern as water pollutants.

Several trace elements are found in polluted water. The most dangerous among them are heavy metals like Pb , Cd, Hg, and metalloids such as Se As and Sb. Heavy metals have great affinity for sulphur and attack sulphur bonds in enzymes and immobilises the latter. Heavy metals binds to all membrane affecting transport process through cell wall. They also tend to precipitate phasphatic bio compounds and catalyse their decomposition. Metals are contributed by domestic sewage and industrial effluents.

Sediments

The natural process of soil erosion gives rise to sediments in water. It represents the most extensive pollutant of surface water. Soil erosion gets enhanced as a result of agricultural development and due to constructive activities. Bottom Sediments are important source of organic and inorganic matter in Stream, fresh water, estuaries and oceans. Sediments and suspended particles are also important store house for trace metals *e.g.* Cr, Cu, Mo, Ni, Co and Mn.

Radio-Active Materials

Radio-active pollution is mainly caused due to the following activities—

(i) Use of radioactive materials in nuclear weapons

(ii) Use of radio-active materials in nuclear power plants

(iii) Mining and processing of ores to produce usable radio-active substances and

(iv) Use of radioactive isotopes in medical, industrial and research applications.

Nuclear weapons testing in air, leakage from under ground nuclear detonations etc. give rise to radio active fall out. During the processing and extraction of uranium large quantities of Uranium tailings are produced which pose the problem of radio active pollution. Nuclear power plants generate the following types of pollutants—

(i) Low level radio active liquid wastes

(ii) Liquid and gaseous wastes

(iii) Fission products and

(iv) Heat.

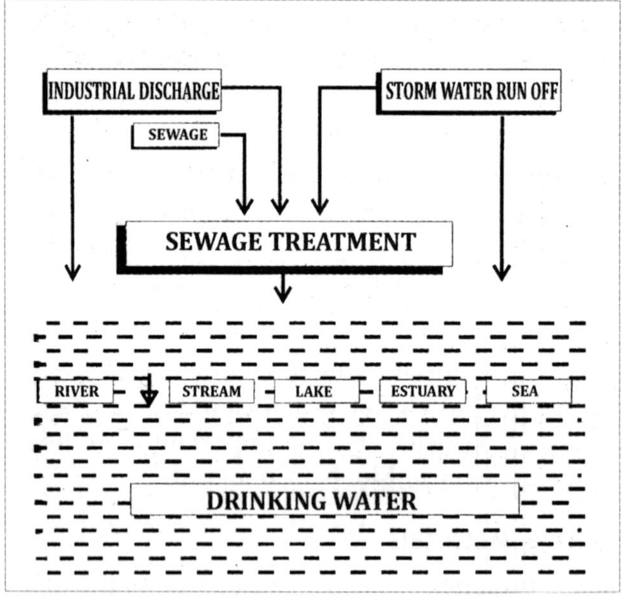

Fig. 5.2. Source of Heavy Metals in Surface Water

The radio active nucleides present in water causing sever water pollution like R-226, K-40, Sr-90, I-131, Cs-137, Ba-140, Cs-141, Kr- 85, Co-60, Mn-54, Fe-55 and Pu-239.

The sources of heavy metals in surface water may be shown by **Fig. 5.2**.

Thermal Pollutants

Coal fire or nuclear fuel fire, Steam, powerplants are associated with the problem of thermal pollution. It is reported that the waste heat from industries raised the temperature of nearby lakes and rivers by 10°C. It decreases the D.O. of water and adversely affects aquatic life. India stands amongst the first 10 heavily industrialized countries of the world. River pollution is a necessary evil of essentially all the developmental activities. This has resulted heavily back log of gaseous, liquid and solid pollution heavy metals *e.g.* Pb. represent an important source of metal input to surface water. Metals are contributed by industrial effluents and domestic sewage. All these sources may be routed by way of sewage treatment works which reduce significantly the amount of metal discharged.

Possible Remedial Measures for the Water Problems

A number of treatment processes have been employed to minimise and cure the serious problems of water pollution. Before making a final choice, it is necessary to describe in brief the different method adopted for such treatment. The treatment method may be classified into following four groups–

(1) Physical Method: Techniques which are generally employed to diffuse out the physical stress may be floatation, filtration, sedimentation and membrane filtration etc. Sedimentation method is used for the removal of suspended impurities. Very fine suspended particles and some bacteria can be removed with the help of sedimentation with coagulants. Flotation method is adopted for the separation of suspended and colloidal impurities by bubling solution. Biological flocks and coagulants can be channelised using filtration methods may also be used for water purification, earlier its disposal into the water.

(2) Biological Methods: These methods are used for the treatment of sewage which are highly potent in municipal wastes Complex organics waste may be recycled in simpler and stable end products can be safely disposed off. Several treatment processes have developed including activated sludge process and tricking filters, septic tanks, detritus tanks, oxidation ponds, oxidation ditches or aerated lagoon before adding to the river water.

(3) Chemical Method: To improve the quality of water, different chemical methods such as precipitation coagulation. Adsorption and ion exchange methods may be used for the removal of various chemicals from water being poured to river.

Precipitation and reduction processes are generally employed for the removal of toxic metallic species from waste water. To remove ionic species from water, ion exchange device can be used. This method is also applicable for the removal and recovery of radioactive materials from waste water of nuclear reactors, laboratories and hospitals:

Different types of inorganic and organic pollutants can be removed by using simple and comparatively economic method called fly ash and slag. The use of activated carbon for the treatment of organic contaminated waste water specially using adsorption techniques has been practically more reliable process. The addition to the methods mentioned above electro deposition, evaporation, cementation, ion floatation, freeze concentration etc. are also employed for the purification of undesirable substances from the water.

(4) Integrated Method: No single method is sufficient for thorough treatment of water but a series of methods are used in combination depending upon the degree of treatment required. The treatment process can be shown in **Fig. 3**.

Because of sludge free operation and easy handling of overall operation adsorption technique was selected for the removal of toxic pollutants from water using some unconventional adsorbents are frequently used.

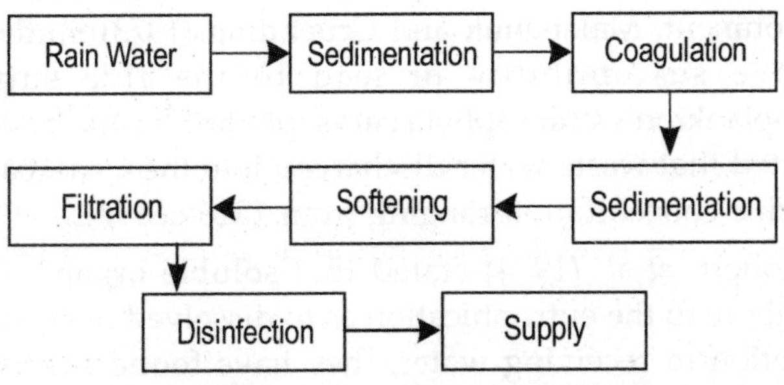

Fig. 5.3. Treatment Process of Water

Review of Literature

The pollution of streams by industrial wastes must have its beginnings at the time of industrial revolution in later half of the eighteenth century. The major pollution problem from industrial waste lies in the disposal of organic wastes, the major source of organic waste are the food processing, paper, textile, petroleum and chemical industry. Pollution from chemical wastes are evolved from plants manufacturing acids, detergents explosives, insecticides, fungicides, plastics etc. Distillation, filtering and screening also produce chemical wastes.

Srivastava (2002) reported that the presence of small amount (0.2 ppm) of free ammonia in natural water is only an indication of recent organic pollution, and in highly saline water ammonia concentration ranges up to 0.05 ppm only (Hood, 1966). First fish mortality was observed in the ponds of reasi and in Nehru Stream in Jammu and Kashmir where D.D.T. was used in city drains (ICAR, 1967). Edward (1977) observed the industrial effluent are perhaps the most important sources of contamination for rivers and estuaries whereas of contamination for rivers and estuaries whereas large scale spraying and run-off water are important contributes of pesticides pollution in ponds and lakes.

Siegel and Eshleman (1975) reported that heavy metals are the leading. Source of contamination of the aquatic environment. Malanchuk and Gruending (1973) Studied the relative susceptibility of lead to the five supp. of phytoplankton's Chlorophyta chrysophyta. Shastry *et. al* (1972) reported that waste water discharged into the Chambal river and zinc concentration ranging from 1316-6689/L.

Robert, *et al.* (1974) stated that soluble organic matter contribute to the eutrophication as to dissolved oxygen (DO), Depletion in receiving water, they have found the average pH, total solids, COD, BOD where 7.14, 358 mg/l,412 mg/l and 260 mg/l respectively and concluded that septik tank treatment of waste water may not be satisfactory for environmental pollution control. CBIPCWP (1985-86), pointed that the organic carbon load in terms of BOD and COD of raw and partially, treated sewage and untreated industrial waste water has shown that the soil can absorb this load without much difficulty. Salim (1983) Studied the effect of chemical composition and particle size of suspended particle in river water on the absorption of lead on to these particle and lead has been determined using the anodic voltametry. Duzzin and Pavoni (1988) Stated that the heavy metal may occur in streams as a result of natural and anthropogenic factors. Concentration of pollutant were found to be related to sediments to be good pollution indicator as they accumulate all metals.

Mcbay *et. al.* (1988) studied the absorption of four pollutants in aquous solution on to activated carbon, the solutes are phenol, P. cholro-phenol, sodium dodecyl sulphate and mercuric ions. Singh (1975) studied the fertilizer tolerance of blue green algae and their effect on heterocyst differentiation.

Millington *et. al.* (1988) investigated the effect of varying growth medium components on the toxicity of four chemicals to three spp. of fresh water green algae by the standard algal growth inhibition test. Genjatulin (1990) study performed which has been based on mathematical method to test culture response to action by a number of chemical water pollutants.

Joy (1989) and Balakrishnan *et al* (1990) study the ecology of phytoplankton production in the river Periyar which receives continuous effluent discharge from a dozen industrial effluent units, industrial zone of river was observed to have a high standing stock of phytoplankton during premonsoon (summer). Khare and Sharma (1979) studied the ecology of solah sugar pond at Ujjain. Palmer (1969) in this valuable review on algae as biological indicators of pollution found certain algae to lerant to relatively organic waste.

Ghazali *et al*, (1988) studied the six sites along the Al-Khair river in Baghdad were allocated for monitoring water pollution, escherichia coli (E.coli) was used as a fecal pollution indicator. This study demonstrated that the Al-Khair river heavily Contaminated with the antibiotic resistance, E. Coli which prove a capability of spreading antibiotics resistance.

Osborne and Davis (1987) Collected physico-chemical and biological samples from 12 sampling stations over a 13-month period to assess the effect of a small town's chlorinated sewage and a thermal discharge on the sheep river's macro-invertebrate communities. Jolley *et al* (1975-85) stated environmental and health concerns associated with chlorination of municipal sewage and industrial discharges were the imputes behind several international water chlorination conferences.

IAWPRE (1985) held a international Singapore conference between (28-31 may) together with (ESS) Engineering Society of Singapore and with (ASEAN) Association of SE Asian Nations. Conference on Industrial Water Technology, Treatment, Re-use and Re-cycling. All are extremely interested industrial development and concerned about the potentially adverse impact of this on the environment. The conference will deal with the range of industries most appropriate to the ASEAN Region. Discussion will centre on optimum techniques for water treatment and re-use.

Eloranta (1983) Studied the effect of cooling water discharge from one small thermal power plant on physical, chemical biological properties of water in a natural closed pond and principal changes in surface water. Davis (1948) carried out some studies on effect of industrial waste pollution in the lower communities with special reference to effect of copper. Kumar (1965) investigated the effect of certain toxic chemicals and mutagens on the growth of the blue green algae. Rao and Rani (1985) studied the effect of Mercuric chloride on photosynthesis and respiration on biopotential while Lackey (1942) studied the effect of distillery wastes on microscopic flora and fauna.

Kovacs *et. al.* (1992) done a survey of the biological and chemical characteristic of effluents without secondary treatment from Canadian news print mills. Webb (1985) describes the cause and prevention of sewage fungus growth in rivers receiving paper and board mills effluents. Abeliovich (1985) work has been done to develop a biological treatment for chemical industry effluent. Riedel *et. al.* (1990) studied a microbial amperometic sensor for the determination of biological oxygen demand BOD using Trichosporn cutaneum cells immobilized in poly vinyl alcohol has been developed. This sensor allows BOD measurement with very short response. The sensitivity and specificity was increased by incubation of the BOD Sensor.

Ubom and Tsuchiay (1988) investigate a simple fast and sensitive method comprising in on chromatography, eluent suppression columns and spectro photometric method was used to determine the iodine concentration in water sample. Rajczyk(1993) treated the waste water formed during the production of citric acid and foder yeast while Kim and

Anderson (1990) studied the effect of biological treatment on COD absorption of waste water containing eight metal cutting fluids. Jusiak *et.al.* (1984) used an algal rotating disk for biological purification of Nitrogen fertilizer industry effluents. Srivastava and Jain (1985) developed a solid membrane electrode selective to sulphate ions has been prepared from hydrous thorium oxide gel with polystyrene as binder for estimation of sulphate ions from industrial waste. Hynning (1996) developed a procedure for the separation, identification and quantification of industrial effluents. Garrote *et.al.* (1995) used a co-agulation/flocculation method for treatment of tannery effluent on which alkaline $FeCl_3$ is used as flocculating agent and $CaOH_2$ as base/precipitant. This method reduces the chemical oxygen demand COD by 87% producing a colourless, odorless waste water from the antibiotics production containing quantities of butyl acetate and butanol installation, heat exchange and stripping column are used and investigation shows a degree of purification of 99-100% at different stages of operation.

Laxen *et. al.* (1983) presented a scheme for the speciation of metals applied to the Pb, Cd and Cu. Suess (1982) gives a book review on Standardized method of water examination and sampling. Horne and Bennison (1987) produced a design for a three channel, recirculating laboratory, stream system, suitable for use in biological experimentation. Olach *et. al.* (1988) Study was performed to evaluate the influence of B-cyclodextrin (B-CD) Complexation on the toxicity of some pesticides and pesticides decomposition products in activated sludge system, Jenke and Frank (1985) modified the computer programme R-EDEQL- FPAK to allow for the production and simulation of chemical effect of mining aquous solution. Byrne *et. al.* (1988) gives an achievement to an adequate dilution. The rate of discharges effluent has been restricted on the basis of calculation made using a formula adopted by International Maritine Organization (IMO formerly IMCO). Srivastava (2002) presented a research review on Physico-chemical and micro biological characters of water mainly Ganga river while Murtaza (1998) carried out research on Physico-Chemical analysis of river water with reference to heavy metal pollution. Kumar (1995) Studied on pollution on river Majurukshi of South Bihar.

REFERENCES

1. Abeliovich, Aharon, 1985: Biological Treatment of Chemical Industry Effluents by Stabilization Ponds, Water Res. Vol. 19, No. 12, pp. 1947-1503.
2. Byrene, C.D, Law, R.J. and Thain, J.E., 1988: Measurement of the Dispersion of Liquid Industrial Waste Discharge in to a Wake of a Dumping Vessel, Water Res. Vol. 22, No. 12, pp. 1577-1584.
3. CBPCWP, 1985: Adsorption of Treated or Untreated Organic Load by the Soil in Term of BOD and COD, Indian Jour, Environ Health, Vol. 8. No. 1: pp. 131-135.
4. Davis, C.C., 1948 : Studies on the Effect of Industrial Pollution on the Lower Patapasco River Area. The Effect of Copper Pollution on Plankton, Chesapeak Biog. Lab. Pub. BO. 72, pp.11-12.
5. Duzzin, B., Pavoni and Doonozolo, R., 1988: Macro-invertebrate Communities and Sediments as Pollution Indicator for Heavy Metal in the River Adige (Italy), Receiving Industrial Effluents, Water, Res. Vol. 22, No. 1, pp. 1353-1358.
6. Edward, C.A., 1977: Persistent Pesticides in the Environment, C.R.C. Press, Cleveland, Ohio.
7. Eloranta, P.V. 1983: Physical and Chemical Properties of Pond Waters Receiving Warm Water Effluent from a Thermal Power Plant, Water Res. 17, pp. 133-140.
8. Garrote, J., Castro, Pablo and Bao, J. Manuel, 1995: Treatment of Tannery Effluents by a Two Step Coagulation Flocculation Process, Wat. Res. Vol. 29, No. 11, pp. 2600-2608.
9. Genjatulin, Valeevich Karl, 1990: Controlling Chemical and Biological Water Pollution by Quantitative, Bioassaying, Wat. Res. Vol. 24, No.5. pp. 539-541.
10. Ghazali, Al. R.M. and Jairwal, F.S., 1988: Antibiotic Resistance among Pollution Indicator Bacteria, Isolated from Al-khair River Bhagdad, Wat. Res. Vol. 22, No. 5, pp. 641.

11. Hood, D.W. 1966: In Fair Fridge, R.W. (ed.), The Encyclopaedia of Oceanography, Van Nostrand, N. Yark.

12. Hynning, Per- Ake, 1996: Separation, Identification and Quantification of Components of Industrial Effluents with Bio-cocentration Potential, Wat. Res. Vol. 30. No. 5, pp. 1103-1108.

13. IAWPRC, 1985: Held a International Singapore Conference on Industrial Water Technology, Treatment and Reuse of Waste Water, Wat. Res. Vol. 19, No. 4, pp. 543-545.

14. ICAR, 1967: Reports of the Special Committee on Harmful Effects of Pesticides, ICAR, New Delhi.

15. Jolley and Jolley, et al, 1975-85: Environmental Hazards due to Excessive Chlorincation Waste Water Treatment, Wat. Res. Vol. 2, No. 6, pp. 233-241.

16. Joy, C.M. 1989: Growth Response of Phyto Plankton Exposed to Industrial Effluents in River Priyar, Ph. D thesis Cochin University of Science and Technology, India.

17. Kolev, N. Semkov, Kr. and Darak Chiev, R., 1996: Butyl Acetate and Butancl Stripping from Waste Water in Antibiotic Production, Wat. Res, Vol. 30, No. 5, pp. 1312-1315.

18. Kumar, A. 1995: Studies on Pollution in River Majurukshi in South Bihar, Indian, Jour, Environ. Poll. 2 (I) pp. 21-26.

19. Kumar, H.D. 1965: Effects on Certain Tonic Chemicals and Mutagens on the Growth of the Blue Green Algal, can. Jour. Bot. Vol. 43, pp. 1523-1532.

20. Laxen H.P., Dunian and Harrison, M. Roy, 1983: Physico-Chemical Speciation of Selected Metals in the Treated Effluent of Lead-acid Battery Manufacture and in the Receiving River, Wat. Res., Vol. 17, pp. 71-80.

21. Malanchuck, J. Land Gruendling, O.K., 1973: Tixicity of Lead Nitrate on Algae Jour of Water, Air, Soil Pollution, Vol. 2, pp. 180-190.

22. Mackay, Goradon and Bino, J. Murad, 1988: Absorption of Pollutants from Waste Water into Activated Carbon based on Eternal Mass Transfer and Pore Diffusion, Wat. Res. Vol. 22, No. 3, pp. 279-286.

23. Millington, L.A. and Adams, N. 1988: The Influence of Growth Medium Composition on the Toxicity of Chemicals to Alage, Wat. Res. Vol. 22, No. 12; pp. 1593-1597.

24. Olach, J. Cserhati, Tibor & Szejti, J. 1988: B-Yclodextvin Enhanced Biological Detoxification of Industrial Waste Water, Wat. Res. Vol. 22, No. 11, pp. 1345-1351.

25. Osborne, L. Lewis and Davis, W. Ronald, 1987: The Effects of a Chlorinated Discharge and a Thermal Outfall on the Structure and Composition of the Aquatic Macro-invertebrate in the Sheep River, Alberta, Canada, Wat. Res., vol. 921, No. 8, pp. 913-921.

26. Palmer, C.M. 1969: A Composite Rating of Algae Tolerating Organic Pollution. Jour. Phycol. No. 5, pp. 78-82.

27. Prasad, G. 1998: Hydrology (in Hindi), Chandra Publication, Gorakhpur, 1st Edition.

28. Rajczyk, J.M. 1993: Fermentation of Food Industry, Water Waste under Dynamic Condition in an Anaerobic Biofilter up flow, Wat-Res. Vol. 27, No. 7, pp. 1257-1262.

29. Rao, J.C. and Rani, Sudha, K., 1985: Effect of Mercuric Chloride on Photosynthesis and Respiration of Scenedesums inci assauflus, Geobios, Vol. 12, pp. 82-83.

30. Riedel, K. Lange, K.P. and Scheller, F; 1990: A microbial Sensor for BOD Wat. Res. vol. 24, No. 7, pp. 883-887.

31. Robert, D., Barshied and Hussan, 1974: Physical and Chemical Treatment of Septic Tank Effluent, Jour. WPCF, Vol. 46, No. 10, pp. 2347-54.

32. Salim, R. 1983: Absorption of Lead on the Suspended Particles of River Water. Wat. Res. Vol. 17, No. 4, pp. 423-429.

33. Sastry, C.A., 1977: Treatment of Waste Water from Small Paper Mill without Soda Recovery, A Case Study, Indian Jour. Environ. Health (19) p. 346.

34. Siegal. S.M. and Eshlcman, A. 1975: Chlorine, Bioaches; A Significant long-term Source of Mercury Pollution. Jour of Water, Air, Soil Pollution, Vol. 4, pp. 355-365.

35. Singh, P.K. 1975; Fertilizer Tolerance of Blue-green Algae and their Effect of Heteroeyst Differentiation, Phykos, Vol. 14, pp. 81-88.

36. Srivastava, K.S. and Jain, K.C. 1985: Estimation of Sulphate ions in Water and Industrial Wastes using a Solid State Membrane Electrode, Wat. Res., Vol. 19, No. 1, pp. 53-56.

37. Srivastava, M.L., 2002: Physico-Chemical and Microbiological Characters of Water, Daya, Publishing House, New Delhi.

38. Ubom, H. Gregory and Tsuchiya, Y, 1988: Determination of Iodine in Natural Water by Jon Chromatography, Wat. Res., vol. 27, No. 11, pp. 1455-1458.

39. Webb, L.J., 1985: An Investigation in to the Occurrence of Sewage Fungus in Rivers Containing Paper Mill Effluents, Wat., Res. Vol. 19, No. 8, pp. 955-959.

CHAPTER

6

Water Resources and Its Management

Shardendu Kislaya and Madhavi Gupta

Introduction

Water resources is the backbone of life. This is not only an essential thing for our survival but also an auspicious factor for the development of country. It is universal truth that water is the most valuable and treated as life supporting resources of the universe. Almost the five elements it is the water corresponding where there is life. Although water is a renewable resource on global earth but its beneficial reserves in nature is limited. Water management in India is the burning aspect of study for the healthy future prospects as well as sustainable development. The major objective of this effort is to examine the occurrence surface and ground water resources along with its availability, utilisation, requirement and the problems raised for the management of water resources in India.

Water Resources in India

India is one of the richest country in water resource on the globe. Mean annual rainfall of the country is about 110 cm. which in turn stored as 3700 Billion cubic meter (BCM) in which 1869 BCM flow in river, 1250 BCM is being used in evaporation and remaining 581 BCM is found in saturated form. The kinds of water resources are treated as surface, ground, atmospheric and oceanic of the country in which surface and ground water is so important for socio-economic development. Another classification of water may be presented as (i) Water in liquid form, which may be seen in ponds, lakes, rivers and seas or oceans. It may be defined as stored water as registered in ponds and lakes and also as moving water draining in river, (ii) water in gaseous form, and it is measured in atmosphere with recognition of water vapour, (iii) Water in solid form, as it is recognised on the top of the high hills and the polar areas in view of ice and (iv) Water in soil saturated form, marked below the ground surface. In all respect water creates like and controls life and natural system. Without water no chance of existence as truly stated 'Bin Pani Sab Soon'.

Surface Water in the Country

Surface water occupies in the rivers and ponds wherein major rivers as the Ganga, Indus, Brahmaputra, Godavari, Krishna, Cauvery, Pennar, Mahanadi, Brahmani, Sabarmati, Mahi, Narmada, Tapi and Suvarnarekha may be nominated in Indian context. These rivers are provided about 690 BCM water potential for use to country (Sharma, S.K., 2003). The total quantity of Indian river water is estimated about 6% of the whole quantity of global river water. Water harvesting capacity in the country is about 147 BCM at present which is 08.47% of whole water of the river basins. Although mean annual rainfall of the country is about 110 cm. yet the distribution of the rainfall is highly adequate (**Figure 6.1**). Northern area of Jammu and Kashmir, Western Rajasthan and Kuchchh shows below to 35 cm. mean annual rainfall. Beside its the humid zone of Meghalaya state shows more than 800 cm. mean rainfall annually. The remaining part of India receives mean annual rainfall between 35 cm to 800 cm. It is notable that about one-third part of the country occupies mean annual rainfall between 100 cm. to 200 cm. and about one-fourth terrain accumulates between 70 cm to 100 cm. The Western coast of Peninsular India and North-eastern India alongwith some scattered areas holds between 200 cm to 400 cm. mean annual rainfall. The Northern Arunachal, Northern Meghalaya along with some areas of Kerala indicates mean annual rainfall between 400 cm to 800 cm. In the last, between 35 to 70 cm. mean annual rainfall represented in Eastern

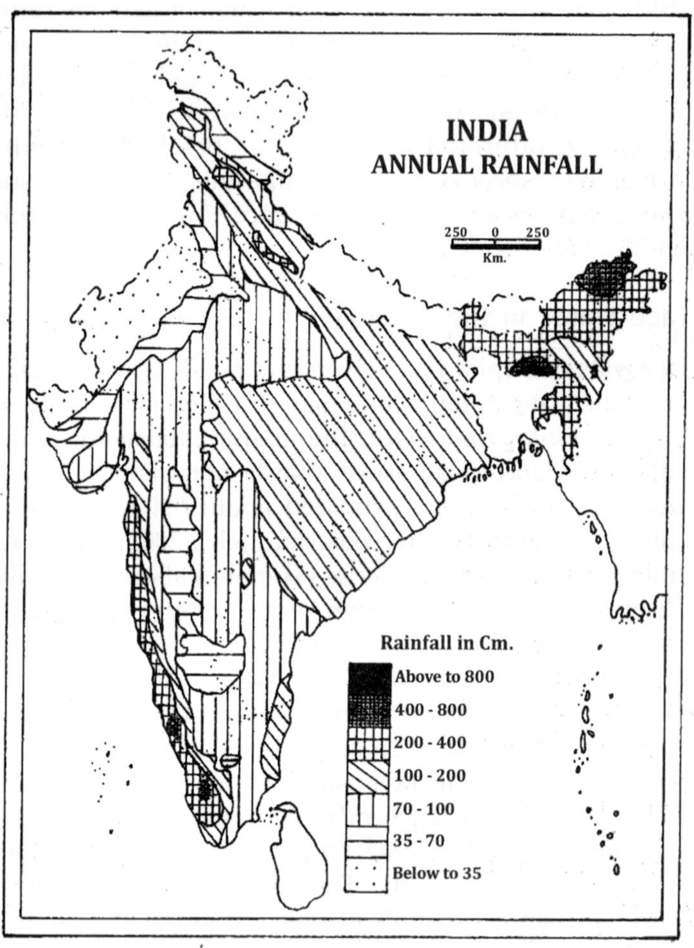

Fig. 6.1.

Rajasthan, Middle Gujarat, Middle Maharashtra and Northern Karnataka states. The discontinuity of rainfall distribution from place to place is greatly responsible for flood and draught hazards as problems of drinking water, irrigational disparities etc.

Ground Water in the Country

Ground water is the major source of drinking water and modern irrigation in India. The annual replenishable ground

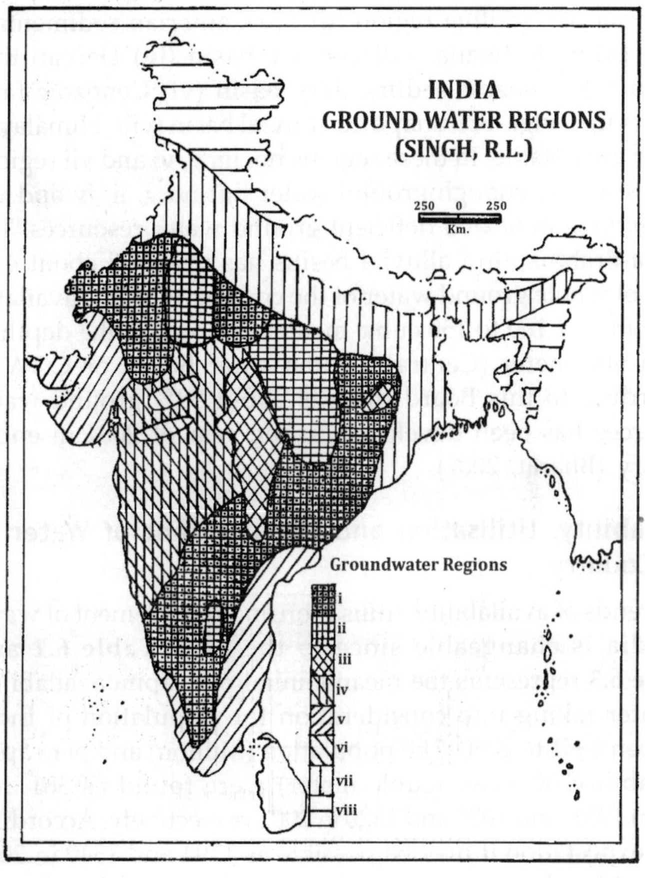

Fig. 6.2.

water resource for the country was expected as 433 BCM in the March 2004 in which 67% share included by rainfall and 33% share included by canal seepage, return flow from the irrigation, seepage from waterbodies and artificial recharge due to water harvesting structures. Notable that the climatic conditions, relief, geological structure and hydrological circumstances are the major responsible factor for ground water resources (Gautam, A., 2007). The ground water regions of India is in nature diversified. Singh, R.L. has divided India into 08 Ground water regions (**Figure 6.2**) in which (i) Pre-Cambrian Crystalline region (ii) Pre-Cambrian sedimentary basin (iii) Gondwana sedimentary basin (iv) Deccan trap region (v) Cenozoic sedimentary basin (vi) Cenozoic fault basin (vii) Ganga-Brahmaputra alluvial basin (viii) Himalayan region are notable. In these regions no. iii, v, vi and vii regions have reserved enough ground water but no. i, ii, iv and viii region have indicated deficient ground water resources. The Ganga-Brahmaputra alluvial basins has reserved about 45% share of whole ground water of the country which is available at the rate of 100 to 150 cubic meter per hour till the depth of about 600 meter (Central groundwater Board or CGWB). According to this Board there is about 58% ground water resources has been developed in the year of 2004 in entire country (Bharat, 2007).

Availability, Utilisation and Requirement of Water in the Country

The trends of availability, utilisation and requirement of water in India is changeable since to the past. **Table 6.1** and **Figure 6.3** represents the mean annual per capita availability of water taking into consideration the population of India between 1951 to 2050. The population (Million) and per capita availability of water (cubic meter) were found as 361 and 5177 in 1951, and 1027 and 1820 in 2001 respectively. According to an expectation it may be possible as 1394 and 1340 in 2025 and, 1640 and 1140 in the year of 2050 (Singh, R.D., Arora, M.

Table 6.1 : Mean Annual Per Capita availability of Water v/s Population of India: 1950-2050

Year	Population (Million)	Mean annual Per capita availability of water (cubic meter)
1951	0361	5177
2001	1027	1820
2025*	1394	1340
2050*	1640	1140

*Expected.

Source: Singh, R.D., Arora, M. and Kumar, R., 'Yojana', July 2010, p. 37 and Bharat, 2007, p. 890.

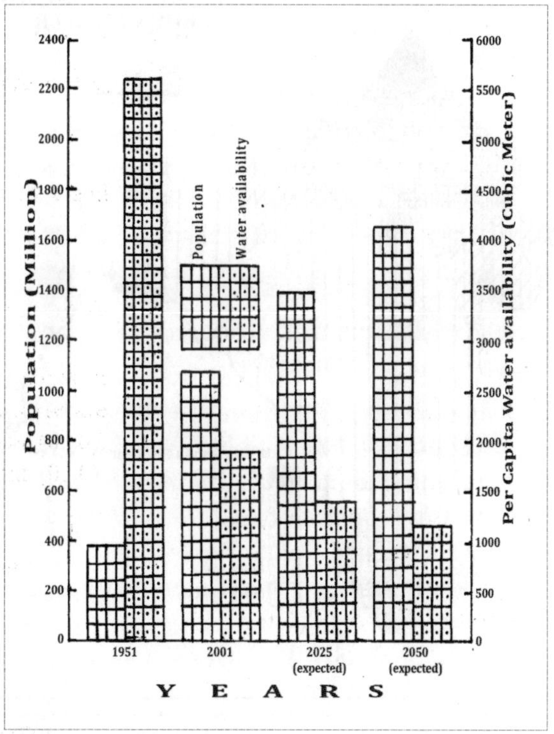

Fig. 6.3. Mean Annual Per Capita Availability of Water and its Relationship with Population of India 1951-2050

and Kumar, R., 2010). In the duration of last 100 years the population will expected about 455 per cent and per capita water availability will be minimised about 455 per cent also. Accent of population growth and descent of water availability in forthcoming future is an aspect of concern.

The **Figure 6.4** indicates the utilisation of potential of groundwater in the states and Union Territories of India. The highest (above to 80%) potential is indicated in Punjab and Delhi, and the lowest (below to 20%) is marked in Jammu

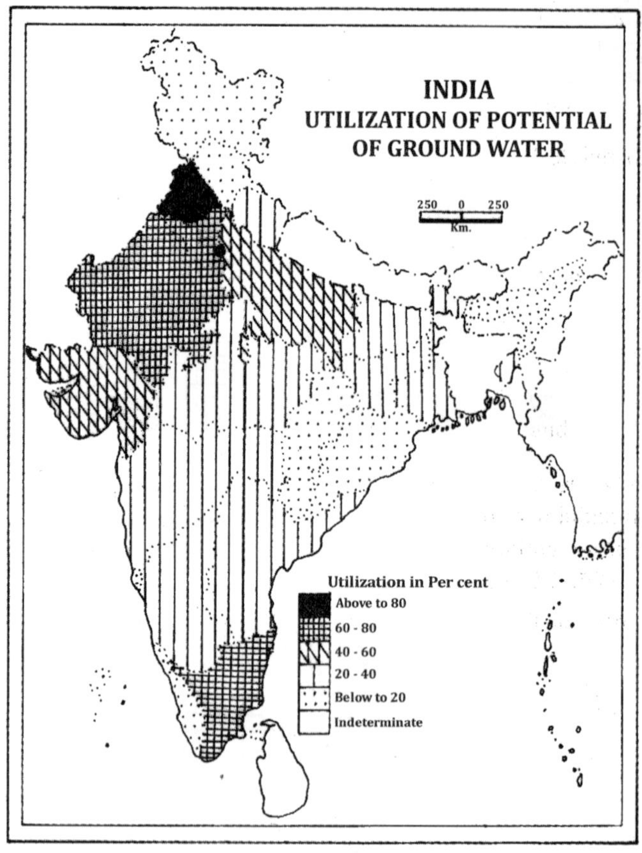

Fig. 6.4.

and Kashmir, Himachal Pradesh, Assam, Chhattisgarh, Odisha, Kerala and Goa. Between 60 to 80% potential of groundwater is highlighted in Haryana, Rajasthan and Tamil Nadu and 40 to 60% is obtained in Uttar Pradesh and Gujarat. Beside its 20 to 40% potential is founded in Uttarakhand, Bihar, Jharkhand, West Bengal, Tripura, Madhya Pradesh, Maharashtra, Karnataka and Andhra Pradesh as the larger part (about one-third) of the country. It is notable that 06 states namely as Arunachal Pradesh, Nagaland, Manipur, Mizoram, Meghalaya and Sikkim are in determined (Sharma, S.K., 2003). The utilisation of water resource is interrelated with various sectors an irrigational domestic, industrial, energy and others.

The sector-wise current and expected annual water requirement in India (BCM) between year of 200 and 2050 is given in **Table 6.2** and **Figure 6.5**. The attached data of year 2000 is upto mark and the year of for 2010, 2025 and 2050, it is expected by compendium of Agricultural Statistics, 2002. In the year of 2000 the whole water requirement in India was

Table 6.2 : Sector-wise Current and Expected Annual Water Requirement in India (B.C.M.) 2000-2050

Sector-wise uses of Water	Year			
	2000	2010*	2025*	2050*
Irrigation	541	688	910	1072
Domestic	42	56	73	102
Industry	08	12	23	63
Energy	02	05	15	130
Others	41	52	72	80
All Total	**634**	**813**	**1093**	**1447**

B.C.M. = Billion cubic meter

*Expected

Source: Compendium of agricultural statistics, 2002, MoSPI by Bordoloi, B. and Bordoloi, E.S., 'Yojana', July 2010, p. 12.

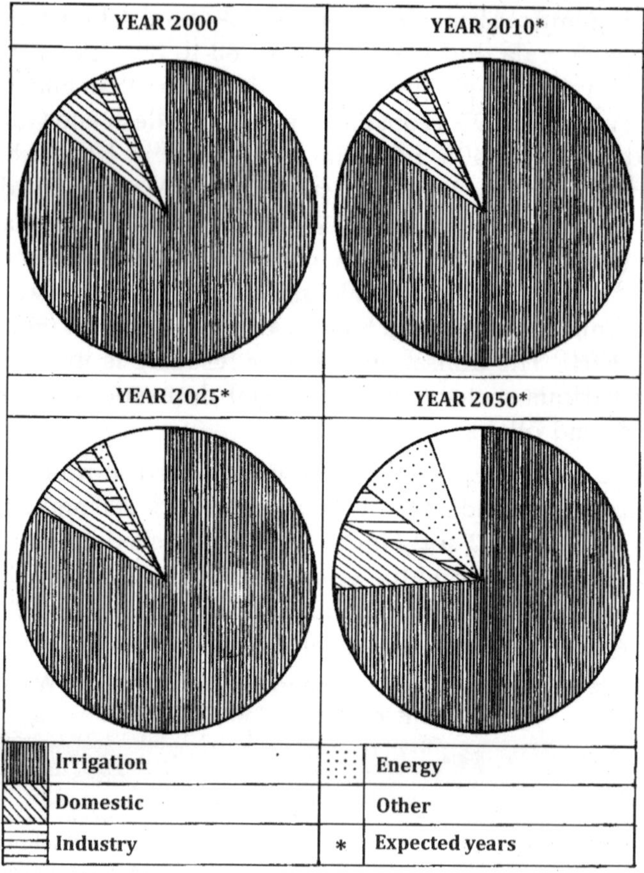

Fig. 6.5. Sector-wise Current and Expected Annual Water Requirement in India (Billion Cubic Meter) 2000-2050

634 BCM in which 541 BCM (85.33%) in irrigation, 42 BCM (06.62%) in domestic, 08 BCM (01.26% in industry, 02 BCM (0.032%) in energy and 41 BCM (06.47% in other sectors have been used. The whole water requirement in the year of 2010, 2025 and 2050 may be possible as 813,1093 and 1447 BCM respectively (Pandey, A., 2007). Time to time increasing of water requirement in India is the indicative of question mark for water supply and other use. Between the duration of 2000

to 2050 it may be increased as 228% touching dangerous level. In these three base expected years (2010, 2025 and 2050) sector wise water requirement in expected in irrigation as 688, 910 and 1072 BCM (84.63%, 83.20% and 74.08%), in domestic use as 56, 73 and 102 BCM (06.89%), 06.68% and 07.05%), in industry as 12, 23 and 63 BCM (01.48%, 02.10% and 04.35%) in energy as 05, 15 and 130 BCM (0.62%, 01.37% and 08.98%) and in other sectors as 52, 72 and 80 BCM (06.40%, 06.59% and 05.53%) respectively. In the duration of the half century (2000-2050) increaseness in water requirement in various sectors like irrigation as 198%, domestic purposes as 243%, industry as 788%, energy as 6500% and in other sectors as 195% is expected. The highest demands in energy sector and lowest demands in other sectors is expected in the duration of base years. The gap between supply and demand of water is expected to rise as about 50% by 2030 with demands doubling from current level of 700 BCM to around 1498 BCM and supply barely reaching 744 BCM (Yojana, July 2010).

Problems of Water Resources

The major problems of water resources are its high consumption, increasing population around the resource base and disturbance in hydrological cycle by global warming. These problems are caused by over population, industrialisation, Green revolution (I) and modernisation. Our country has covered 02.45 per cent of landed area and 04 per cent of water resources of the global volume with respect to 16.87 per cent population as a whole (Pandey, A. and Pandey, V., 2007). According to annual population growth rate of 01.93 per cent of 2001 census the population in advance is expected as 1640 million with respect to water requirement expected as 1447 BCM by year 2050. According to decadal estimate between 1995-2004 of Central Ground Water Board (CGWB) of India there were 839 units of 'over critical', 226 units of 'critical' and 550 units of 'semi critical' category of exploitation in all 5723 estimated units by Blocks/Mandals/

Talukas of India which is the indicator of water problems of the present and future (Bharat, 2007). Although India is saturated with 110 cm. of annual rainfall but about half part of total area of the country is declared as water deficient region (**Figure 6.6**) in which cold region (arid and semi arid) and hot region (arid and semi arid) is located in the north and west part of the country. In the water deficient region

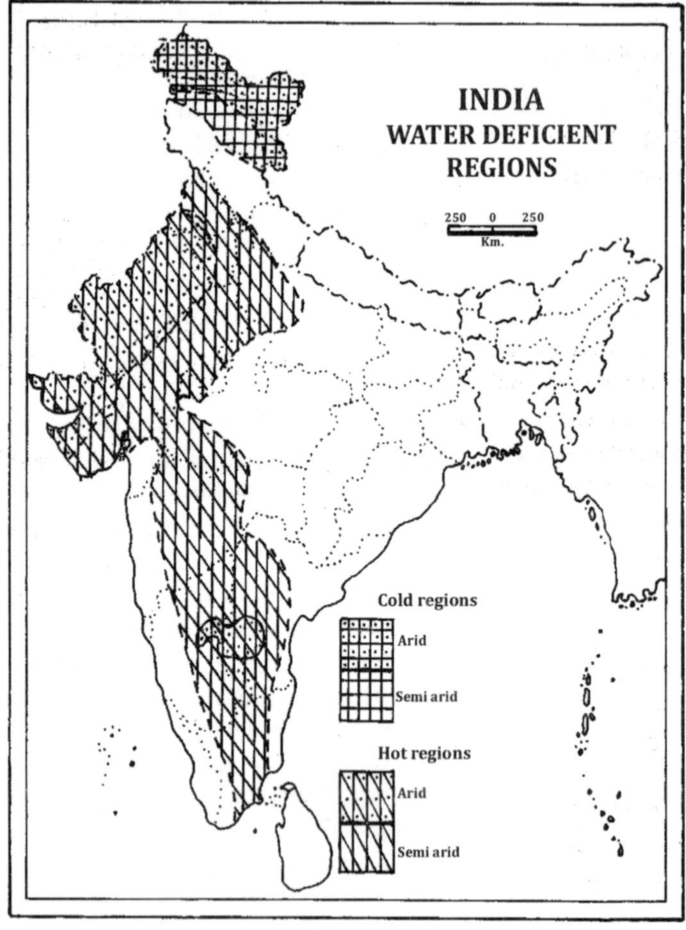

Fig. 6.6.

North-east Jammu and Kashmir, Haryana, Punjab, Chandigarh, Delhi, Western U.P., Rajasthan, Gujarat, South-Western M.P., Middle Maharashtra, Eastern Karnataka, South-Western Andhra Pradesh and Middle Tamil Nadu states/U.Ts. are enclosed (Sharma, S.K., 2003).

Pollution is one of the most burning problems of the water. The United States Department of Health, Education and Welfare has divided the water pollutants into 08 principal categories as (i) sewage and waste (ii) infections agents (iii) plant nutrients (iv) particulates (v) mineral and chemical substances (vi) heat (vii) radio active substances and (viiii) organic chemical exotics (Franke and Franke, 1975). According to experts and scientists about 70 per cent water in the whole available water of India is to be polluted. At present, more or less all major rivers are polluted by the interferes of population and their activities. Although Central Pollution Control Board (CPCB) has established a network of 1700 monitoring stations in 27 states and 06 U.Ts. yet the problems of water pollution in river is not being solve. Notable that the monitoring networks of CPCB, covers 353 rivers with 979 stations, 107 lakes with 117 stations, 44 ponds, 09 tanks, 14 canals, 15 creeks/sea water, 18 drains and 491 wells in the country (Bharat, 2007).

The global warming is also a prime problem of water which in turn has caused uncertainity of rainfall, deglaciation and sea level change. It is well known that India is a monsoony country so the continuity and regularity of monsoon is the most important factor for the future of the nation. According to the latest report of the intergovernmental Panel on Climatic Change (IPCC) a 20 per cent rise in rainfall during summer monsoon over all states of India except Punjab, Rajasthan and Tamil Nadu is recorded which show the slight decrease and increase in extremes of highest and lowest precipitation particularly over Western Coasts and Central-Western part of the country. Deglaciation on the crown of India (Himalaya) is rapidly due to warming the existence of atmosphere of glaciers. Himalayan region has about 10 thousand glaciers covering an area of about 38 thousand square km. (Geological Survey of India, 2007). The glaciated area of 2077 square km. measured in 1962 has been reduced due to global warming and currently it has been noticed as 1628 square km. The melting of glaciers percentage thus noted as 21. Sea level change is also the result of global warmings well as climatic change. At present, sea level rise could be raise a wide range of issues in the coastal areas. According to 'The Energy and Resources Institute (TERI), the potential impact the one meter sea level rise include inundation of 5763 square km. in India (Singh, R.D., Arona, M. and Kumar, A., 2010). It is estimated that odisha, Andhra Pradesh, Tamil Nadu, Karnataka, Kerala, Goa, Maharashtra, Gujarat, West Bengal etc. States may be affected with waterprone hazard in near future and about 10 crores of population may be migrated from there.

Management of Water Resources

The management of water resources is compulsory on two dimensions *e.g.* qualitative and quantitative. The qualitative management is performed under the provision of 'The Water (Prevention and control of Pollution) Act, 1974. To maintain and restore the wholesomeness of national aquatic resources by prevention and control of pollution in the fundamental objectives of the water Act, 1974, the CPCB is designated the best use of primary water quality criteria (**Table 6.3**). The primary water quality criteria for designated best uses is classified into 5 classes as A, B, C, D and E in which Class A denotes the drinking water source without conventional treatment but after disinfections, Class B indicates the outdoor bathing (organised), Class C highlights the drinking water source with conventional treatment followed by disinfections, Class D follows the propagation of wildlife and fisheries, and Class E inaugurates the irrigation, industrial cooling and control of waste disposal (Gautam, S.P. and Bhardwaj, R.M., 2010).

Table 6.3 : Primary Water Quality Criteria for Designated Best Uses

Class	Designated best use	Criteria
A.	Drinking water source without conventional treatment but after disinfections	pH between 6.5 and 8.5 Total coliform organism MPN/100 ML shall be 50 or less Dissolved oxygen 6 MG/1 or more Biochemical oxygen demand 2 MG/1 or less
B.	Outdoor bathing (organised)	pH between 6.5 and 8.5 Total coliform organism MPN/100 ML shall be 500 or less Dissolved oxygen 5 MG/1 or more Biochemical oxygen demand 3 MG/1 or less
C.	Drinking water source with conventional treatment followed by disinfections	pH between 6.0 and 9.0 Total caliform organism MPN/100 ML shall be 5,000 or less Dissolved oxygen 4 MG/1 or more Biochemical oxygen demand 3 MG/1 or less
D.	Propagation of wild life, fisheries	pH between 6.5 and 8.5 dissolved oxygen 4 MG/1 or more Free ammonia (as N) 1.2 MG/1 or less
E.	Irrigation, industrial cooling, controlled waste disposal	pH between 6.0 and 8.5 Electrical connectivity less than 2250 micro MHOS/CM Sodium absorption ratio less than 26 Boron less than 2 MG/1

Source: Central Pollution Control Board (C.P.C.B.), Gautam S.P. and Bhardwaj, R.M., 'Yojana', July 2010, p. 14.

The holistic responsibility of water resource management for irrigational, domestic, industrial, hydropower potential and other needs with prudence is essential for everybody in India. It is writable that about 75 per cent share of whole mean annual rainfall (110 cm) is precipitated in 300 hours of 3 months, whose 85 per cent of rainwater is flowed into the sea/ocean by the tributaries and rivers (Madhujyotsna, 2006).

It is an unwanted result churing by mismanagement. India has about 5 lakhs tanks and ponds most of them are dumped by deposits. Renovate all the ponds is demand of today for water harvesting as well as recharging. In this way, it is an unique news that 'Mahatma Gandhi National Rural Employment Guarantee Act (MGNREGA) is being implemented for the above purpose. During the 11th Five Yearly Plan, artificial recharge projects of the Government are being taken up by the CCWB under the ongoing central sector scheme of the ground water management and regulation in priority areas as over-exploited and critical areas, urban areas showing steep grand water level decline draught prone and water deficient areas, coastal areas and submountainous/ hilly areas (Jha, B.M. and Jain, R.C., 2010).

In our country, the water management techniques follow subsidized micro-irrigation, mandatory rain water harvesting, community based watershade management, promotion of water conserving practices as system of the rice intensification (Bordoloi, B. and Bordoloi, E.S., 2010). The several Non-Governmental Organisations (NGOs) and Voluntary Organisations (VOs) have presented the vital role for water resources management programmes. It is good news that those organisations are actively engaged in artificial recharges and rainwater harvesting techniques with respect to underground water resource management. The role of symposiums, workshops, Seminars, Conferences, rallies and Public movement are also the most impressive efforts for water resource management.

Conclusion

The water resource is an unique gift of the Nature. It is lifeline element. In view of increasing population the decreasing trend of water resources is unhealthy for coming/future generation of mankind. The deviation between water demand and availability have resulted low level of per capita availability of water resources. These problems have become barrier before sustainable development of country. In all respect the management of water resources should be practised on a priority basis.

REFERENCES

1. Bharat, 2007: Director, Publishing Division, Ministry of Information and Broadcasting, Govt. of India, C.G.O. Complex, Lodhi Road, New Delhi-110 003, pp. 890-901.
2. Bardoloi, B. and Bordoloi, E.S., July 2010: '*Water Security in India*', a Paper Published in 'Yojana' Monthly Journal, Ministry of Information and Broadcasting, Yojana Bhawan, Sansad Marg, New Delhi, pp. 9-12.
3. Central Pollution Control Board (C.P.C.B.), Arjun Nagar, Delhi.
4. Compendium of Agricultural Statistics, 2002, MoSPI.
5. Franke, R.G. and Franke, D.N., 1975: *Man and the Changing Environment*, Holt, Rinehart and Winston, New York, p. 311.
6. Gautam, A., 2007: *Bharat ka Vrihad Bhoogol*, Sharda Pustak Bhawan, 11, University Road, Allahabad-2, pp. 66-67.
7. Gautam, S.P. and Bhardwaj, R.M.; July 2010: 'Vigil Over Water Quality' a Paper Published in 'Yojana' Monthly Journal, Ministry of Information and Broadcasting, Yojana Bhawan, Sansad Marg, New Delhi, p. 14.
8. Geological Survey of India, 2007, Kolkata.
9. Jha, B.M. and Jain, R.C.; July, 2010: 'Artificial Recharge of Groundwater—the Indian Experience' a Paper Published in 'Yojana' monthly Journal, Ministry of Information and Broadcasting, Yojana Bhawan, Sansad Marg, New Delhi, pp. 19-20.
10. Madhujyotsna, March-April, 2006: 'Ghatta Pani-barhti Marg', a Paper Published in 'Bhoogol Aur Aap' Journal, IRIS Publication Pvt. Ltd. 111/9 Aruna Asaf Ali Marg, Kishangarh, Vasant Kunj, New Delhi-110 070, pp. 17-18.
11. Oxford School Atlas, 2000: 'Annual Rainfall', Oxford University Press, YMCA Library Building, Ji Singh Road, New Delhi-110 001, p. 25.
12. Pandey, A.; 2007: Bharat Ka Jansankhya Bhoogol, Discovery Publishing House Pvt. Ltd., 4831/24, Ansari Road, Daryaganj, New Delhi-110 002, pp. 194-195.

13. Pandey, A. and Pandey, V., 2007: 'Vishwik tapan' a Paper Published in 'Manav Evam Paryawaran', Ed. Prasad G., Pandey, A. and Kislaya, S., Discovery Publishing House Pvt. Ltd., 4831/24, Ansari Road, Daryaganj, New Delhi-110 002, pp. 56-58.
14. Sharma, S.K., July, 2003: Bharat: Log Aur Arthvyawastha, Ed. Mishra, R.P., N.C.E.R.T. Sri Arvind Marg, New Delhi-110 016, p. 67-70.
15. Singh, R.D., Arora, M. and Kumar, R., July 2010: 'Impact of Climatic Change on Water Resources' a Paper Published in 'Yojana' Monthly Journal, Ministry of Information and Broadcasting, Yojana Bhawan, Sansad Marg, New Delhi, pp. 37-39.
16. The Energy and Resources Institute (T.E.R.I.), New Delhi.
17. Yojana, July 2010: A Development Monthly Journal, Ministry of Information and Broadcasting, Yojana Bhawan, Sansad Marg, New Delhi, p. 3.

CHAPTER

7

Physico-Chemical Analysis of The River Water

Introduction

The present research paper elucidates the physico-chemical analysis of Gomti river (tributary stream of River Ganga) water specially in district Sultanpur, Uttar Pradesh wherein Physico-chemical parameters like temperature, PH, Alkalinity, BOD, COD, dissolved oxygen and suspended solids and heavy metals like lead and chromium have been measured in river water Gomati at Chandipur, Isauli and Gola Ghat sampling stations located along the river. The causes and effects of these components appeared in river water is shown through tables and diagrams.

Introduction to Area Surveyed

The study area Sultanpur lies on the both sides of river Gomati between latitude 25° 59′ north and 24°40′ north and longitude 81°32′ East and 42′ East. The extreme length of the district (avoiding nearly framed district CSM nagar) is about 129 km. and the extreme breadth from north to south about 61 km. The main channel of the district is the Gomati (Fig. 7.1). The three sampling stations like Chandipur Ghat (S1), Isauli Ghat (S2) and Gola ghat (S3) are located along the right flank of the river between Musafirkhana Tahsil head quarter and sudar

Sultanpur of about 35 km away to each others. The river is one of the meandoring river (Ghoomati Nadi) and restores too much physico-chemicals and heavy metals from its neighbouring states. Most of the pollutants join the said river near Lucknow city.

Result and Discussion

Water quality deterioration causing pollution is the greatest crime of mankind against himself with the rapid pace of industrialisation. Effluents have posed a serious threat to the vast and varied resources of the country. Water quality of major river system is getting rapidly deraded due to massive discharges of municipal waste and industrial waste of diverse origin.

Impurities in traces are universal in water. We are concerned with the quality of water when its physical- chemical characteristics or its quality deteriorates and become harmful to man, his household needs or other aquatic ecosystem, such a situation is referred to as aquatic pollution.

In the light of above effective management and control of water pollution and becoming increasingly important for sustainable development and human welfare, because industrial effluent discharged into water bodies are responsible for a number of mortalities and incapacitations in the world.

The character of effluent studies included river water temperature, pH, alkalinity, Bio Chemical Oxygen Demand (B.O.D.) Chemical Oxygen Demand (C.O.D.) dissolved oxygen (D.O.) and suspended solids respectively. Heavy metals like lead and chromium were also observed. Sampling was done from January 2002 to December 2003 by months. The observations showing monthly variations in Physico-chemical parameters have been depicted by **Table 7.1** to 3-9 and **Fig. 7.1** to 3-9 respectively.

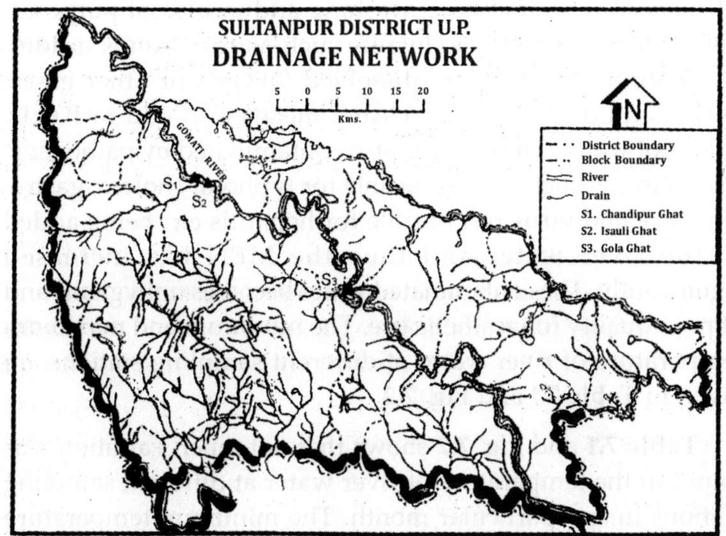

Fig. 7.1.

The physico-chemical analysis of river water is also mentioned in the previous research works of Ambush (1990), Clesari (1989), Das and Pandey (1978) De (1984), Gujral, Sharma and Yadav (1992), Hasan (1992), Mishra, Singh and Maladean (1990), Murtaza (1998), Ray, Singh and Sehgal (1966), Shukla, Tripathi, Rajanikant and Pandey (1989), Sikaandar and Tripathi (1984), Singh and Singh (1994), Singh, Choudhry and Kalchaur (1982), Singh and Singh (1995), Sinha and Banerjee (1987), Srivastava (2002) Tiwari, and Trivedi and Goel (1984) respectively.

The Physico-Chemical characteristics of Gomati river water may be discussed in the following manner–

Analysis of Physico-Chemical Parameters

1. ***Temperature:*** Temperature is one of the most important physical aspect of water pollution which may be harmful as a primary pollution and indirectly through driving out the D.O. and causing fish death. The physico-chemical properties of water contributes in the increase of B.O.D. value. The water become unfit for drinking, washing and industrial purposes. The chemical aquatic pollutants such as total solids, acidity or alkalinity, pH change, dissolved Oxygen or other gases, metals and other ions etc. Heavy metals also add in B.O.D. values of water. The water is also contaminated by pathogenic microbes *e.g.* bacteria responsible for typhoid, cholera, gastro, dysentry and virus responsible for hepatitis etc. being added to the river water and thus the MPN has increased significantly. The contaminated water becomes unhygienic and of poor quality for aesthetic use. The minimum and maximum temperature of river water at different sampling stations are given in **Table 7.1** and **Fig. 7.2**.

Table 7.1 and **Fig. 7.2** shows that not much variation was found in the temperature of river water at different sampling stations in any particular month. The minimum temperature as 20.50°C is recorded in the month of January and December 2002, and 2003 at S_3 and S_1, S_2 and S_3 respectively. The maximum temperature was recorded in the month of June 2002 at S_1, S_1 and S_3 as 27.3°, 27.5° and 28.5°C respectively.

Table 7.1: Range of Temperature at different Sampling Stations

Sampling Stations	Temperature (in O°c)			
	Minimum		Maximum	
	2002	2003	2002	2003
S_1 Chandipur Ghat	20.6 (Jan.)	20.5 (June)	27.3 (June)	28.6 (June)
S_2 Isauli Ghat	21.0 (Jan & Dec)	20.5 (Jan & Dec.)	27.5 (June)	28.9 (June)
S_3 Gola Ghat	20.5 (Jan. & Dec.)	20.5 (Dec.)	28.5 (June)	28.7 (June)

During the session 2003, it is found as 28.5°C, 28.9°C and 28.7°C in the month of June at Chandipur Ghat, Isauli Ghat and Gola Ghat respectively. Thus, the maximum temperature (28.9°C) was recorded at 82 in the month of June 2003.

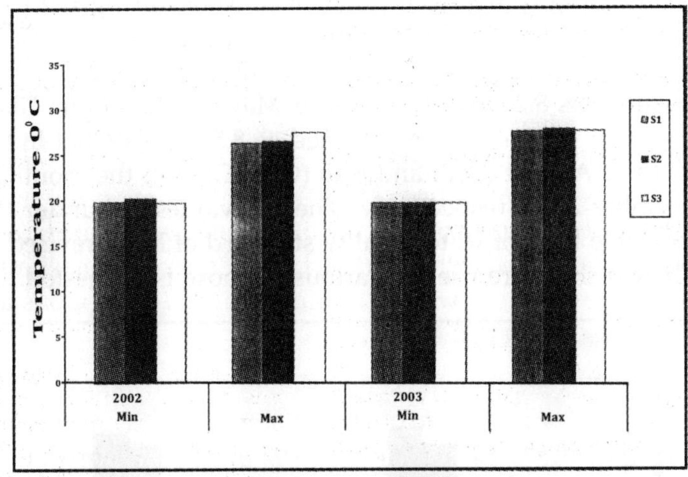

Fig. 7.2. Range of Temperature

2. pH: pH measurement is one of the most important and frequently used test in water chemistry. Every phase of water supply and waste water treatment *e.g.* acid base neutralization, water softening, precipitation, coagulation, disinfection and corrosion control is pH dependent. The minimum and maximum values of pH have been given in **Table 7.2** and **Fig. 7.3**.

Table 7.2 : Range of pH value at different Sampling Stations

Sampling Stations	Temperature (in O°c)			
	Minimum		Maximum	
	2002	2003	2002	2003
S_1 Chandipur Ghat	7.55 (June)	7.15 (Feb)	8.22 (May)	8.20 (Nov)
S_2 Isauli Ghat	7.83 (July)	7.35 (Feb)	8.35 (April)	8.30 (Dec)
S_3 Gola Ghat	7.80 (Jan)	7.20 (March)	8.58 (Aug)	8.40 (Dec)

The above discussion reveals the fact that the pH of river water was usually on alkaline side. It was observed generally in increasing order from January to May during both the years. During the year 2002, the minimum pH value (7.55) was observed at S_1 in June while in the year 2003, it is measured as 8.22 in the month of May at Chandipur Ghat. Maximum pH values are recorded as 8.58 (Gola Ghat in the month of August 2002) and 8.40 (Gola Ghat in the month of December 2003) respectively. The pH values are under the acceptable limit of water quality standard of India revised in 1975 and therefore use for various purpose is suggested.

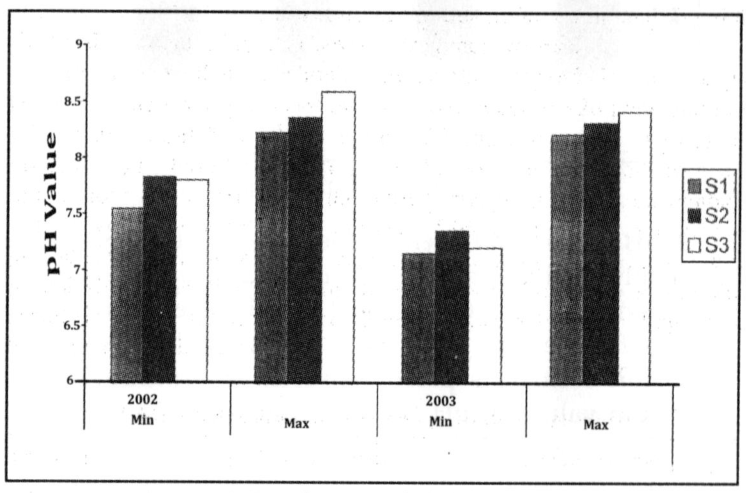

Fig. 7.3. Range of pH

3. ***Alkalinity:*** Alkalinity of water is its acid, neutralizing capacity. It is a measure of an aggregate property of water. The minimum and maximum values are given in **Table 7.3** and **Fig. 7.4.**

On the basis of the after description, it is pertinent to point out that the alkalinity of river water is increasing day by day. Mimimum alkalinity was observed as 1500 (Sept. 2002) at Chandipur Ghat and 1510 (September 2003) at Isauli and

Chandipur Ghat. The maximum alkalinity (2195) during the months of May 2002 and June 2003 was recorded at Gola Ghat and Isauli Ghat respectively. Lower value of alkalinity was observed in rainy season probably due to addition of rain water in the river. It was found to be maximum in the month of May & June at most of the sampling stations. Gola Ghat shows maximum alkalinity during both the year of Study period.

Table 7.3 : Range of Alkalinity at different Sampling Stations

Sampling Stations	Alkalinity (µg/L)			
	Minimum		Maximum	
	2002	2003	2002	2003
S_1 Chandipur Ghat	1500 (Sept.)	1510 (Sept.)	2165 (June)	2180 (May)
S_2 Isauli Ghat	1505 (Sept)	1510 (Sept)	2175 (June)	2195 (June)
S_3 Gola Ghat	1510 (Sept.)	1580 (Sept)	2195 (May)	2195 (May)

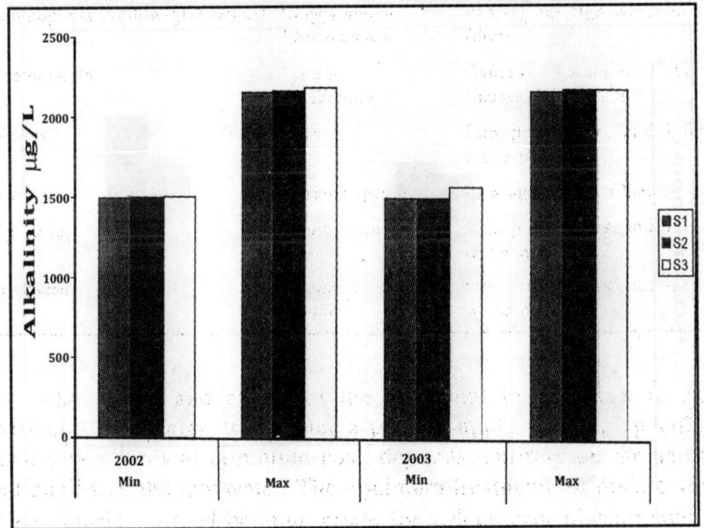

Fig. 7.4. Range of Alkalinity µg/L

4. Bio Chemical Oxygen Demand (B.O.D.): BOD is the measure of organic matter present in a water sample and can be defined as the amount of Oxygen required by the micro-organic in stabilizing the biologically degradable organic matter under aerobic condition. **Table 7.4** and **Fig. 7.5**. Show the minimum and maximum values of BOD.

Table 7.4 : Range of Bio-Chemical Oxygen Demand (B.O.D.) at different Sampling Stations

Sampling Stations	B.O.D.			
	Minimum		Maximum	
	2002	2003	2002	2003
S_1 Chandipur Ghat	5.15 (Sept.)	5.45 (Dec.)	6.35 (June)	6.80 (June)
S_2 Isauli Ghat	5.22 (Sept. & Dec.)	4.30 (Sept.)	6.65 (June)	7.80 (Oct.)
S_3 Gola Ghat	5.33 (Sept.)	5.45 (Aug.)	6.65 (June)	7.00 (July)

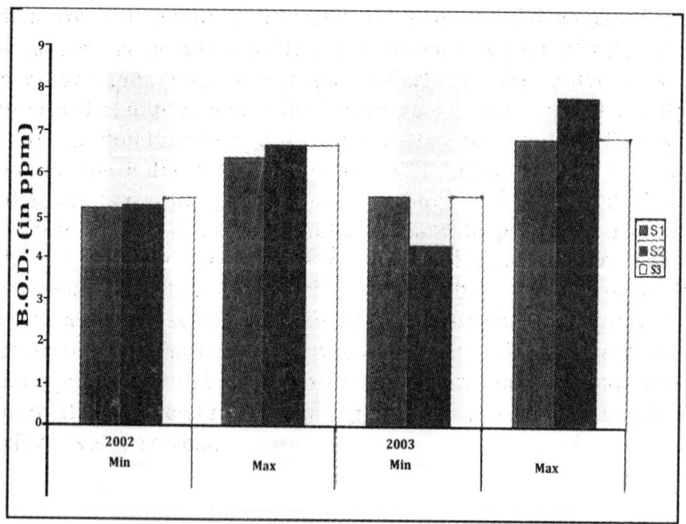

Fig. 7.5. Range of Biological Oxygen Demand

It is clear from **Table 4** and **Fig. 5** that the B.O.D. values of river water were comparatively lower in winter months. The values were found to increase gradually in Summer months attains the peak in June and then decreases gradully in summer months. The minimum BOD value was recorded as 4.30 in the month of September 2003 at Isauli Ghat while the maximum BOD value was observed as 7.8. in the month of October 2003 at Isauli Ghat. The B.O.D. values of all the sampling stations were found to be higher than the maximum permissible value for drinking, bathing and washing water. In general the B.O.D. values have gone higher at all the sampling stations in all the seasons. This is an indication for the alarming conditioned to be attained in near future.

5. *Chemical Oxygen Demand (C.O.D.):* COD is a measure of Oxygen consumed during the oxidation of oxidizing agent. The minimum and maximum values of Chemical Oxygen Demand (C.O.D.) of Gomati river are given in **Table 7.5** and **Fig. 7.6.**

Table 7.5: Range of Chemical Oxygen Demand (in ppm) at Different Sampling Stations

Sampling Stations	COD (in ppm)			
	Minimum		Maximum	
	2002	2003	2002	2003
S_1 Chandipur Ghat	99.40 (Feb.)	100.70 (Feb.)	150.80 (July)	147.50 (June)
S_2 Isauli Ghat	103. 05 (June)	104.60 (June)	150.40 (March)	148.10 (May)
S_3 Gola Ghat	93.80 (Feb.)	96.50 (Feb.)	135.50 (July)	144.00 (July)

Table 7.5 and **Fig. 7.6** illustrates the fact the lower C.O.D. values are generally found during winter months. The minimum values of C.O.D. during the session 2002 and 2003 are observed as 93.80 and 96.50 in the month of February at Gola Ghat (S_3). The maximum C.O.D. values were

recorded as 150.80 (July 2002 at Chandipur Ghat) and 148.10 (May, 2003 at Isauli Ghat) respectively. It is apparent that the maximum values of C.O.D. are observed in summer months. The mimimum values of C.O.D. as observed in the month of June 2002 and 2003 at Isauli Ghat show contradictory result.

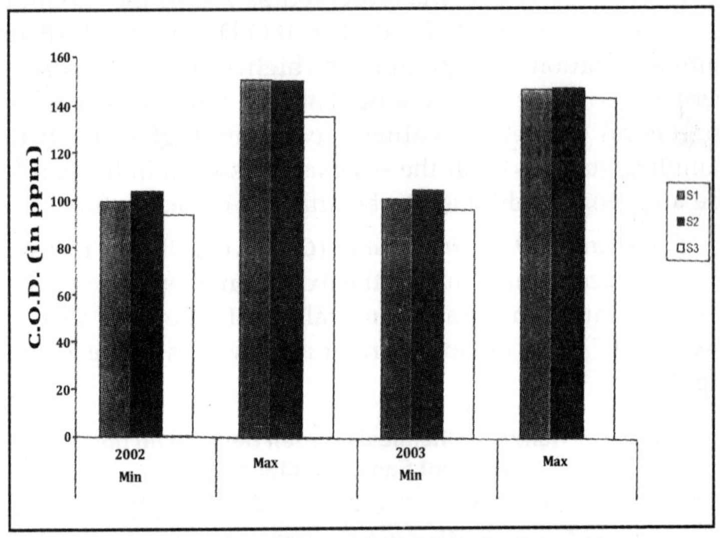

Fig. 7.6. Range of Chemical Oxygen Demand

*6. **Dissolved Oxygen (D.O.):*** Dissolved Oxygen is the measure of Oxygen concentration in the given water sample. **Table 7.6** and **Fig. 7.7** also illustrates the range of dissolved Oxygen in the Gomati river water during the year of 2002 and 2003.

On the basis of **Table 7.6** and **Fig. 7.7**, it may be explained that the D.O. values of Gomati river water during the corresponding years 2002 and 2003 were found to be lower in rainy and summer months when temperature was high. The minimum values were recorded as 5.95 (September 2002 at Isauli Ghat) and 5.68 (September 2003 at Isauli Ghat) respectively. During the year 2002, the maximum value (8.53) of D.O. was measured at GolaGhat in 2003 it was found as

8.60 in the month of March at Isauli Ghat. The minimum and maximum values of D.O. were marked the higher in 2003 than that of the values measured during 2002. The values of dissolved Oxygen at all the three sampling Stations were found to be higher than permitted value.

Table 7.6: Range of Dissolved Oxygen (D.O.) at different Sampling Stations

Sampling Stations	D.O. (in ppm)			
	Minimum		Maximum	
	2002	2003	2002	2003
S_1 Chandipur Ghat	6.0 (July, Sept.)	5.70 (Sept.)	7.55 (April)	8.20 (March)
S_2 Isauli Ghat	5.95 (Sept.)	5.68 (Sept.)	7.92 (April)	8.60 (March)
S_3 Gola Ghat	6.15 (Sept.)	5.70 (August)	853 (Jan.)	8.10 (March)

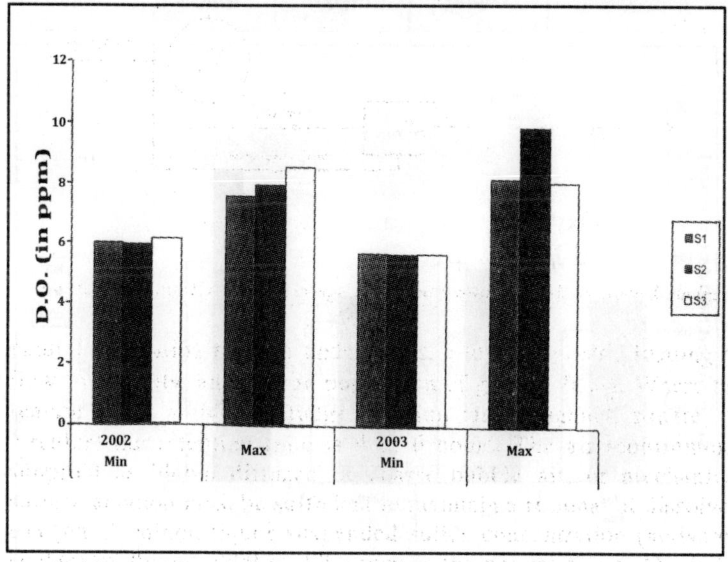

Fig. 7.7. Range of Dissolved Oxygen

7. ***Suspended Solids:*** Suspended solids were determined as the residue left after evaporation of unfiltered sample. It indicates the quantity and presence of solid pollutants dissolve or undissolved in water. **Tables 7.7** and **Fig. 7.8** depict the monthly variations and minimum and maximum values of suspended solids found in Gomati river water sampled in Sultanpur district.

Table 7.7: Range of Suspended Solids at different Sampling Stations

Sampling Stations	Suspended Solids (in ppm)			
	Minimum		Maximum	
	2002	2003	2002	2003
S_1 Chandipur Ghat	120.60 (Jan.)	124.0 (Jan.)	140.0 (Nov.)	162.60 (Sept.)
S_2 Isauli Ghat	120.70 (Feb)	123.0 (Jan)	141.30 (Aug.)	206.50 (Sept.)
S_3 Gola Ghat	100.75 (April)	106.50 (May)	145.80 (Aug.)	146.00 (Sept.)

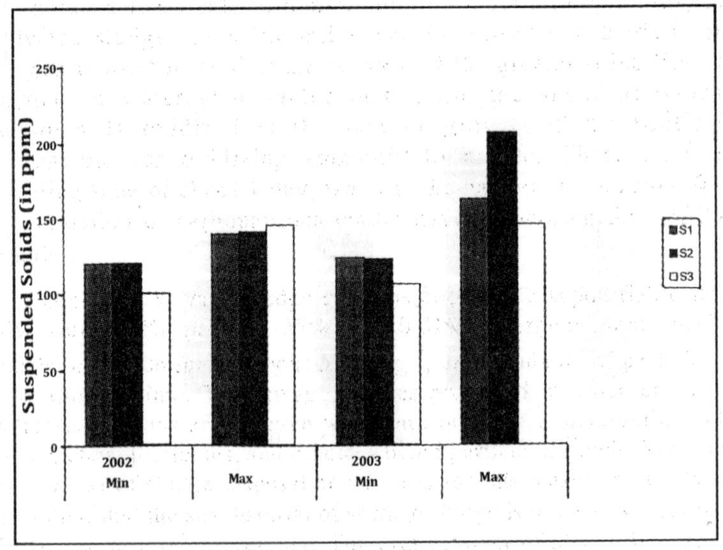

Fig. 7.8. Range of Suspended Solids

On the basis of the above observations, it may be said that the minimum values of suspended solids were marked during winter and summer seasons while the maximum values were registered during rainy months. The concentration of suspended solids in the river water was found in increasing order. During the year 2002, the minimum values (100.75) was observed in April 2002 at Gola Ghat. The maximum value of suspended solids was observed as 206.50 (September 2003) at Isauli Ghat.

HEAVY METALS

1. Lead (µg/l): Lead is highly poisonous element used in industries and as antiknock agent in automobile fuels. It has a property of getting accumulated in increasing concentrations over a period of time in the body of organism. Chemicals containing lead have shown a high rate of miscarriages. They affect skin, gastro, intestinal track, lungs and cause respirattory diseases. The range of minimum and maximum concentration of lead in river water is represented through **Table 7.8** and **Fig. 7.9**.

Table 7.8: Range of Lead (µg/L) at different Sampling Stations

Sampling Stations	Lead (µg/L)			
	Minimum		Maximum	
	2002	2003	2002	2003
S_1 Chandipur Ghat	11 (Feb.&Mar.)	22 (Jan.)	155 (Jan)	75 (Nov.)
S_2 Isauli Ghat	60 (Sept.)	72 (Sept.)	275 (Jan.)	185 (March)
S_3 Gola Ghat	75 (Sept.)	66 (Sept.)	223 (April)	(May)

The above description reveals the fact that the concentration of lead is minimum as 11.0 (February and March 2002) and 22 (January 2003) at Chandipur Ghat. It is also marked Lowest as 60.0 (September 2003) and 66.0 (September 2003) at Isauli Ghat and Gola Ghat respectively. The maximum concentration of Pb in the year 2003 was marked as 275.0 at Isauli Ghat and in 2003, it was registered as 185.0 at the same sampling station. During the sampling session 2003, Chandipur and Gola Ghat represent the maximum concentration of lead as 155.0 (January) and 223.0 (April) respectively.

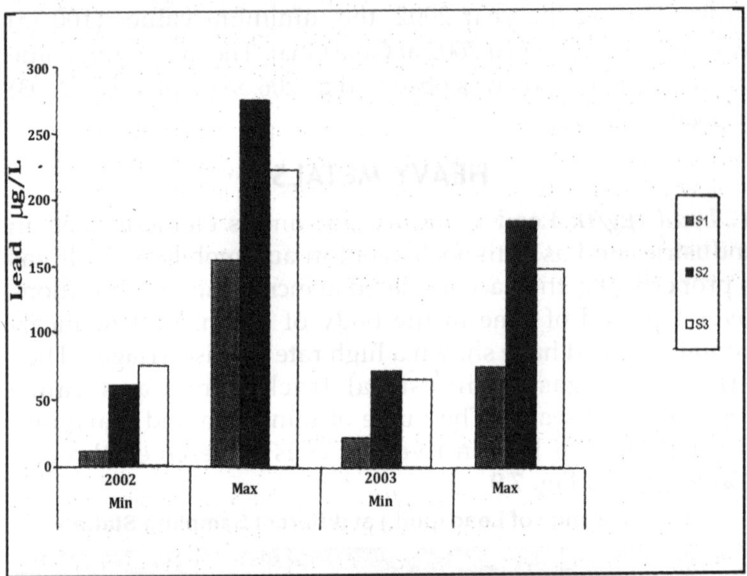

Fig. 7.9. Range of Lead

The maximum allowed limit of lead is 50, ug/L = 0.05 ppm. At most of the sampling stations, the values observed were much higher than that of the maximum allowed limit. The expected source of such high values are automotive products, caulking compounds, cosmetics, fuels, pesticides, lubricants paints, photography, pigments and preservatives etc. Lead plumbing of water pipes are a few common source to add minute concentrations in the river water. As the values have exceeded the maximum permissible limit of WHO, at most of study period and hence removal is needed before use of water for various purposes.

2. ***Chromium (µg/L):*** Chromium is an essential nutrient for plant and animal metabolism (glaucose metabolism, amino

acid and nucleic acid synthesis). Like lead, chromium is also poisonous if present in high concentration in the water.

The high level concentration of chromium in water can generate serious trouble and diseases (nausea, skin ulceration, lung cancer) and as the concentration reaches 0.1 mg (100 ppm), it can becomes lethal. Chromium (VI) is the most toxic form for bacterial plants and animals. The minimum and maximum concentration of chromium is also represented by **Table 7.9** and **Fig. 7.10** respectively.

Table 7.9 : Range of Chromium (µg/L) at different Sampling Stations

Sampling Stations	Chromium (in µg/L)			
	Minimum		Maximum	
	2002	2003	2002	2003
S_1 Chandipur Ghat	30 (Sept.)	18 (Jan.)	155 (Jan.)	72 (Nov.)
S_2 Isauli Ghat	40 (Nov.)	68 (Sept.)	290 (Feb.&M.)	180 (April)
S_3 Gola Ghat	55 (Nov.)	69 (Sept.)	218 (April)	150 (May)

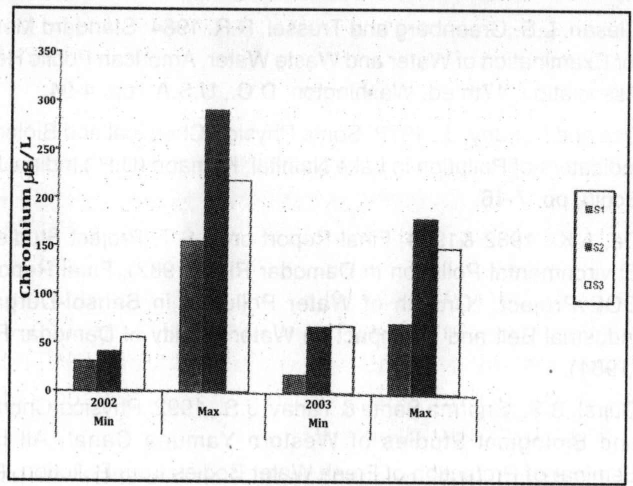

Fig. 7.10. Range of Chromium

It is apparent from **Table 7.9** and **Fig. 7.10** that the concentration of chromium is much higher than that of the permissible limit. During the sampling year of 2002, the minimum concentration of chromium (30mg/L) was recorded in the month of September at Chandipur Ghat while the maximum concentration was observed as 290 mg/L during the months of February and March as 290.0 mg/L at Isauli Ghat. During 2003 the minimum and maximum concentration of chromium in Gomati river water were marked as 18 ug/L (January 2003) and 180 mg/L (April 2003) at Chandipur and Isauli Ghat respectively.

The high concentration of chromium at various Sampling Stations is probably due to steel work, chrome plating, leather Tanning and other industrial effluents. Therefore, the control of high concentration of Cr in aquatic system is of major concern.

REFERENCES

1. Ambush, R.S., 1990: Environmental Pollution, Student Friend's & Co. 5th Edition, Lanka, Varanasi, p. 40.
2. Clesari, L.S. Greenberg and Trussel, R.R. 1984: Standard Method for Examination of Water and Waste Water, American Public Health Association, 17th ed. Washington, D.C., U.S.A., pp. 4-94.
3. Das and Pandey, J., 1978: Some Physico-Chemical and Biological Indicators of Pollution in Lake Nainital, Kumaon (U.P.) Indian Jour. Ecol5, pp. 7-16.
4. De, A.K., 1982 &1984: Final Report on D.S.T. Project Studies of Environmental Pollution in Damodar River(1982), Final Report of DOE Project. "Growth of Water Pollution in Sansol-Durgapur Industrial Belt and its Impact on Water Quality of Damodar River (1984).
5. Gujral, B.S., Sharma Sarita & Yadav, J.S., 1992: Physico-Chemical and Biological Studies of Western Yamuna Canal, All India Seminar of Protection of Fresh Water Bodies from Pollution, April, 92, Varanasi, pp. 77-80.

critically from an economic viewpoints and water is provided of a quality such that risk of disease is minimal.

In the developing countries like India, the position may, be quite different in the following manner—

(i) The people of developing countries are often too poor to pay for a supply providing completely safe water through a multiple tap system in the home.

(ii) Governments or private agencies providing funds will require clearer evidence of the health benefits to be expected, since their hope of financial returns will be smaller.

(iii) The funds made available may be inadequate for an ideal water supply so that difficult choices between differing incomplete sorts of improvement have to be made. If these decisions are not made consciously, the situation usually arises where a very few people get excellent water supplies and the vast majority do very badly indeed.

(iv) The diseases formed by water supplies are more numerous, more important and more diverse than other country lands and effects of improved supplies are more complex.

Due to all these causes, the engineers as well as the administrators need to have a much clearer understanding of the diseases associated to water and the health consequences of improved supplies if they are to make the best use of the funds made available to them.

Human health is an important question in developing countries and it is in poorer form. The health reports may be obtained by death conditions and the sorts of disease from which people suffer. In rich countries, the human survival rate is higher due to essential facilities. There are excellent water supplies and sewerage systems and water related disease is in consequence rare. Due to infectious diseases and malnutrition the health aspects in the developing country is much more gloomy.

The polluted water supplies cause intestinal infections related to water increase malnutrition in developing countries which in turn predisposes to severe infections.

There are several examples noted in surgical and medical departments where infections are most common among in patients. It is higher in developing countries. Skin infections are also noted in those patients waiting outside the hospitals. Most of the patients (more than 10%) are found serious by water borned diseases. A large number of misery, sickness and earth due to infections disease related to water supplies are common factors in developing countries.

Water Supplies v/s Public Health

The relationship between water supplies and public health has been recorded from the time of Hippocrates. Snow (1855) has studied a precise relation of a disease to water in his pioneer work on cholera similarly as Budd demonstrated the spread of typhoid through water supplies. Manson (1877) studied filariasis and Ross for malaria which was indirectly related to surface water. Some other water formed diseases are recognised in nineteenth century. Water causes disease in many ways. Warmth and poverty are the principal cause which initiate generally vector borne diseases as malaria, schistosomiasis, guinea worm and yellow fever. The hazards from bad water are too much common. Poverty is much more serious for many areas, specially in the rural areas. Where most people live and around the edges of the cities, which are the fatest growing communities, most people can not afford a conventionally good water supply at present, and the choice in the short run may be between doing nothing and providing a somewhat improved supply, (Bradley, 1977). The chemical quality of waters also affects health. Water causes infections. Some groundwater has very high floride levels which may affect bone growth adversely, while various types of chemical pollution of surface water may occur. These chemical risks are on a small scale compared with the hazards from microfial pollution of water.

Water-Related Infections

Various infective diseases may be affected by changes in water supply. Diseases are usually classified as viral, bacterial, protocol and helminthic. There are four main categories of diseases (**Figure 8.1**) of water supplies.

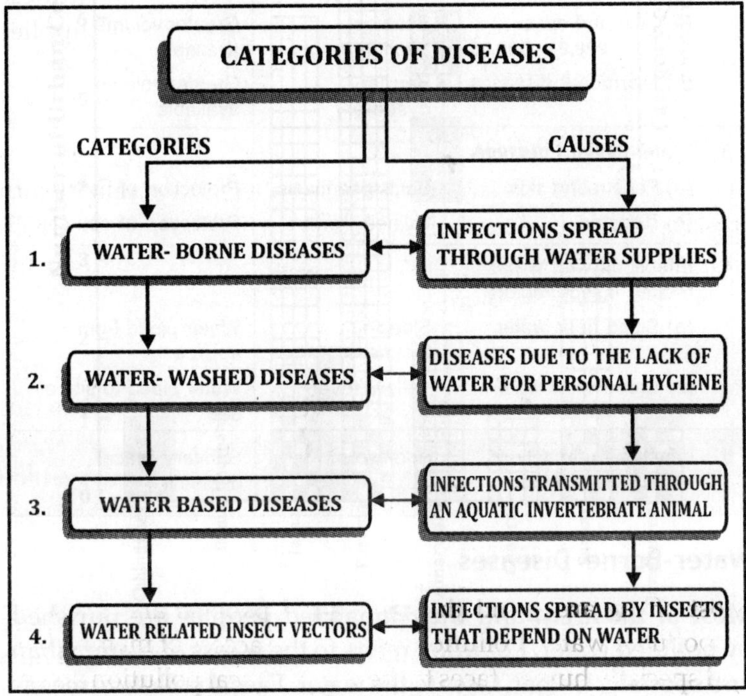

Fig. 8.1.

Bradley, 1974; white, Bradley and White (1972) have diseases about the classification of infective disease in relation to water supplies which is mentioned in **Table 8.1**.

Table 8.1 : Classification of Infective diseases in relation to Water supplies

Category	Examples	Relevant Water Improvements
1. Water-borne Infections		
(a) Classical	Typhoid, Cholera	Microbiological sterility
(b) Non-classical	Infective hepatitis	Microbiological improvement
2. Water-washed Infections		
(a) Skin and eyes	Scabies, trachoma	Greater volume available
(b) Diarrhoeal diseases	Bacillary dysentery	Greater volume available
3. Water-based Infections		
(a) Penetrating skin	Schistosomiasis	Protection of user
(b) Ingested	Guinea worm	Protection of source
4. Infections with water related insect vectors		
(a) Biting near water	Sleeping Sickness	Water piped from source
(b) Breeding in water	Yellow fever	Water piped to site of use
5. Infections primarily of defective sanitation	Hookworm	Sanitary faecal disposal

Water-Borne Diseases

Most of the areas and their inhabited peoples are nurished by polluted water. Pollution refers to the access of mammalian and specially human faces to the water. Faecal pollution means that if those who pollute the water are suffering from intestinal infections, those who drink the water will ingest the organisms and may also get the infections. Faecal pollution may allow the organisms which cause such diseases as typhoid, where the infecting dose of bacteria to some one who drinks the water is extremely low, to be spread through the water supply and cause a large outbreak of typhoid among the many people who drunk the water. Such infections can clearly be accurately described as water borne diseases where the pathogenic organisms are carried passively in the water supplies and they are prevented by attention to water quality.

Some localities are also marked where little water supply is available for bathing, washing the clothes, for agricultural as well as other domestic uses. Lack of water generally generates intestinal and skin infections. This type of infections are closely related to water washed infections. This is resulted from lack of water for washing or personal hygiene. The prevention of these infections depend on water availability, access to and quantity of domestic water rather than its quality.

Some infections cause by biting insects. Most of these, most notably the mosquitoes, breed in water bodies, sometimes as small as household domestic water containers. Yet other insects capable of transmitting disease, the tretse flies, in some cases only bite near water, to which those lacking piped supplies must of necessity come. These water related insect vectors may sometimes be affected by improvements in domestic water supplies.

The classifical water-borne diseases are due to highly infective organisms where only rather few are needed to infect someone, relative to the levels of pollution that readily occur. The two chief ones have a high mortality if untreated and are diseases which a community is very anxious to escape: typhoid and cholera. Both are relatively fragile organisms whose sole reservoir is man.

Typhoid is the most cosmopolitan of the classical water-borne infections. In man it produces a severe high fever with generalized systematic, more than intestinal symptoms. There is a considerable typhoid mortality in developing countries, though early diagnosis and adequate therapy with expensive antibacterial drugs can greatly reduce this.

Cholera is in some ways similar to typhoid, but its causative bacteria are more fagile and the clinical course is extremely dramatic. Several other infections are water-borne but are less important than typhoid and cholera. Leptospirosis, due to a spirochaete, has its reservoir in wild rodents which pollute the water. Leptospires can penetrate the skin as well as being ingested. They produce jaundice and fever, called 'Weils disease' which is severe but not common.

A large group of enterobacteria related to typhoid may cause diarrhoea or dysentery. The most important of the genus 'Shigella' can be spread through water supplies, but often are not. Recently the role of a new group of viruses, the rotaviruses, as causes of childhood diarrhoea is beginning to emerge. The mode of transmission is not yet known, but most high intensities of diarrhoeal diseases have been associated with defective water supplies.

During the summer season, most part of the Indian peninsula realizes very hot day and night and thus cholera, Jaundice and diarrhoea exist as dangerous diseases in urban as well as rural areas. Singh, T. (198), Singh, N.K. (2000), Singh P.K. (2000), Singh B. (2000), Singh, P.K. (2001) Singh P. (2001), Vishwakarma, R. (2001) and Gitanjali (2009) have studied the different areas of eastern Uttar Pradesh and found that during the hot summer and rainy seasons the above diseases have affected about 90% of the rural and urban population of the area. These areas are economically backward and basically agriculture based. The medical facilities are not properly available here while the uses of water are also traditional in manner. The concerned population is innocent about good health and the quality of water. During rainy season, suddenly causing flood which in turn initiate water lodging and pollution that creates seasonal diseases.

Water-washed Diseases

Hollister (1955) and Stewart (1955) have studied about the water-washed diseases in Southern United States. These two workers have noted that infections spread from one person to another by way of water supplies may also be more directly transmitted from faeces to mouth or by the way of dirty food. Dirty food causes diarrheal diseases due both to bacteria and to viruses as well as protozoa. Van Zijl (1966), Scrimshaw, Taylor and Gordon (1968) have stated diarrhoeas as the most important water-washed diseases in South America and South-East Asia.

Cook (1967) has surveyed in Ankola Uganda the second main group of water-washed diseases like the infections of the body surface, the skin and the eyes. The author have also marked the most common diseases like diarrhoeas, skin and eye infections in most of the areas of Ganga valley in north India. Feachem (1973) in his village sample from Ankole, Uganda has expressed that over 90 per cent of the people suffered from skin infections. White, Bradley and White (1972) and Praftt-Johnson and Wessels (1958) have also presented some pioneer works on watershed diseases.

Water-based Diseases

Water-based diseases are all worm infections. Several are due to flickes or thrematodes whose larvae depend on aquatic snails. The importance of guinea worm is great. It produces arthritis of joints adjacent to the active worm and effectively disables those infected for a couple of weeks which because of the timing of the infection, fall at the short planting season.

Water-Related Insect Vectors of Disease

David J. Bradley (1977) has noted several virus diseases like yellow fever, lethal jaundice, dengue and an acute influenza like illness in the Caribbean, West Africa and in many Asian cities. The author has marked influenza, Jaundice and dangerous dengue impact in eastern Uttar Pradesh. Recently dengue has seriously influenced most of the population of eastern Uttar Pradesh and several deaths are noted in hospitals.

Diseases of Defective Sanitation

If it is already clear that many diseases in the water borne, water washed and water based categories depend on access of human wastes to water or people mouths, so that they all may be reduced by measures aimed at improving waste disposal as well as water supply (Bradley 1977). Some theoretical reasons have been advanced (Macdonald, 1965) for water being more likely to be effective than sanitation against some water based diseases; but the chief practical reason is that the use of new water supplies presents for fewer difficulties than does persuading people to use new sanitary facilities.

A number of infections, however are only affected by the latter-human hookworms penetrate the skin from damp contaminated soil and certain flukes encyst in food items unaffected by changes in water supply. Flookworms which are a major problem live in the small intestine and cause major blood losses into it, acting as a cause of anaemia specially in populations where dietary iron is lower poorly absorbed.

The common roundworm or 'Ascaris' lays very numerous eggs which escape in the faeces and nature in the ground before becoming infective to man if ingested. They usually get in on fingers or food and both water supply and sanitation reduce transmission. Broadley (1977) has stated that all infections can be controlled by through cooking of food or by sanitation either standard sewage treatment approaches or leaving faces in pit latrines or adequate storage at appropriate temperatures prior to their use as an agricultural fertilizer.

Conclusion

The above discussion clarifies that water is very important and essential for life. Water is life. To maintain the quality of water is closely related to public health. The mismanagement of water may cause several diseases which in turn make difficult the life system. Use fresh water make healthy living environment. Precautions may safe the system and some scientific treatment of water supply can easily solve the entire hazardous conditions. We will march positively to collect some drop of pure water for happy and healthy long life.

REFERENCES

1. Bradley, D.J. 1974: Water Supplies : The Consequences of Change, in Human Rights in Health (Ed. K. Elliott and J. Knight), Amsterdam, ASP North-Holland; pp. 81-98.
2. Bradley, D.J. 1977: Health Aspects of Water Supplies in Tropical Countries, (Ed. Richard Feachem, M. McGarry and D. Mara) John Wiley and Sons Chickester, pp. 1-1).
3. Cook, R. 1967: The Ankole Pre-school Protection Programme, Kampala, Uganda (Mimeographed).
4. Feachem, R.G. 1973: Environment and Health in a New Guinea Highlands Community, Ph.D. Thesis, Sydney, University of New South Wales.
5. Gitanjali, 2009: Economic Analysis of Demographic Structure and Family Planning Programmes of Kerakat Tahsil Distt. Jaunpur, U.P. Ph. D. Thesis of Commerce Submitted to Dr. R.M.L. University Faizabad.
6. Hollister, A.C. Beck, M.D. Gitted Sohn, A.M. and Hemphill, E.C., 1955: Influence of Water Availability on Shigella Prevalence in Children of Farm Labour Families, American Journal of Public Health, 45, pp. 354-362.
7. Macdonald, G. 1965: The Dynamics of Helminth Infections with Special Reference to Schistosomes; Transactions of the Royal Society of Tropical Medicine and Hygiene, 59 pp. 489-506.
8. Pratt-Johnson, J.A. and Weggels, J.H.W. 1958: Investigation into the Control of Transchoma in Sekhu Kuniland, South African Medical Journal, 32, pp. 212-215.
9. Singh, Babita, 2000: Population Growth and Family Planning Programme in Machhali Shahar Tahsil of Distt. Jaunpur, Ph.D. Thesis in Geog. (Unpublished) Supervised by G. Prasad Submitted to VBS Purvanchal University, Jaunpur, U.P.
10. Singh Nand Kumar; 2000: Dimension of Population Resources and Population Planning of Chhindwara Distt. M.P. Ph. D. thesis

in Geog. Published and Submitted to VBS Purvanchal University Jaunpur, U.P.

11. Singh, P.K. 2000: Socio-economic Transformation of Hoshangabad Distt. M.P., Ph.D. Thesis in Geog. Supervised by G. Prasad and Submitted to VBS Purvanchal University, Jaunpur, U.P.
12. Singh, Priyambada 2001; Problems and Prospects of Child and Female Labours in Jaharia Block Distt. Ghazipur, U.P. Ph.D. thesis in Geog. Supervised by G. Prasad and Submitted to VBS Purvanchal University Jaunpur, U.P.
13. Singh, T. 1998: Population Resources and Environment: A Geographical Study of Kerakat Tahsil Distt. Jaunpur, U.P. Ph.D. Thesis in Geography Supervised by G. Prasad and Submitted to VBS Purvanchal University Jaunpur, U.P.
14. Snow, J. 1855. On the Mode of Communication of Cholera, 2nd ed. London: J. Churchill.
15. Schrimshaw, N.S. Taylor, C.E. and Gordon J.E., 1960: Interactions of Nutrition and Infection, World Health Organisation, Geneva.
16. Stewart, W.H. McCabe I.J. Hemphill E.C. and Decapito T. 1955: Diarrhoeal Disease Control Studies, IV, the Relationship of Contain Environmental Factors to the Prevalence of Shigella Infection, American Journal of Tropical.
17. Van Zijl, W.J. 1966: Studies on diarrhoeal diseases in seven countries by the WHO diarrhoeal diseases advisory team. Bulletin of the World Health Organisation, 35, pp. 249-261.
18. Viswakarma, R. 2000: Panchayati Raj and Socio-Economic Problems of Ambedkar villages of Chandauli distt. U.P. Ph.D. Thesis supervised by G. Prasad and submitted to VBS Purvanchal University Jaunpur, U.P.
19. White, G.F. Bradley, D.T. and White A.U. 1972: Drawers of Water, Domestic Water use in East Africa, Chicago and London: University of Chicago Press.

CHAPTER

9

Urban Development

Anupam Pandey

Introduction to Physico-Cultural Background of the Study Region

Chhindwara District is located in the lap of Satpura Range of Vindhyachal-Baghelkhand region in Jabalpur Zone of Madhya Pradesh. It extends between the parallels of latitude 21°27′30″ and 22°47′45″ North and longitude 78°15′10″ and 79°24′30″ East with a geographical area of 11815 square kilometres. The physical shape of the study area is equilateral-elongated from South to North direction. The Hoshangabad and Narsimhapur Districts make Northern, Nagpur and Amarawati Districts (Maharashtra) delimit Southern, Seoni and Betul Districts perform its East and West boundaries respectively (**Figure 9.1**). There are 8 Tahsils as Chhindwara, Tamia, Jamai Parasia, Amarwara, Chaurai, Sausar, Pandhurna and 11 Development Blocks (Chhindwara, Tamia, Jamai, Parasia, Amarwara, Chaurai, Sansar, Pandhurna, Bichhua, Harrai and Mohkher) in the study region (Prasad, G. and Pandey, A., 2009).

Based on Census Abstracts, 2001, the total population of the study area is estimated as 1849283 wherein Male and Female population is recorded as 946582 and 902300 respectively. The decadal population growth rate (17.86%), population density (157 person per square kilometre), sex ratio

(952 Female per thousand Male population), Scheduled Castes and Scheduled Tribes population of the total population (11.58% and 31.65% respectively) and literacy rate (65.81%) have been measured in the region.

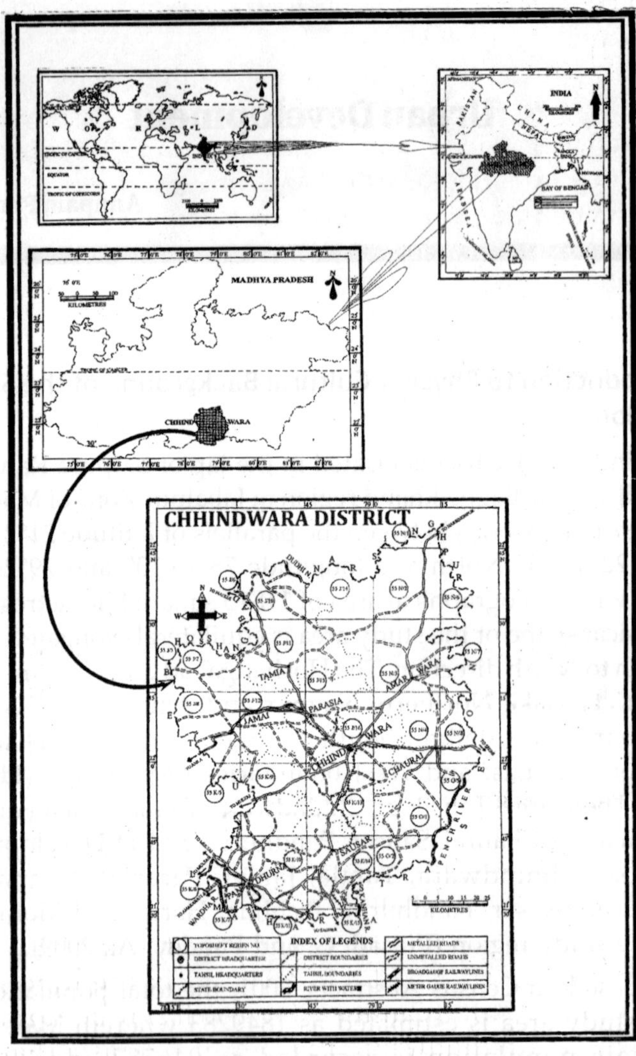

Fig. 9.1. Location Map

Urbanisation

The 'Urban' word is nominated on 'curbs' or urbis (city) of Latin language (Darling Kindersley, Oxford Dictionary, 2003). The increase in the proportion of population residing in towns, brought about by migration of rural population into towns and cities, and the higher urban levels of natural increase resulting from the greater proportion of people of child bearing age in cities which in turn, reflects pattern of migration. Urbanisation indicates a change of employment structure from rural to urban and cottage industries to mass production and service industries (Mayhew, S., Oxford Dictionary of Geography, 2005). The urbanisation is a shift of people from village to city (Taylor, G., 1964). The rate of urbanisation is the per cent increase over a given period in the proportion of total population living in urban communities (Trewartha, G.T.) Urbanisation refers to the proportion of total population concentrated in urban settlements or else to arise in the proportion (Davis, K.). Urbanisation is a process in which the rural society and its functional, migrational, demographical and socio-cultural attitudes change into the urban society (Pandey, A., 2007).

According to Census Abstracts of 2001, about 25 per cent of the total population of the region have consumed in urbanisation processes. About 452203 persons (24.45% of the total population) are residing in urban areas of the District wherein Male and Female contribution exist as 234916 and 217287 respectively. The area around a town which it serves and from which it draws customers for its shops and users of its various services is called by urban area or field of influence (Leong, G.C. and Morgan, G.C., 1982).

As regards the evolution and growth of urban areas, there were only 3 towns in 1951 A.D. but now it has been increased a 24 in the District (Census, 2001) which may be registered namely as Chhindwara, Pandhurna, Parasia, Sausar, Junnardeo, Chandemata, Damua, Amarwara, Jamai, Newton

Chikhli, Badkuli, Kali Chhapar, Mohgaon, Harrai, Lodhikhera, Iklehra, Sirsaura, Dighawani, Pala Chaurai, Almada, Santhia, Panara, Bhamori, Jata Chhapar in descending order in view of population (**Table 9.1** and **Figure 9.2**).

Table 9.1 : Chhindwara District: Urban Centres/Towns and Population—2001

Sl. No.	Urban centres/Towns	Total Population	Sexwise population		Sex ratio (Female per thousand male)
			Males	Females	
1	2	3	4	5	6
1.	Chhindwara	1,53,552	79,889	73,663	922
2.	Pandhurna	40,931	21,299	19,632	922
3.	Parasia	37,863	19,418	18,445	950
4.	Sausar	24,312	12,594	11,718	930
5.	Junnardeo	22,440	11,605	10,835	934
6.	Chandameta	16,937	08,755	08,182	935
7.	Damua	15,857	08,185	07,652	935
8.	Amarwara	12,096	06,333	05,763	910
9.	Jamai	11,394	05,968	05,426	909
10.	Newton Chikhli	10,850	05,649	05,201	921
11.	Badkuhi	10,773	05,599	05,174	924
12.	Kali Chhapar	10,692	05,561	05,131	923
13.	Mohzaon	09,892	05,126	04,766	930
14.	Harrai	09,430	04,850	04,580	944
15.	Lodhikhera	09,381	04,769	04,612	967
16.	Iklehra	09,197	04,768	04,429	929
17.	Singaura	08,481	04,406	04,075	925
18.	Dighawani	07,928	04,217	03,711	880

1	2	3	4	5	6
19.	Pala Chaurai	07,262	03,807	03,455	908
20.	Almada	06,852	03,707	03,185	859
21.	Santhia	04,559	02,461	02,098	852
22.	Panara	04,143	02,078	02,065	994
23.	Bhamori	03,932	02,048	01,884	920
24.	Jata Chhapar	03,449	01,788	01,661	929

Source: Census-2001, District Stat. Handbook (HIndi), Chhindwara, 2007, Table 2.7, pp. 16-17.

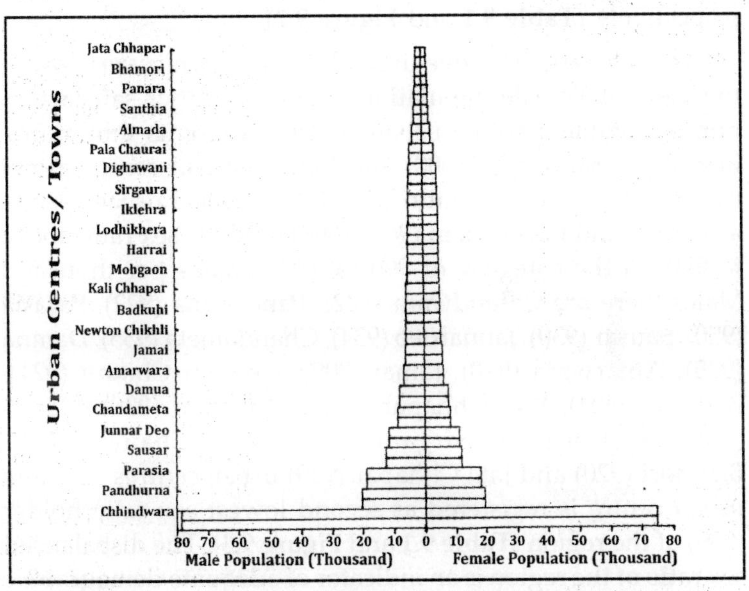

Fig. 9.2. Chhindwara District: Sex-wise Population in Urban Centres/Towns-2001

Chhindwara headquarter is the largest urban centre of the region denoting 122247 population wherein Male and Female population have been calculated as 63584 and 58663 respectively. The total population (Male and Female) of other

Urban Centres and town are as Pandhurna 40931 (21299 and 19632), Parasia 37863 (19418 and 18445), Sausar 24312 (12594 and 11718), Junnardeo 22440 (11605 and 10835), Chandameta 16937 (8755 and 8182), Damua 15857 (8185 and 7652) Amarwara 12096 (6333 and 5763), Jamai 11394 (5988 and 5426), Newton Chikhli 10850 (5649 and 5201), Badkuhi 10773 (5599 and 5174), Kali Chhapar 10692 (5561 and 5131), Mohgaon 9892 (5126 and 4766), Harrai 9430 (4850 and 4580), Lodhikhera (9381) (4769 and 4612), Iklehra 9197 (4768 and 4429), Sirgaura 8481 (4406 and 4075), Dighawani 7928 (4217 and 3711), Pala Chaurai 7262 (3807 and 3455), Almada 6852 (3707 and 3185), Santhia 4559 (2461 and 2098), Panara 4143 (2078 and 2065), Bhamori 3932 (2048 and 1884) and Jata Chhapar 3449 (1788 and 1661) respectively (**Table 9.1** and **Figure 9.2**).

The sex ratio in above urban centres/town is very low in the view of Female papulation which is neither satisfactory nor acceptable. Santhia urban centre represents minimum/lowest sex ratio (852/1000) and Panara urban centre shows maximum/highest sex ratio (994/1000). Only 2 urban centres as Panara and Lodhikhera (967/1000) hold the sex ratio above to 950. In the category of 900 to 950 females per thousand Males there are Chhindwara (922), Pandhurna (922), Parasia (950), Sausar (930), Jannardeo (934), Chandameta (935), Damua (935), Amarwara (910), Jamai (909), Newton Chikhli (921), Badkuhi (924), Kali Chhapar (923), Mohgaon (930), Harrai (944), Iklehra (929), Sirgaura (925), Pala Chaurai (908), Bhamori (920) and Jata Chhapar (929) urban centres. Almada urban centre is registered as second lowest sex ratio holder (859) of the region (**Table 9.1** and **Figure 9.3**). The disbalanced sex ratio of the region is an indicator of adequate demographic composition which is generated the various type of moral and socio-cultural problems in concerned urban societies and communities. It is a weak aspect of perfect development of urban societies like a cancer in the body.

According to Census report of 2001, there are 24 urban centres in which 05 categories are founded of town based on

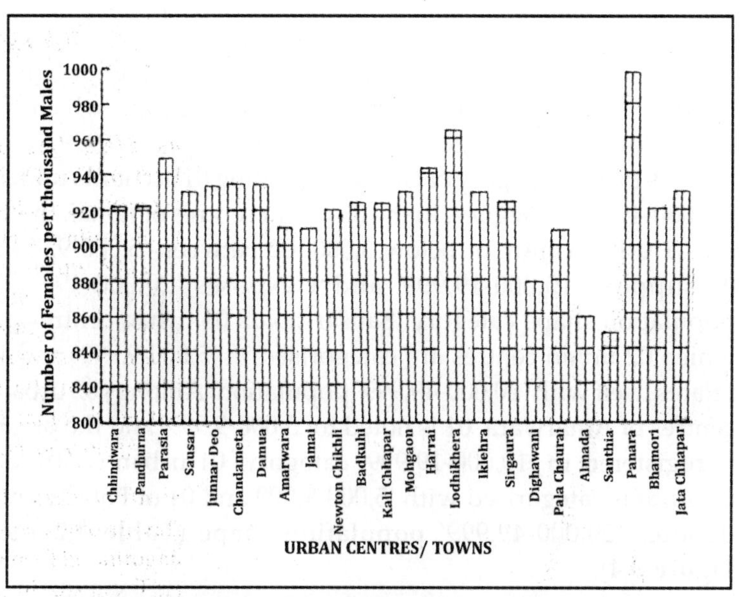

Fig. 9.3. Chhindwara District: Sex Ratio in Urban Centres/ Towns-2001

census standard. In the category of 'below 5,000' there are 04 urban centres (Jata Chhapar, Bhamori, Panara and Santhia), and in the category of '5,000-9,999' 08 urban centres (Almada, Pala Chaurai, Dighawani, Sirgaura, Iklehra, Ladhikhera, Harrai and Mohgaon). The 07 urban centres (Kali Chhaper) Badkuhi, Newton Chikhli, Jamai, Amarwara, Damua and Chandameta) exist between '10,000-19,999' category, and 04 urban centres (Junnardeo, Sausar, Parasia and Pandhurna) follow '20,000-49,999' category. Another category of population 'above 1,00,000' highlights 01 urban centre (Chhindwara) who is the headquarter of the District. Notable that no any urban centre have been founded in the category of '50,000-99,999' population.

Tahsilwise distribution of number of urban centres is not equal. Maximum 10 urban centres are located in Parasia. Beside it, Tamia is entirely unurbanised. The Chhindwara, Chaurai and Pandhurna hold only one urban centre respectively.

Remaining Jamai occurs 06, Sausar 03 and Amarwara 02 urban centres. Chhindwara holds 01 urban centre having population 'above 1,00,000'. Parasia locates 10 urban centres in which 03 fall 'below 5,000' category, 03 stand under '5,000-9,999' and '10,000-19,999' category each and remaining 01 accounts under '20,000-49,999' category. In the 06 urban centres of Jamai, there are 01 urban centre of below 5,000' 02 between '5,000-9,999', 02 support '10,000-19,999' and 1 exposes '20,000-49,999' population shape category. Sausar holds 03 urban centres in which 02 urban centres are categorised in '5,000-9,999' and 1 relates itself with '20,000-49,999' population. Amongs 02 urban centres of Amarwara, 01 is noted to '5,000-9,999' and the other is registered in '10,000-19,999' category. 01 urban centre of Chaurai is categorised with '5,000-9,999 and 01 of Pandhurna denotes '20,000-49,999' population shape (**Table 9.2** and **Figure 9.4**).

Table 9.2: Chhindwara District: Tahsilwise Number and size of Urban/Centres/Towns 2001

Sl. No.	Name of Tahsil	Number of Urban centres	Categories of Urban centres Towns according to population size				
			Below to 5,000	5,000-9999	10,000-19999	20,000-49999	Above to 1,00,000
1.	Chhindwara	01	—	—	—	—	01
2.	Tamia	—	—	—	—	—	
3.	Jamai	06	01	02	02	01	—
4.	Parasia	10	03	03	03	01	—
5.	Amarwara	02	—	01	01	—	—
6.	Chaurai	01	—	01	—	—	—
7.	Sausar	03	—	02	—	01	—
8.	Pandhurna	01	—	—	—	01	—
	Entire District	24	04	09	06	04	01

Source: Census-2001, District Stat. Handbook (Hindi), Chhindwara, 2007, Table 2.12, p. 23.

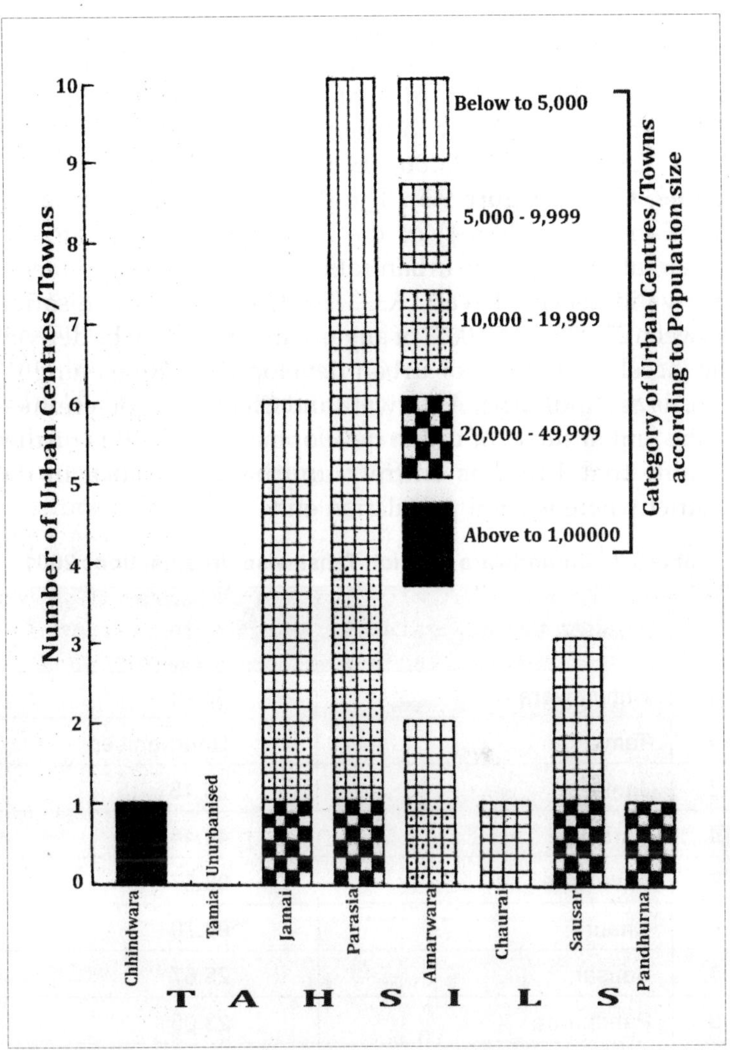

Fig. 9.4. Chhindwara District Tahsil-wise Number of Urban Centres/Towns-2001

The present urbanisation rate of entire District is 24.45 per cent (2001) which is the indicative of 'initial stage' of urbanisation cycle' Tahsilwise crux and clues of urbanisation is also adequate. Parasia is an extremely urbanised (44.44% Tahsil of the District. The percentage of urbanisation processes in descending order of Chhindwara, Jamai, Sausar, Pandhurna, Amarwara and Chaurai Tahsils are illustrated as 35.61, 28.18, 25.67, 23.06, 08.67 and 06.70 respectively (**Table 9.3** and **Figure 9.5**). The Parasia, Chhindwara, Jamai and Sansar tahsils (04) of the District may be treated in 'acceleration stage' of urbanisation cycle. The above fact is also validated by Tiwari, R.C. (2003) that the urbanisation between 25.00% to 50.00% of any urban centre may be derived the 'accelation stage' of urban development. Remaining 03 Tahsils as Pandhurna, Amarwara and Chaurai are determined in the 'initial stage' of urban development/cycle. It is further notable that Tamia is entirely unurbanised Tahsil in the District where is rural population only.

Table 9.3 : Chhindwara District: Tahsilwise Urbanisation : 2001

Sl. No.	Name of Tahsils	Urbanisation in per cent
1.	Chhindwara	35.61
2.	Tamia	Unurbanised
3.	Jamai	28.18
4.	Parasia	44.44
5.	Amarwara	08.67
6.	Chaurai	06.70
7.	Sausar	25.67
8.	Pandhurna	23.05
	Entire District	24.45

Source: Census-2001, District Stat, Handbook (Hindi), Chhindwara, 2007, Table 2.4, p.13.

The initial stage of urbanisation cycle basically elucidates the primary production based econo-urban society. It is pertinent to point out that Tamia Tahsil as well cultured on primary production and primitive social attitudes, is untouched with urbanisation. Amarwara and Chaurai Tahsils are also less urbanised due to primary activities, primitive econo-social base and A to Z cropped traditional folkways.

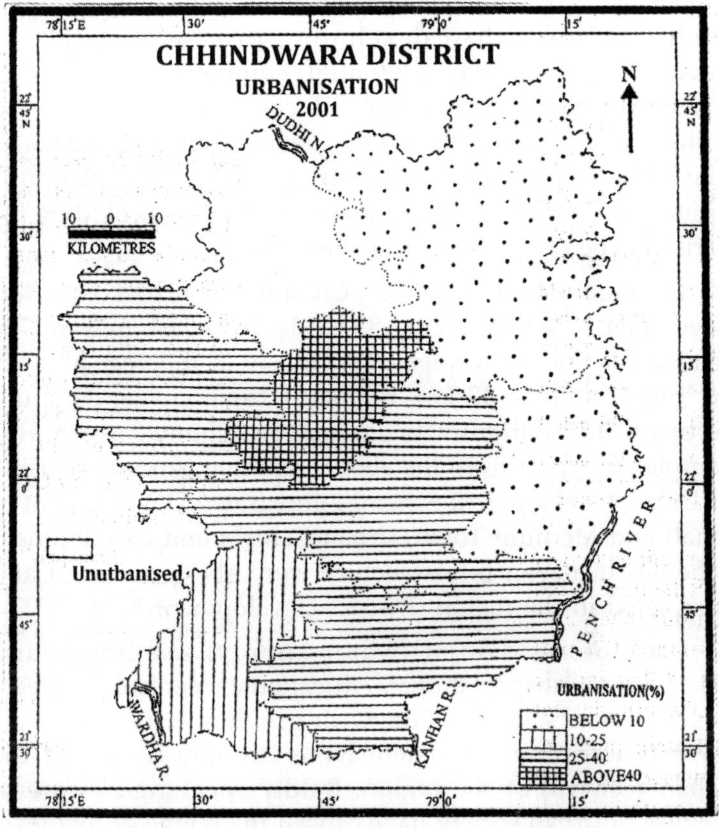

Fig. 9.5.

Urban Development

Urban development is a relatively recent process in the region. It is more rapid than general population growth specially where the largest agglomerations grow most rapidly. Urban development depends upon urban planning. The idea of urban planning is the welfare of the citizens and to rise the standard of living of the people (Stamp, L.D., 1950). Urban planning is simply the exercise of a city and its environs along rational lines with due regard for health, amenity and convenience and commercial and industrial advancement (Lewis, N.P.).

In view of urban developing process and related developing areas like residential, commercial, industrial, transportured, administrative, educational, medical, social, cultural and religions the region stands in developing stage. The CBD (Central business district) of the study region is located at Chhindwara headquarter—which is providing the various type of facilities of business based.

During the year of 2006-07, Chhindwara urban centre has developed 1 Park, 45 shops, 89 roads, 1630 flash toilets, 1750 road-lights and 29 sewages. Previously in the year of 2005-06, public toilets, 37 km. roads, 01 town curve, 05 slum-reforms, 175 community insurance schemes were also completed. Apart from the above planning process, revision of Urban Development Schemes, Integrated Development of Small and Medium Town/Urban Centres and Development Schemes of urban Infrastructure were also proceeded and completed in the region (District Development Book, 2007).

Lack of residential (water supply, sewerages and electricity), transportational, educational, medical, and eco-development schemes alongwith growing crime, hazards, poverty and unemployment have strongly degraded the urban scenario of the region. Boldly speaking no care of welfare of urban society have caused the region at low level of urban accommodation.

Conclusion

The region is marked in 'initial stage' of urbanisation. The primary activities demerit the shadow of urbanisation with depressed society. Major urban facilities/amenities are residential commercial, industrial, transportational, administrative, educational, medical, social, cultural and religions have been marked below standard of urban development. Poverty, unemployment, crime, blightness and environmental degradation are thought to be as the business problems of the study region in making the urban circumference up to mark. It will be fruitful to make an effort of sustainable development in the existing urban society flowering some many gift of public awareness and Governmental–Non Governmental beneficial efforts. Traditional approach must be minimized and adopting recent techniques.

REFERENCES

1. Census Abstract Report; 2001.
2. District Development Book (Hindi), 2007: District Statistical Office, Chhindwara, M.P., Table No. 96, pp. 49-50.
3. District Statistical Hands (Hindi) Book; 2007: District Statistical Office, Chhindwara, M.P., Table 2.6 and 2.12, pp. 16-17 and 23.
4. Darling Kindersley, S Oxford Dictionary; 2003: Darling Kindersley Limited, London, U.K., p. 917.
5. Gazetteer of India, Chhindwara; 1995: Edited by Sinha, A.M., Gazette Unit, Directorate of Rajbhasha Evam Sanskriti, Deptt. of Culture, Govt. of M.P., Bhopal, p. 69.
6. Leong, G.C. and Morgon, G.C., 1982: *Human and Economic Geography*, Oxford University Press, New Delhi, pp. 89-90.
7. Mayhew, S.; 2005: *Oxford Dictionary of Geography*, Oxford University Press, YMCA Library Building, Jai Singh Road, New Delhi; p. 515.
8. Pandey, A; 2006: Population, Environment and Public Health, published research paper (Hindi), Ed. by Prasad, G., Pandey, A. and Kislaya, S. in '*Population and Environment*', Discovery Publishing House, Daryaganj, New Delhi. p. 28.
9. Pandey, A., 2007: *Population Geography of India* (Hindi), Discovery Publishing House, Daryaganj, New Delhi, pp. 153-155.
10. Pandey, A., 2010: Geomorphological Analysis of Chhindwara Plateau, Satpura Range, M.P., unpublished Ph.D. thesis, Dr. R.M.L. Awadh Univ. Faizabad, U.P.

11. Prasad, G. and Pandey, A; 2009: Measurement of Drainage Density on Chhindwara Pleateau (Satpura Range), M.P., published research paper, Ed. by Tripathi, R.D., Vol. 16, No. 2 Indian Research Journal of Social Sciences, Basti, U.P., p. 123.
12. Rao, B.P. and Sharma, N.; 2000-01: Urban Geography (Hindi), Vasundhara Prakashan, 236, Daudpur, Gorakhpur, U.P., pp. 52-59.
13. Stamp, L.D.; 1950: Planning and Agriculture, Journal of Town Planning Institute, London (U.K.), p. 141.
14. Taylor, G.; 1964: Urban Geography, London, U.K.
15. Tiwari, R.C.; 2003: *Settlement Geography* (Hindi), Prayag Pustak Bhawan, 20-A, University Road, Allahabad, U.P., pp. 189-90 and 324.

CHAPTER

10

Socio-Economic Characteristics of Scheduled Tribes

Anupam Pandey and Chhaya Pandey

Introduction to the Study Area

Chhindwara District is physically located on Satpura range of Central India and politically in Jabalpur Division of M.P. State. It extends between the parallels of latitudes 21°28′ and 22°48′ North and longitudes 78°15′ and 79°25′ East. Hoshangabad and Narsimhapur Districts touch Northern, Nagpur and Amrawati (Maharashtra) Districts flank Southern, Seoni locates Eastern and Betul District delimits western boundary of the study region 'Chhindwara District' (Pandey, A, 2010). The total Geographic area of region is as 11815 square kilometre which is divided into 09 sub-Districts as Tamia, Amarwara, Chaurai, Jamai, Parasia, Chhindwara, Sausar, Bichhua and Pandhurna and 11 Development Blocks (Tamia, Amarwara, Chaurai, Jamai, Parasia, Chhindwara, Sausar, Bichhua, Pandhurna, Mohkher and Harrai). Chhindwara is fourth largest District in Geographical area and sixth largest District in population shape (18,49,283 persons) of M.P. State (Census, 2001).

Scheduled Tribes Communities

Article 342 of Indian Constitution provides for specification of tribes or Tribal communities or parts of or groups within Tribes or Tribal communities which are deemed to be for the purposes of the Constitution the Scheduled Tribes in relation to that state of Union Territory. In pursuance of these provisions, the list of Scheduled Tribes are notified for each state or Union Territory and are valid only within the jurisdiction of that State or Union Territory and not outside (Census, 2001). 'Gond' shows the largest Scheduled Tribes population existed as 5,30,485 persons in the region (Census, 2001). Similarly Mawasi (66,420 persons), Bharia, Bhumia, Korku, Pardhan, Kol, Halba or Halbi, Kharia Pardhi, Baiga, Bhungia, Munda, Oraon, Ninhal Bhil, Birhul or Birhar, Dhanwar Bhunjia, Kawar or Kanwar and Praja are also registered as Scheduled Tribes of District (Gazetteer, 1995).

Demographic Composition of Scheduled Tribes

The demographic composition is an essential aspect to analyse the socio-economic conditions of Scheduled Tribes population because it depicts the social, economical and cultural interrelationships between concerned societies. The major parts of demographic composition like population shapes and sex ratios are analysed as follows:

Population Shapes of Scheduled Tribes

Above to one third (34.68%) population of the District consists of persons belonging to Scheduled Tribes. In the total Scheduled Tribes population (6,41,142 persons) about 92.60% (5,93,956 persons) are settled in rural areas and remaining 07.40% (47,186 persons) are inhabited in urban areas. Sub-Districtwise distribution of total Scheduled Tribes population is registered in Tamia as 67,943 person, in Amarwara as 1,34,028 persons, in Chaurai as 33,135 persons, in Jamai as 97,350 persons, in Parasia as 81,518 persons, in Chhindwara as 98,146 persons, in Sausar as 28,823 persons, in Bichhua as 42,243 persons, and in Pandhurna as 58,235 persons. Sub-Districtwise share of percentage of total Scheduled Tribes population in Tamia, Amarwara, Chaurai, Jamai, Parasia, Chhindwara, Sausar, Bichhua and Pandhurna have been noticed as 10.60, 20.89, 05.17, 15.17, 12.71, 15.31, 04.50, 06.58 and 09.07 respectively. Amarwara sub-district holds the largest number of Scheduled Tribes population and population percentage of the entire region (**Table 10.1** and **Figure 10.1A**).

In the view of percentage of total population of Scheduled Tribes of Sub-District, Tamia is on highest place. Beside the above Bichhua (54.47), Amarwarà (53.98), Jamai (45.42), Pandhurna (32.79), Parasia (29.95), Chhindwara (22.76), Chaurai (19.55) and Sausar (17.00) are successively categorised. Notable that Tamia, Bichhua and Amarwara hold above to half population in Scheduled Tribes category in their total population (**Table 10.1** and **Figure 10.1B**).

Table 10.1 : Chhindwara District: Sub-Districtwise Population and Percentage of Population of Scheduled Tribes-2001

Sl.No.	Sub-Districts	Population of Scheduled Tribes	Percentage of S.T. Population in total S.T. population of District	Percentage of S.T. population in total population of Sub-District
1.	Tamia	67943	10.60	76.10
2.	Amarwara	134028	20.90	53.98
3.	Chaurai	33135	05.16	19.55
4.	Jamai	97350	15.17	45.42
5.	Parasia	81518	12.71	29.75
6.	Chhindwara	98146	15.31	22.76
7.	Sausar	28823	04.50	17.00
8.	Bichhua	42243	06.58	54.47
9.	Pandhurna	58235	09.07	32.79
	Total District	**641421**	**100.00**	**34.68**

Sources: Census, 2001; and District Statistical Handbook (Hindi), 2007.

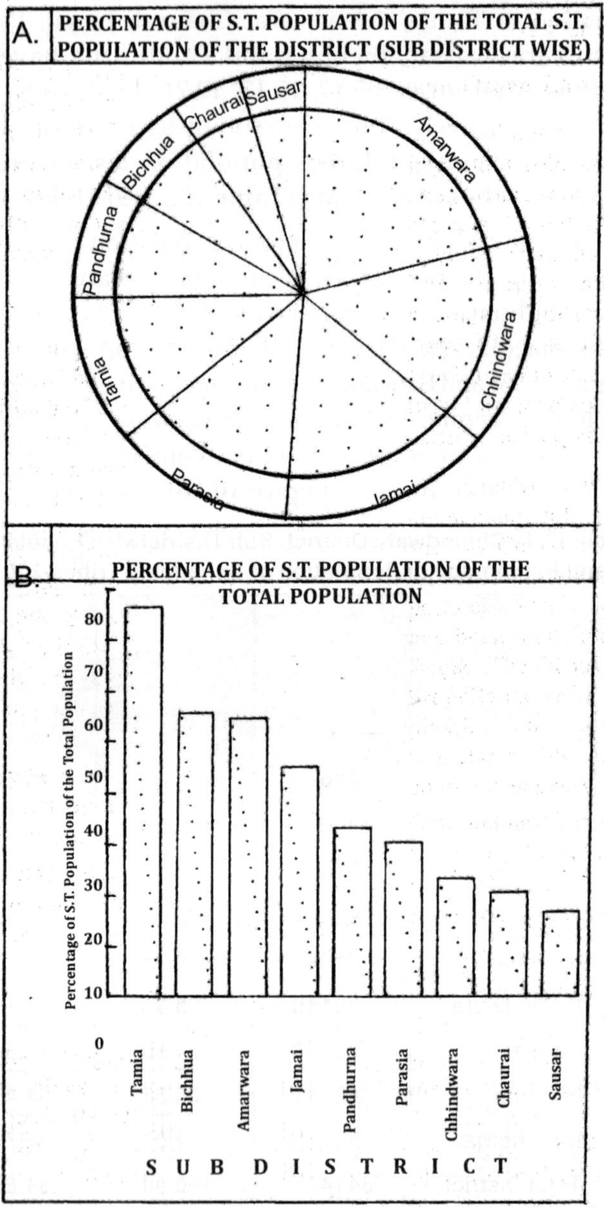
A.
PERCENTAGE OF S.T. POPULATION OF THE TOTAL S.T. POPULATION OF THE DISTRICT (SUB DISTRICT WISE)
Sausar
Chaurai
Bichhua
Pandhurna
Tamia
Parasia
Jamai
Chhindwara
Amarwara
B.
PERCENTAGE OF S.T. POPULATION OF THE TOTAL POPULATION
Percentage of S.T. Population of the Total Population
80
70
60
50
40
30
20
10
0
Tamia
Bichhua
Amarwara
Jamai
Pandhurna
Parasia
Chhindwara
Chaurai
Sausar
S U B D I S T R I C T

Fig. 10.1A & B.

Sex Ratios of Scheduled Tribes

In all over India, sex ratio has been defined as the number of Females per thousand Males of existing population. It is presented as 'number of Females per thousand Males' as follows:

$$\text{Sex ratio} = \frac{\text{Number of Females}}{\text{Number of Males}} 1000$$

The sex ratio of the total population of the District exists as 952/1000 (Pandey, A; 2007) but in the case of Scheduled Tribes population, it is as high as 989/1000. Notable that total 3,22,458 Males and 3,18,963 Females are inhabited in the District. As regards the sex ratio of Amarwara sub-district stands at highest position which presents 1007. Females per thousand Males. In the same context Bichhua 997, Jamai 996, Chhindwara 991, Pandhurna, 985, Parasia 980, Tamia 974,

Table 10.2 : Chhindwara District: Sub-Districtwise Sex Ratio of Scheduled Tribes—2001

Sl. No.	Sub-Districts	Sex ratio (No. of Females per thousand Males)		
		Total	Rural	Urban
1.	Tamia	974	974	—
2.	Amanwara	1007	1009	934
3.	Chaurai	969	971	911
4.	Jamai	996	1000	957
5.	Parasia	980	982	974
6.	Chhindwara	991	1000	946
7.	Sausar	959	965	894
8.	Bichhua	997	997	—
9.	Pandhurna	985	987	932
	Total District	**989**	—	—

Sources: Census, 2001.

Chaurai 969 and Sansar show 959 Females per thousand Males (**Table 10.2** and **Figure 10.2**). It is fact that rural areas of every sub-districts indicate high sex ratio with comparison of Females per thousand Males of urban areas. Sub-District-wise sex ratio in rural and urban areas is as Amarwara 1009 and 934, Jamai 1000 and 957, Chhindwara 1000 and 946, Pandhurna

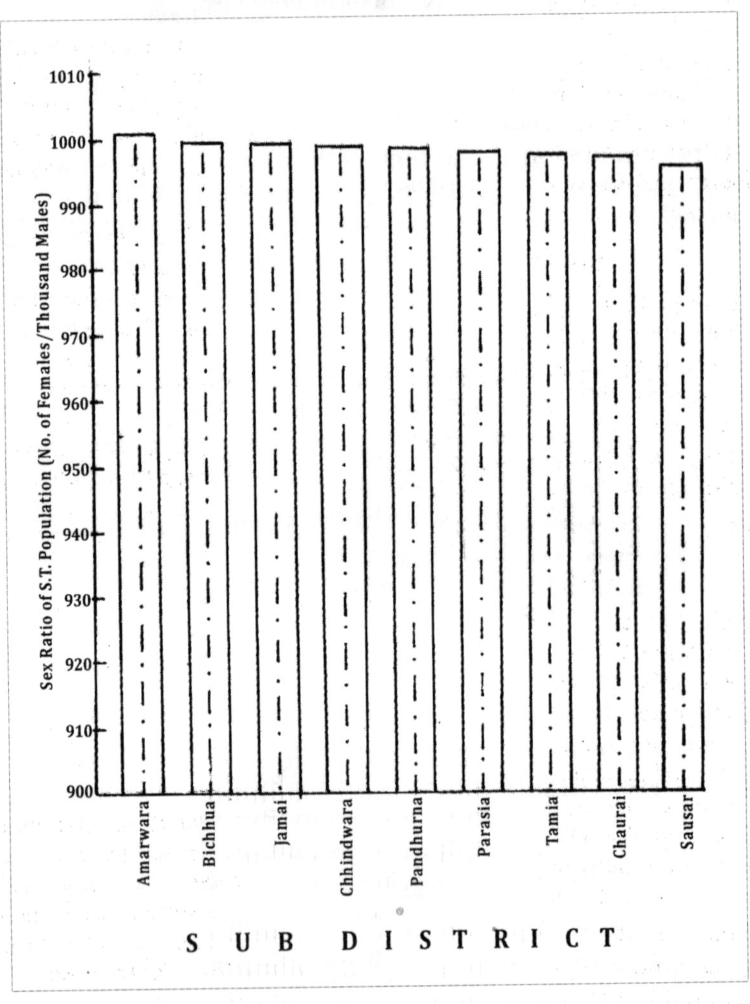

Fig. 10.2. Sex Ratio of Scheduled Tribes Population, 2001

987 and 932, Parasia 982 and 974, Chaurai 971 and 911, Sausar 965 and 894 Females per thousand Males respectively. It is necessary to present that Tamia and Bichhua Sub-Districts are entirely rural as well as unurbanised whose sex ratio of Scheduled Tribes population are found better than that of Chaurai and Sausar urbanised sub-districts.

Socio-Economic Characteristics of a Scheduled Tribe 'Gonds'

'Gonds' is the largest populous Scheduled Tribe of the Study region so this is selected to study of socio-economic characteristics. According to Census 2001, the total population of Gonds is recorded as 82.70% of the total population of Scheduled Tribes. It is observed by National Council of Applied Economic Research, New Delhi that the slopes of Satpura mountain ranges, about 55 miles from Chhindwara, there is a cupshapped valley sheltered by high hills and inhabited by the Bharias and the Gonds. For centuries, this valley had been cut off from outside contacts and modern socio-economic changes taking places elsewhere in M.P. have not made of an impact on this area. Even today the valley is not easily accessible, the only access to it being through several hundred stone steps which on has to climb down to reach the valley.

The major socio-economic characteristics of 'Gonds' of Chhindwara District are given in the following manners:

(*i*) ***Physical Traits***: The Gonds have solid body structure. They are of black and solid dark brown colour. Thick, black curly hair, round head, oval face, flat nose, black eyes, wide nostrils and mustaches with less hair are the main physical tracts of the body structure of the Gonds. Female Gonds are found shorter and fairer than Male Gonds in the study region.

(*ii*) ***Colonies***: The rural houses of Gonds traditionally, even now are mostly of mud. On 'kachcha' mud walls, a proof of bamboo with local tiles and watch is laid. The floor of house is also of mud, but it is well made and plastered with cowdung. Normally, a small three room house is constructed by those who can afford. One of the room becomes for general use. The other one as kitchen and stores, and the last one for the cattles. In the 'badi' behind the house a 'mandha' is constructed on which grass etc. are stored. The compound wall in this region is built all around and rooms run around. The inner wall without a break. But the urban houses of Gonds are made not only traditionally but also in recently model and generally constructed by bricks or stones.

(*iii*) ***Habitat***: The settlement of villages are generally small with 40 to 60 huts. On hills, villages are very small. Raw bricks, straw and mud are used to make habitat. The walls are also made of grasses and slides of timber. The shape of huts is like a rectangular nature. The huts are made in parallel pattern and gape between two huts remains 5 to 10 metres. The figure of man and animals are made on the walls (outer) of the rooms. Corridors, kitchen, bedroom and rooms for the pigs are important parts of a hut. Gonds keep same beds, mats, baskets, grinders of stone and other things of basic needs in their habitats.

(*iv*) ***Food and Drinks***: Gonds eat kutki, mahua, bajra, sanwa, dodma etc. as staple food. They also eat fish and meat of titar-bater and other wild animals and birds. Tea has become a popular beverage of morning and is available even in houses of Gonds. Smoking (locally manufactured 'bidi') is the popular hobby among those who enjoy smoking. Ganja, bhang, tobacco, supari and pan are also used with great interest and hobby. Flesh of cow is prohibited and can beaten in no case.

(*v*) ***Economical Conditions***: The main occupation of Gonds in recent time is fishing, hunting and gathering. Fishes are planted in the ponds but hunting is being practised but prohibited by the local and Central Environment. Forest based things like fruits, vegetables, honey, herbs, flowers, mahua, gular, semal-cotton, amaltas, gums, date, tad, lakh, jamun, sabudana, mango, amrood, tendu patta are generally collected by Scheduled Tribes whom they sell in the local markets. They keep the cow, buffaloes and goats for milk based things, oxes for ploughing and carrying goods, and pigs, pigeons and hens for flesh. Beside above, the occupations of Gonds are handcrafts and agriculture. They make basket, mat and bag by timber. The participation rate in agriculture is very high in Gonds. In the ancient times 'Jhuming Cultivation' was in practice after slashing and burning the vegetational groups. This kind of cultivation was named as 'Dippa'. On the slope of hills cultivation is called as 'Penda', kulhadi and kudali are used in this cultivation. Lack of facilities of irrigation, seeds, fertilizers and technology have caused very low productivity in the said region. Mining is another occupation of Gonds after agriculture.

(*vi*) ***Social System*** : Gonds are freely permitted for polygamy but polyandry is not at all in volgue even exceptionally. The lower category of the society generally marriages between the sons and daughters of the maternal uncle and aunt is not taboo. Cross cousin marriage in the preferential form of marriage. Among those Gonds who are not Hinduised, the 'barat' goes from the girl's house to the bridegoom, and marriage takes place there. The Gonds have their own priest, the 'bumka' who performs the marriage. Child marriage, dowry and divorce are the social evils of Gonds society but the marriage of widows is continued traditionally until now as the name of 'patkarna' and 'Gandharwa Vivah'. Both joint and separate families of Gonds are until traditional. All the member of family of Gonds generally engaged himself in hunting, fishing, gathering and agriculture. The believe in black magic (Jadu-tona) and in spirit (bhut-pret badha) is measured to a large extent. All clans of Gonds worship their individual shrine of 'Baradeo' who is equated with 'Mahadeo', 'Bhimsen' or 'Bhime' is another God of Gonds. Educationally the Gonds and their women are still very backward in comparison to agglomerating population and the Scheduled Castes (Gazetteer, 1995).

Problems of Scheduled Tribes Population

The following types of problem of Scheduled Tribes population are noted in Chhindwara District:

(*i*) Demographic problem

(*ii*) Food and malnutritional problem

(*iii*) Drinking water problem

(*iv*) Residential problem

(*v*) Poverty problem

(*vi*) Unemployment problem

(*vii*) Illiteracy problem

(*viii*) Communicational problem

(*ix*) Energy problem

(*x*) Medical problem

(*xi*) Environmental problem

(*xii*) Social problem

(*xiii*) Other problems.

The analysis of the above problems are given below:

(i) Demographic Problem: Areal disparities of population distribution, density, growth rate (birth rate and mortality rate) and sex ratio are the major demographic problems of Scheduled Tribes population of the

District. Maternal mortality rates and infant mortality rates are thought as the most important aspects which are measured very high. Amarwara Sub-District holds maximum (1,34,028) population and Sausar Sub-District shows minimum (28,823) population of Scheduled Tribes of the total population of the Scheduled Tribes (6,41,421). Tamia (974/1000), Chaurai (969ϕ1000), Jamai (996/1000), Parasia (980/1000), Chhindwara (991/1000), Sausar (959/1000), Bichhua (97/1000) and Pandhurna (985/1000) Sub-Districts specially designated below numbers of Females per thousand Males. The minimum females per thousand Males have been recorded in Sausar Sub-District which is an indicative of disbalance sex ratio.

(ii) ***Food and Malnutritional Problem:*** The problem of food and malnutrition are serious in Scheduled Tribes society. The scheme of P.D.S. (Public distribution system) is not fully succeeded because of too much corruption in administrative and supply system. The standard of minimum calories is not available to Scheduled Tribes families in daily meal. The malnutritional problems exist dominant in children and women. Low weight and less hight according to age in children, and low working capabily with various type of diseases are seen in tribal communities due to malnutrition and food crisis.

(iii) ***Drinking Water Problem :*** The fresh drinking water is an essential need and human right. It is hardly available along tribal communities due to uneven terrain and compact stony surfaces of surroundings. Underground water is not easily available and drilling of wells in stony structure of rocks is also a critical task. For the removal of drinking water supply, governmental projects for constituting hand pumps, tubewells and other sources are properly managed but not sufficient.

(iv) ***Residential Problem:*** Residence or habitat is one of the most important needs of mankind, basically. The houses of Scheduled Tribes of the study region traditionally, even now are mostly made of mud with proof of bamboos and Grasses. These type of houses are not safeguard by the attack of wildlife and thiefs. A large number of Scheduled Tribes population are found houseless. The governmental colonies are just like a drop in the ocean. Sewerages create problem but meaningless.

(v) ***Poverty Problem:*** Poverty is like a curse of human life. Only low families of Scheduled Tribes stand upto B.P.L. (below to poverty line) standard. Low level of agricultural activities and food gathering processes have caused the population to maintain the life system, below poverty line. Crux of poverty may be traced in Tamia Sub-District where lack of life supporting system creates problem and daily wages towards work done is provided minimum.

(vi) ***Unemployment Problem:*** Unemployment is the roof of poverty. The economy of Scheduled Tribes is mainly agrobased and the workers are treated as cultivators, agricultural labourers and other workers. Traditional household industries give low income and outputs. The non-workers and marginal workers are also seen maximum. Very high dependency rate in Scheduled Tribes population shows unemployment problem with poverty.

(vii) ***Illiteracy Problem:*** Illiteracy is also a curse of society. According to Census Abstract, 2001 about 61.94% population is noticed illiterate where in 70.75% population corresponds to Female population of Scheduled Tribes. More than half (50.53%) Male population of Scheduled Tribes is also illiterate. The low literacy rate is observed in Tamia (37.54%), Amarwara (37.79%), Chaurai (37.47%), Jamai (26.17%),

Parasia (40.01%), Chhindwara (46.37%), Sausar (48.98%), Bichhua (44.58%) and Pandhurna (42.96%).

(viii) ***Communicational Problem:*** Communicational development is the backbone of modern development of mankind. The study area is dominated with plateaux and mountainous counting so that the connectivity and accessibility of road transport is minimized where except valley region where human inhabitation is most common. Metalled roads are mostly available in urban and sub-urban areas where rural areas are established with unmetalled roads. The telicom, information technology and postal amenities are not found satisfactory in the Scheduled Tribes population areas.

(ix) ***Energy Problem:*** Energy resources are the lifeline for human agglomeration. Although study region is rich with respect to coal production yet elastic supply is not in proper way. For cooking the food, traditionally people used the lumbar and waste material of agricultural products. L.P.G. (Liquified petroleum gas) connections are not available in tribal areas, satisfactory. The awareness and application about solar energy system is also absent.

(x) ***Medical Problem:*** Use of medicine is beneficial for long and healthy life. Scheduled Tribes believe in black magic (jadu tona) and in spirit (bhut-pret badha) to a large extent and thus their medicinal approach is highly associated with these activities, proper medical services are also not available there. They are relied upon to curve the common disease by the use of mantras (jhad-funk). A large number of Tribal population is depended on Ayurvedic (Desi) medicines inspite of modern medical facilities.

(xi) ***Environmental Problem:*** Environment is the basis of origin the most responsible factor of human society. The Tribal societies generally used dirty and polluted

water which gives rise to various type of diseases as cholera, typhoid, dysentry, diarrhoea, ascarisis, jaundice etc. The quarrel, broil and enmity is also affected to peaceful environment of the tribal societies.

(xii) ***Social Problem:*** Polygamy, polyandry, dowry, child marriage, divorce are burning marital problems of tribal society. Beside its drinking, gambling and smoking are the other notable social problems of tribes. Low living standard, illiteracy, unawareness and folkways have promoted them.

(xiii) ***Other Problems:*** The superstitional, moral and cultural bigotry are other problems as vibrant in tribal societies. It makes an unwanted environment of disconnectivity to the main stream of national development and of modern and general social system.

Conclusion

As a matter of fact about one-third (34.68%) population of the total population of District Chhindwara, is Scheduled Tribes and totally avoided to modern development. Problems as demographic, malnutritional, drinking water, residential, poverty, unemployment, illiteracy, communicational, energy, medical, environmental, social and cultural have deeply abstracted the modern development of Tribes. The awareness in tribal societies with the governmental and non-governmental supports and faithful implementation of development policies by the District administration can give the sustainable development of tribal societies which will be the most important factor in equity based society.

REFERENCES

1. Census of India, 2001.
2. *District Development Book* (Hindi), 2007: District Statistical Office, District Chhindwara, M.P., pp. 1-3.

3. *District Statistical Handbook* (Hindi), 2007: District Statistical Office, District Chhindwara, M.P., Table 2.9, p. 19.

4. Gazetteer of India, 1995: District Gazetteer, Chhindwara, Gazetteer Unit, Directorate of Rajbhasha Evam Sanskriti, Department of Culture, Government of M.P., Bhopal, pp. 78-85.

5. Pandey, A; 2007: Population, Environment and Public Health, Chhindwara M.P. (Hindi), a Research Paper Published in Population and Environment (Hindi), Ed. by Prasad, G., Pandey, A. and Kislaya, S.; Discovery Publishing House, 483/24, Ansari Road, Daryaganj, New Delhi, pp. 24-38.

6. Pandey, A.; 2007: *Population Geography of India* (Hindi), Discovery Publishing House, 4831/24, Ansari Road, Daryaganj, New Delhi, pp. 191-192.

7. Pandey, A.; 2010: Recent Trends of Geomorphological Analysis (Hindi), Discovery Publishing House, 4831/24, Ansari Road, Daryaganj, New Delhi.

CHAPTER

11

Tragedy of Crimes

Anupam Pandey

Introduction

The Crime is like a cancer in healthy body of any happy human-society of any geographical area. It is handicapped the human culture, civilisation, moral and holistic values and a peaceful environment of the concerned scenario. In fact, crime is an unwanted incidence for humanity as well as mankind. The tragedy of burning crimes in Chhindwara District, M.P. is indicated as never lasting and most injurious. The control and prevention of crime is first aid need of present for reinstatement of humanity and reformation of fearless society of the study region.

Geographical Background of the Study Region

Chhindwara District (M.P.) is located in Satpura Range of Vindhyachal-Baghelkhand Region of Peninsular India. Chhindwara is one of the largest district of Jabalpur Division of Madhya Pradesh. It extends between the latitude of 21°27′30″ and 22°47′45″ North and longitudes of 78°15′10″ and 79°24′30″ East (Pandey, A., 2007). The total geographical area of the study region is 11815 square kilometres. The Districts of Hoshangabad and Narsimhapur make the Northern boundary, and Nagpur and Amrawati Districts of Maharashtra State demark the Southern boundary of the

District. Beside its Seoni and Betul Districts make the East and West boundary respectively. There are 08 Tahsils and 11 Development Blocks in the region (**Figure 11.1**).

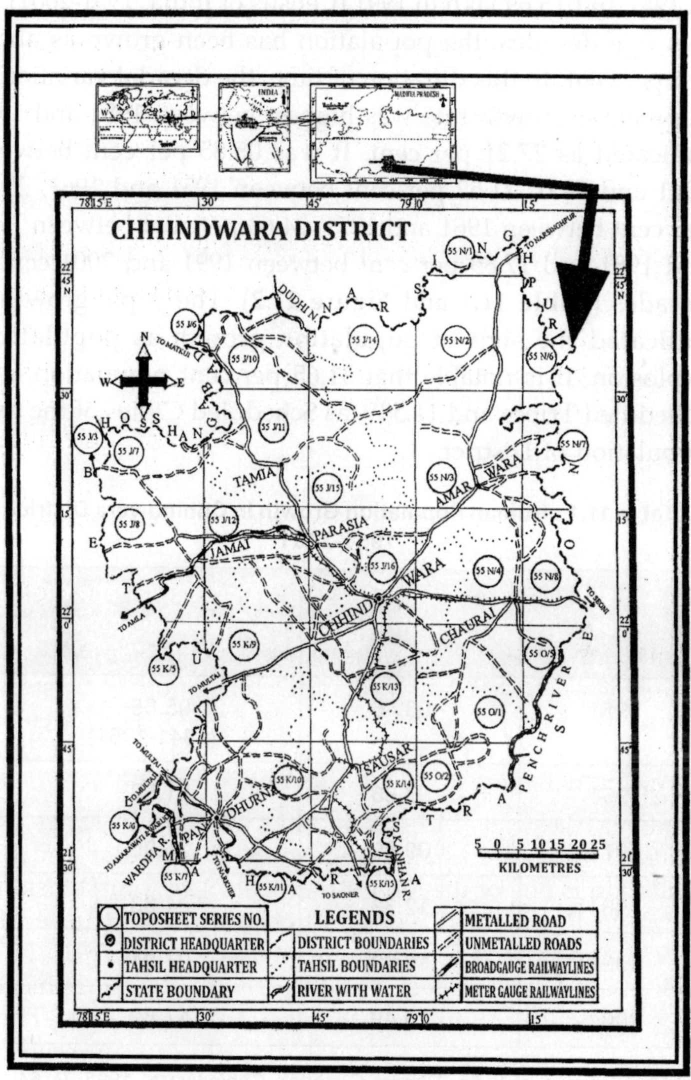

Fig. 11.1. Location Map

On the basis of Census 2001, the total population of District is 1849283 persons (Pandey, A., 2010). It was 06.46 lakh in 1951, 07.86 lakh in 1961, 09.89 lakh in 1971, 12.33 lakh in 1981 and 15.69 lakh in 1991 (Census of India, 1951-2001). In this five decades, the population has been grown as about 286 per cent. In this duration of time, the decadal variation in population growth rate was highest between 1981 and 1991 indicated as 27.21 per cent. It was 05.85 per cent between 1941 and 1951, 21.52 per cent between 1951 and 1961, 25.95 per cent between 1961 and 1971, 24.63 per cent between 1971 and 1981 and 17.89 per cent between 1991 and 2001 census decades (**Table 11.1** and **Figure 11.2**). The triple growth is indicated the sign of population growth as population-explosion. It is notable that 31.65 per cent population is as Scheduled Tribes and 11.58% as Scheduled Castes of the total population of District.

Table 11.1 : Human Population Growth in Chhindwara District: 1951-2001

Census Year	Population growth (Lakh)	Decadal variation in Population growth (Per cent)
1951	06.46	05.85 (1941-1951)
1961	07.86	21.52
1971	09.89	25.95
1981	12.33	24.63
1991	15.69	27.21
2001	18.49	17.89

Source: Census of India, District Gazetter, Chhindwara, 1995, P. 64, Zila Sankhyiki Pustika, 2007, p. 9 and self calculated.

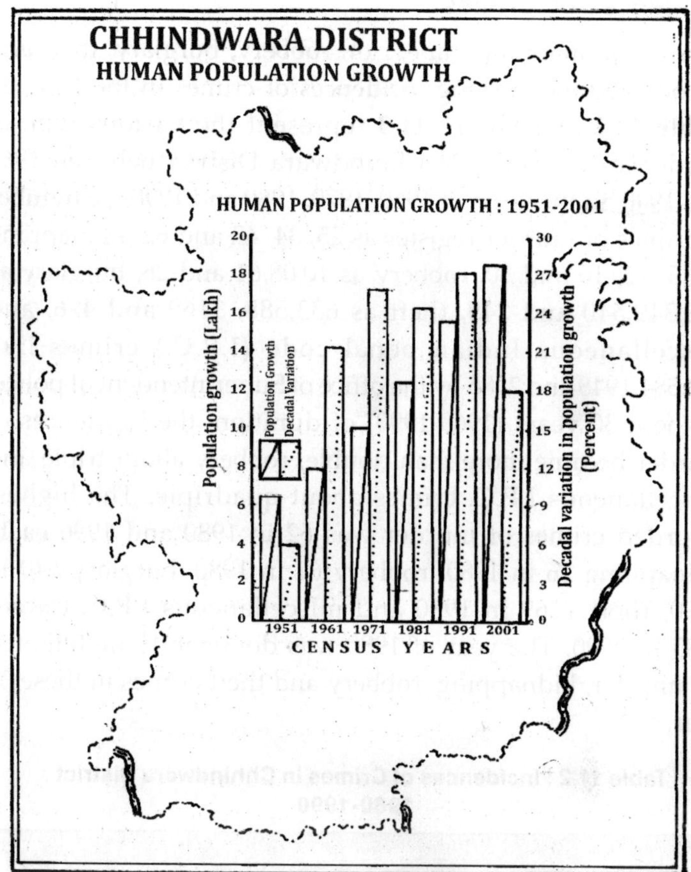

Fig. 11.2.

Circumstances of Crimes

Although the human population of the District needs peaceful environment of living but crime has been cropped out due to some defaulters of low mentalities. The unwanted and immoral activities of these criminals have badly puzzled the human habitation. Children and womens are the main victim of these criminals. So, the various type of crimes are represented in the study area.

Incidences of Crimes

Murder, kidnapping, rape, riot, robbery, burglary, theft and dacoity are the burning incidences of crimes in the District. **Table 11.2** and **Figure 11.3** represent the various type of incidences of crimes in Chhindwara District between 1960 and 1990. In the years of 1960, 1970, 1980 and 1990 the number of crimes of murder register as 25, 34, 42 and 62, kidnapping as 13, 12, 16 and 10, robbery as 10,08,61 and 28, burglary as 248,349,540 and 245, theft as 633,588, 1169 and 476, and miscellaneous Indian penal code (I.P.C.) crimes like 652,584,1948 and 2385 by the office of Superintendent of police. In these 30 years (1960-1990) of duration, the incidences of murder became more than double, robbery about triple and miscellaneous I.P.C. crimes about quadriple. The highest recorded crimes of murder was 62 in 1980 and 1990 each, kidnapping 16 in 1980, robbery 61 in 1980, burglary 540 in 1980, theft 1169 in 1980 and miscellaneous I.P.C. crimes 2385 in 1990. The year of 1980 was dominantly highlighted for murder, kidnapping, robbery and theft crimes in these 30 year.

Table 11.2 : Incidences of Crimes in Chhindwara District : 1960-1990

Year	Type of Crimes					
	Murder	Kidnapping	Robbery	Burglary	Theft	Misc. I.P.C. Crimes
1960	25	13	10	248	633	652
1970	34	12	08	349	588	584
1980	62	16	61	540	1169	1948
1990	62	10	28	245	476	2385

Source: Superintendent of Police, Chhindwara, District Gazetter, Chhindwara, 1995, p. 254.

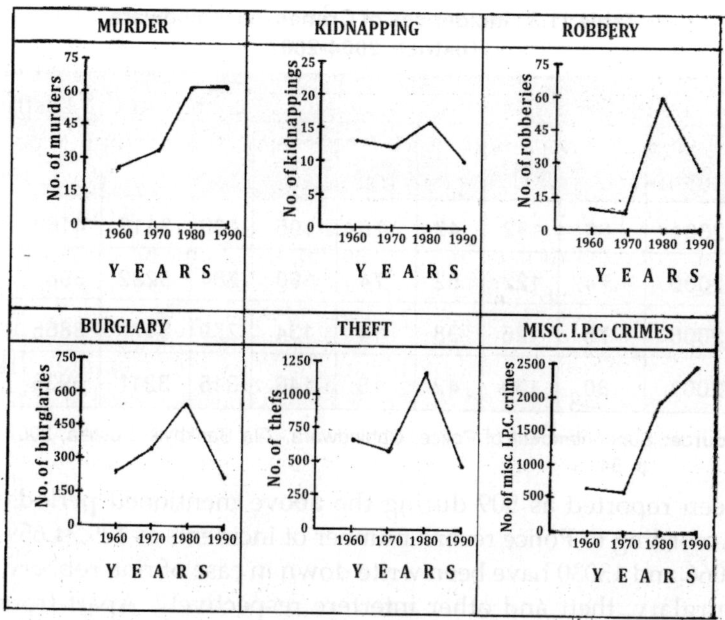

Fig. 11.3. Incidences of Crimes in Chhindwara District 1960-1990

Table 11.3 and **Figure 11.4** depict the current incidences of crimes in Chhindwara District between the year of 2004 and 2007. In this period the murder, rape, riot, robbery, burglary, theft and other type of crimes are recorded in the office of S.P. in Chhindwara. All types of crime in total has been recorded as 4162 in 2004, 3963 in 2005, 3855 in 2006 and 3936 in 2007 respectively. These numbers of crime has presented the dangerous crime of criminal's activities. In the year of 2004, 2005, 2006 and 2007 the number of murder 66, 74, 76 and 80, rape 132, 122, 125 and 130, riot 47, 52, 38 and 42, robbery 28, 14, 14 and 18, burglary 195,190,134 and 140, theft 188,284,279 and 315, and other interferes 3410, 3232, 3177 and 3211 are recorded in the region. Murder is the most dangerous incidence of crime which is increasing day by day. During the year of 2004 and 2007 total 296 cases of murder has been recorded. Maximum 80 cases of murder have shocked out the region in 2007. The heart rending events of rape have

Table 11.3 : Incidences of Crimes in Chhindwara District: 2004-2007

Year	Type of Crimes							
	Murder	Rape	Riot	Robbery	Burglary	Theft	Other Interferes	Total Crimes
2004	66	132	47	28	195	188	3410	4162
2005	74	122	52	74	190	284	3232	3963
2006	76	125	38	14	134	279	3177	3855
2007	80	130	42	18	140	315	3211	3936

Source: Superintendent of Police, Chhindwara, Zila Sankhyiki Pustika, 2007, p. 84.

been reported as 509 during the above mentioned periods. According to Police record number of incidents as 179,74,659, 1066 and 13030 have been write down in case of riot, robbery, burglary, theft and other interfere respectively. Apart from the above years it is apparent to point out that several cases have been happened but not registered.

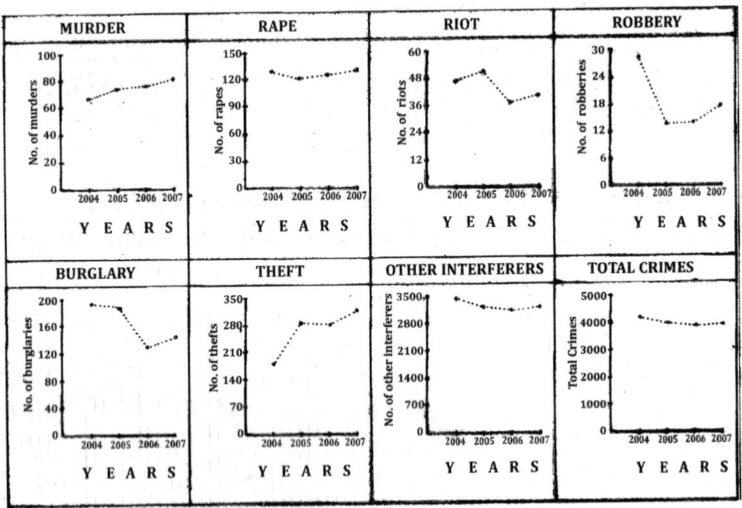

Fig. 11.4. Current Incidences of Crimes in Chhindwara District, 2004-07

Criminal Cases

The details of criminal cases in Chhindwara District during the year of 1975 and 1993 have been given in **Table 11.4** and **Figure 11.5** is divided in three types (i) Indian Penal Code (I.P.C.) (ii) Special and Local Laws (S.L.L.) and (iii) Criminal Procedure Code (C.P.C.) by Office/Court of Hon'ble District Judges and Sessions Judges of Chhindwara. Criminal cases under the I.P.C. was registered as 1779 in 1975, 2828 in 1980, 2853 in 1985, 3252 in 1990 and 3661 in year 1993. In 1993, maximum criminal cases of I.P.C. were noted. Criminal cases of special and local laws were reported as 5040 in 1975, 4979 in 1980, 5750 in 1985, 7788 in 1990 and 5426 in year 1993 in which 7788 cases of 1990 were recorded as highest. Apart from the above number of C.P.C. cases as 508 in 1975, 354 in 1980, 1015 in 1985, 1048 in 1990 and 1444 in year 1993 were denoted in which 1444 cases of year 1993 highlight the highest number of criminal cases. Total criminal cases including with I.P.C., S.L.L. and C.P.C. were registered as 7327 in 1975, 8161 in 1980, 9816 in 1985, 12088 in 1990 and 10531 in year 1993. The highest number of total criminal cases as 12088 have been recorded in the year of 1990 which is the indicative of dangerous growth of crimes in the District. Notable that in

Table 11.4 : Criminal Cases in Chhindwara District: 1975-1993

Year	Type of Criminal Cases			Total Criminal cases
	Indian Penal Code (I.R.C.)	Special and local laws (S.L.L.)	Criminal Procedure Code (C.P.C.)	
1975	1779	5040	508	7327
1980	2828	4979	354	8161
1985	2853	5750	1015	9816
1990	3252	7788	1048	12088
1993	3661	5426	1444	10531

Source: District Judge and Sessions Judge, Chhindwara, District Gazetteer Chhindwara, 1995, pp. 263-264.

this duration of 18 years (1975-1993) the criminal cases under the I.P.C. and C.P.C. have increased double to triple times. Special and Local Laws cases were also increased similarly in this base periods.

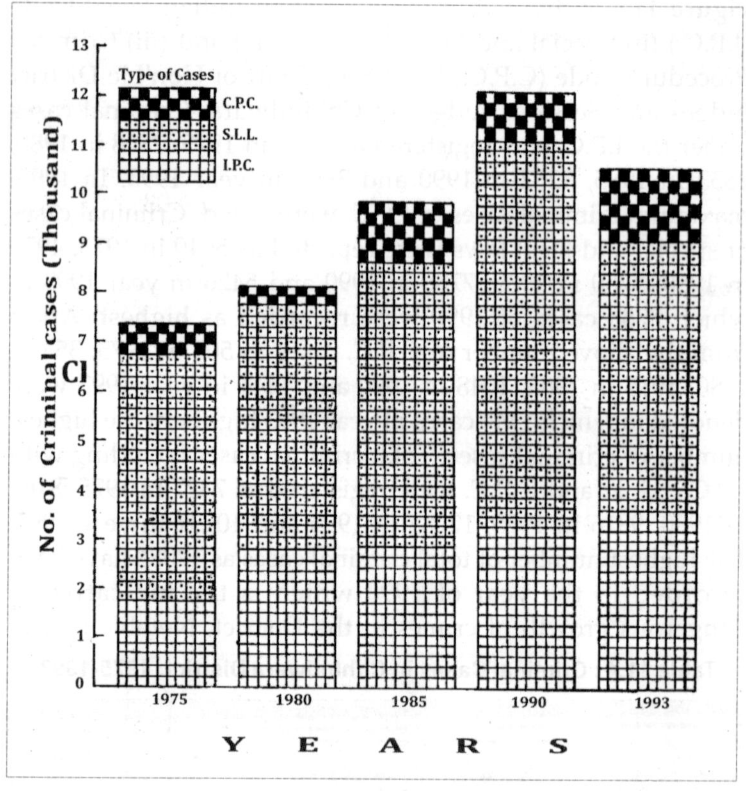

Fig. 11.5.

Convicted Persons

Table 11.5 and **Figure 11.6** represent the convicted persons in Chhindwara District between the year 1975 and 1993 in the various offences as (i) affecting human body (ii) affecting public health and (iii) against property. There are recognized on the basis of decision of the court of Hon'ble District Judges and Sessions Judges of Chhindwara. Number of convicted

Table 11.5 : Convicted Persons in Chhindwara District: 1975-1993

Year	Type of Offences			Total Convicted Person
	Affecting Human body	Affecting Public health	Against property	
1975	397	—	201	588
1980	445	320	473	1238
1985	306	443	277	1026
1990	199	305	91	595
1993	809	140	1127	2076

Source: District Judge and Sessions Judge, Chhindwara, District Gazetteer, Chhindwara, 1995, p. 265.

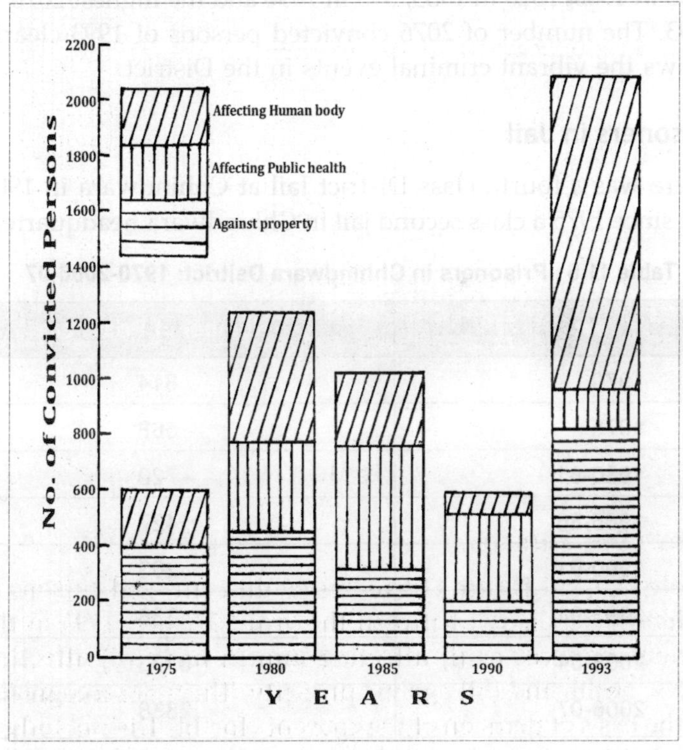

Fig. 11.6. Convicted Person in Chhindwara District, 1975-1993

person in 'offence of affective human body' was presented as 397 in 1975, 445 in 1980, 306 in 1985, 199 in 1990 and highest 809 in 1993. In the duration of 18 yers it has been increased more than double. Convicted persons in 'offence of affecting public health' were calculated as 320 in 1980, 443 in 1985, 305 in 1990 and 140 in 1993. Beside the above, the convicted persons under the 'offence of against property' was nominated as 201 in 1975, 472 in 1980, 277 in 1985, 91 in 1990 and the highest 1127 in 1993. The highest number of convicted persons under the offence of against property as 1127 in 1993 with in the duration of past 18 years are indicated a very high increasement. The number of total convicted persons in afforesaid three type of offences was noted as 588 in 1975, 1238 in 1980, 1026 in 1985, 595 in 1990 and the highest 2076 in 1993. The number of 2076 convicted persons of 1993 clearly shows the vibrant criminal events in the District.

Prisoners in Jail

There was a fourth class District Jail at Chhindwara in 1906 but since 1975 a class second jail in Chhindwara headquarters

Table 11.6 : Prisoners in Chhindwara Dsitrict: 1970-2006-07

Year	Number of Prisoners
1970	814
1975	568
1980-81	720
1985-86	427
1990-91	263
1993-94	338
2003-04	3333
2006-07	2838

Source: Superintendent of Jail, Chhindwara, District Gazetteer, Chhindwara, 1995, p. 261 and Zila Sankhyiki Pustika, 2007, p. 88.

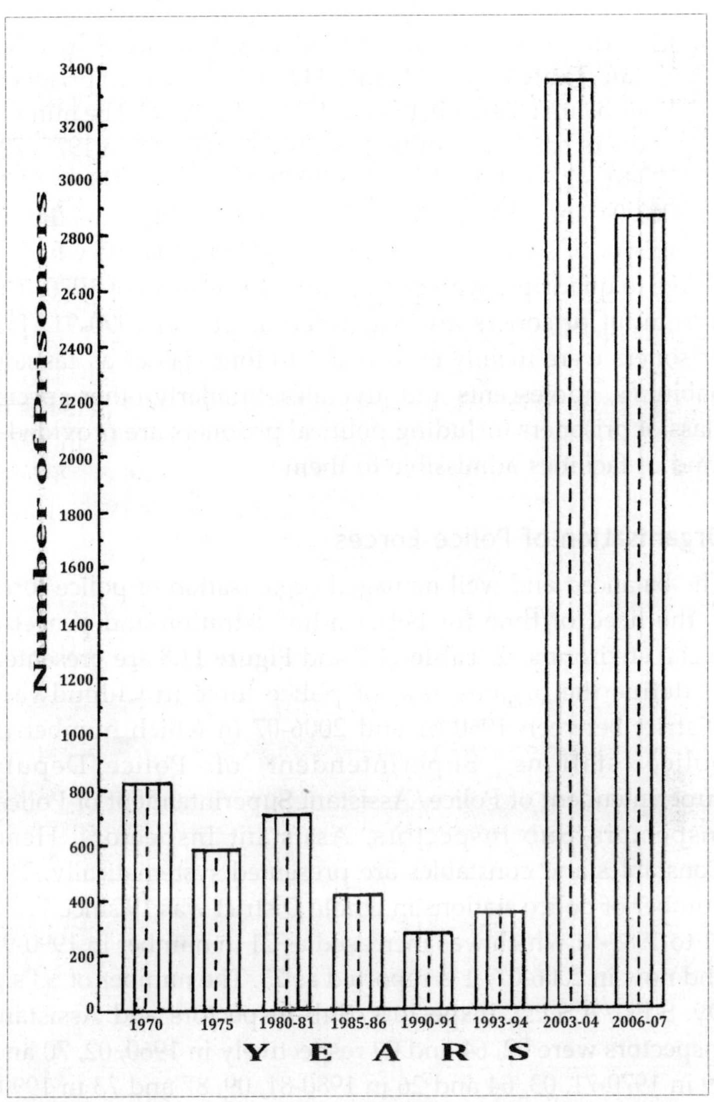

Fig. 11.7. Prisoners in Chhindwara District Jail 1970—2006-07

and two judicial lockups at Sausar and Amanoara were located. According to the District Gazetteer, 1995, the jail was under the charge of Superintendent and had accommodation for 178 prisoners. The Superintendent was assisted by other usual staff. **Table 11.6** and **Figure 11.7** is shown about prisoners in Chhindwara District between 1970 and 2006-07. The number of prisoners has been notified as 814 in 1970, 568 in 1975, 720 in 1980-81, 427 in 1985-86, 263 in 1990-91, 338 in 1993-94, 3333 in 2003-04 and 2838 in 2006-07 respectively. The maximum number of prisoners is registered as 3333 in 2003-04 which is above to quadriple with respect to 814 prisoners of 1970. The minimum prisoners are registered as 263 in 1990-91. The prisoners were mainly classified into four classes as casuals, habituals, adolescents and juveniles. Similarly other special class of prisoners including political prisoners are provided a kind of facilities admissible to them.

Organisation of Police Forces

The balanced and well managed organisation of police force is the need of time for better administration and peaceful social environment. **Table 11.7** and **Figure 11.8** are presented to define the organisation of police force in Chhindwara District between 1960-61 and 2006-07 in which number of police stations, Superintendent of Police/Deputy Superintendent of Police/Assistant Superintendent of Police. Inspectors/Sub Inspectors, Assistant Inspectors, Head Constables and constables are presented systematically. The number of police stations in whole District was 19 since 1960-61 to 1980-81 which was increased as 21 in number in 1990-91 and now in 2006-07, it is reported as 23. The number of S.Ps./ Dy. S.Ps./A.S.Ps., Inspectors/Sub Inspectors and Assistant Inspectors were 02, 64 and 09 respectively in 1960, 02, 70 and 09 in 1970-71, 03, 64 and 26 in 1980-81, 09, 87 and 73 in 1990-91, and 08, 57 and 60 in the year of 2006-07. Beside its the number of Head Constables and constables were 111 and 585 in 1960-61, 124 and 639 in 1970-71, 137 and 741 in 1980-81, 211 and 900 in 1990-91 and now reported as 148 and 612 in 2006-07. The highest numbers of above posts of police department

Table 11.7 : Organisation of Police Forces in Chhindwara District 1960-61—2006-07

Year	Diversified organisation of Police Force					
	Police Staes	S.Ps./Dy. S.Ps. /A.Sps.	Inspectors/ S.Is.	Assistant Inspectors	head Constables	Constables
1960-61	19	02	64	09	111	585
1970-71	19	02	70	09	124	639
1980-81	19	03	64	26	137	741
1990-91	21	09	87	73	211	900
2006-07	23	08	57	60	148	612

Source: Superintendent of Police, Chhindwra, District Gazetteer, Chhindwara, 1995, p. 259 and Zila Sankhyiki Pustika, 2007, p. 87.

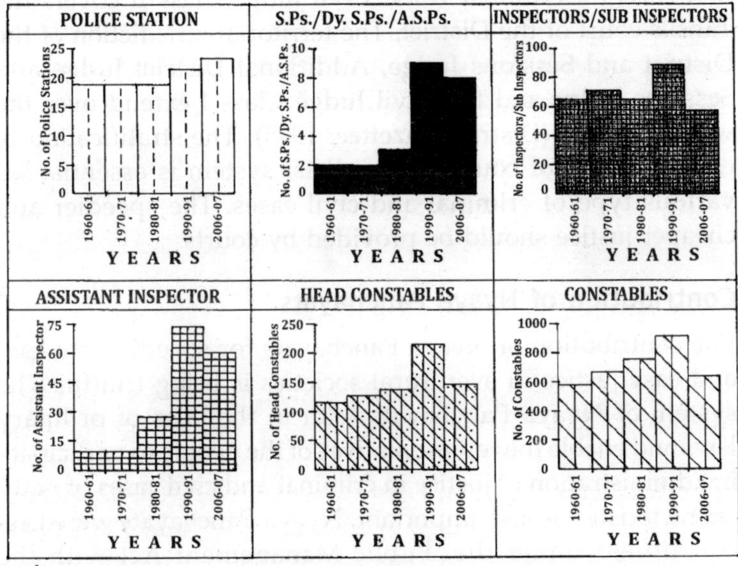

Fig. 11.8. Organisation of Police Forces in Chhindwara District 1960-61—2006-07

as well as organisations is marked in 1990-91. Taking into consideration of existing population and unwanted crimes of the region the aforesaid police force is that like drop of ocean. The qualitative and quantitative requirement of police force is compulsory with modern technology. It is also necessary the large number of Home Guards with recruitments should be provided for District police organisation. According to District Gazetter the number of Home Guards trained in 1980 and from 1985 upwards to 1992 was shown to be 310 for every year.

Establishment of Courts

The Chhindwara Civil District and Sessions Division was created and established in the year of 1961 under the 'Madhya Pradesh Civil Courts Act, 1958'. The Civil and Criminal powers is exercised by all courts of the District. Civil Judges Class I and Class II are designated as Judicial Magistrates, first class for criminal work. Civil Judge Class II covers the Tahsils court of the District. The territorial jurisdiction of the District and Sessions Judge, Additional District Judge and Sessions Judge and the Civil Judge Class I extend over the whole District (District Gazettee, 1995). The stratification of establishment of courts and judicial system is essential for various type of criminal and civil cases. The speedier and cheaper justice should be provided by courts.

Contribution of Nyaya Panchayats

The contribution of Nyaya Panchayats for speedier, cheaper and easy justice in even rural societies is being fruitful. The system of Nyaya Panchayats with in the base of ordinary laws and enable the representatives of the people to participate in administration of justice in criminal and civil cases of petty characteristics is also important. Nyaya Panchayats were first constituted under the 'Public Management Act with the Central Provinces and Berar Village Sanitation, 1920', but it were organised under the 'Madhya Pradesh Panchayats Act, 1962'. There was 64 Nyaya Panchayats exist in 1970 and 67 in 1971 in the District. The number of criminal cases and civil cases stands as 122 an 104 in 1972, 139 and 35 in 1973, 167 and 30 in 1974, and 428 and 40 in respectively generally decided by Nyaya Panchayats of the District. Notable that about half share of the total District population is jointly as Scheduled Tribes and Scheduled Castes so that the importance of Nyaya Panchayats is too much necessary to maintain the social disorder of the communities because they are traditional also today as coarse.

Conclusion

Day by day increasing incidences of burning crimes in Chhindwara District is like the painful tragedy for affected population as well as mankind. Never lastings frequency of most sensitive as murders and rapes are thought to be as serious socio-calamities of the country. A large strength of criminal cases, convicted persons and prisoners are highlighted as the red indicates of increasing crimes on a large scale. The organisation of Police forces and the establishment of courts are as little in number and shape in counting with respect of over population of the District. The upgradation and innovation of Police forces and courts with more number and quality is the present need to the study area. The contribution of Nyaya Panchayats for social justice is also important at present time.

REFERENCES

1. Census of India, 1951-2001: Edited by District Gazetteer, Chhindwara, 1995, p. 65, and Zila Sankhyiki Pustika, 2007, p. 9.
2. District Gazetteer, Chhindwara, 1995: Gazetteers Unit, Directorate of Rajbhasha Evam Sanskriti, Department of Culture, Edited by Sinha, A.M., Government of M.P., Bhopal, pp. 253-255, 258-266 and 269-270.
3. District Judge and Sessions Judge, Chhindwara, 1975-1993; Edited by District Gazetteer, Chhindwara, 1995; pp. 263-265.
4. Pandey, Anupam, 2007: Population, Environment and Public Health (Chhindwara, M.P.), Edited by Prasad, G., Pandey, A. and

Kislaya, S. in 'Population and Environment' DPH, Daryaganj, New Delhi, pp. 24-26.

5. Pandey, Anupam, 2010: Recent Trends of Geomorphological Analysis, Discovery Publishing House Pvt. Ltd. 4831/24, Ansari Road, Darya Ganj, New Delhi-110 002, p. 64.
6. Superintendent of Jail, Chhindwara, 1970-1986: Edited by District Gazetteer, Chhindwara, 1995, p. 261, and Zila Sankhyiki Pustika, 2007, p. 88.
7. Superintendent of Police, Chhindwara, 1960-2007: Edited by District Gazetteer, Chhindwara, 1995, p. 254 and 259, and Zila Sankhiyiki Pustika, 2007, p. 84 and 87.
8. Zila Sankhyiki Pustika, 2007: Zila Sankhyiki Karyalaya, Chhindwara, p. 9, 84, 87 and 88.

PART-B

MODERN DEVELOPMENT OF AGRICULTURE

CHAPTER

12

Techniques of Agricultural Research

Govind Prasad and Santosh Kumar Singh

Introduction

The present chapter highlights the summary account of carrying capacity of agricultural lands intensity of cropping, cropping diversity, rotation of crops, demarcation of crop combination region and agricultural regions systematically. The matter of the concern topic is reviewed from various books and journals previously advocated by pioneer workers of said discipline. The subject matter is closely concerned with agricultural Geography and too much useful for socio-economic planners. Agricultural research is very much important in developing countries of the world.

Introduction to a carrying Capacity of the Agricultural Land

In subsistence economy, it is the agricultural land that has to provide sustenance to the population even though it is increasing at a faster rate. The term carrying capacity is the maximum number of people that a given land area will maintain in perpetuity under a given system of uses without land degradation setting (Steet, 1969). Professor L.D. Stamp had raised two important questions in which first is the maximum number of people can support in terms of food in a sq. mile/km. of productive land. The second question is the population needed to secure maximum production with maximum efficiency. Many scholars have tried to assess the production of land and its man bearing capacity. Mukherjee (1938) has stated that in a country like India one acre of agricultural land would be indispensable for the nourishment of one person. Shafi (1969) has also studied about the carrying capacity of land of India to bear the burden of five times of existing population. According to Kumar (1986), the carrying capacity of land depends upon the nature of land like Bhit land, dhanhar land, gaurha land (most productive land) etc. as studied in Nalanda district, Bihar.

Measurement of Intensity of Cropping

The intensity of cropping may be defined as the degree of cropping or the number of crops grown in the same plot during one agricultural year. If is an indication of the total cropped area as distinguished from the net area sown. The difference between the two is brought about by the area on which more than one crop is grown during the one agricultural year. It may be stated as Net area sown + area sown more than once is equal to total cropped area. In case when only one crop is grown during the whole agriculture year, the net area sown and the total cropped area will be equal and crop intensity will be only one. But, on the other hand, a portion of the cultivated area is sown more than once. *e.g.* Out of 10 acres if 2 acres are sown more than once, the total cropped area would get increased to that extent, *i.e.*, it becomes 10 + 2 = 12 acres and the crop intensity also increases (the same land during the same agricultural year) yields more than one crop) to 1:2. The data become very useful because these data exhibit the nature of the cropping pattern and productive capacity of the land. Such data also highlights about the possibilities or otherwise of intensification of agriculture or enhancing of production through expansion of double cropping.

The intensity of cropping may be calculated with the help of following formula:

$$I = \frac{TCA}{NAS} \times 100$$

where I = Intensity Index of Cropping

TCA = Total Cropped Area

and

NAS = Net Area sown

In case where only one crop in one agriculture year is grown then the degree of intensity index will be 1 and the index number of crop intensity will be 100 per cent while in the other hand, the degree of intensity will be 1 : 2 and the index number of crop intensity will be 120 per cent. Thus, the index number of crop intensity increases with the increase in the area sown more than once. The intensity of cropping may be classified as high, medium and low categories according to intensity percentage.

It is pertinent to point out that areas hairing high index of intensity reveal the dominance of productive soils, developed irrigation facilities and developed agricultural practices. Similarly, the areas indicating low index of intensity may produce less crops either due to unsuitable land, water-logging land, non-agricultural use of land and less developed irrigational facilities. Kumar (1986) has calculated three categories for example A-High intensity index (above 180 per cent) B-Medium intensity index (between 160-180 per cent) and C-low intensity index (between 150-160 per cent) in the Nalanda districts of Bihar, India.

Measurement of Cropping Diversity

A thick blanketing of productive soil, easily available irrigational facilities and suitable eco-climatic conditions in respect of growing crops of the region causes intensive agriculture which in turn shows cropping diversity in the region. Climatic change is the major factor for cropping diversity. The cropping diversity denotes more than one crop specially three or four crops in one agricultural year in most productive piece of land. The scientific use of agricultural land necessitates more work and provides employment to more inhabitants. Recent scientific techniques, and recent varieties of seeds are also responsible for cropping diversity.

The index of multiple cropping can be used as a yardstick for measuring the intensity of agricultural land use and also diversity of cropping. The cropping characteristics reveals the fact of too much diversification in cropping pattern in the region. The index of cropping diversification may be statistically calculated with the help of following formula:

$$X = \frac{\text{Percentage of TCA under N crops}}{N}$$

where X = Crop Diversification

TCA = Total Cropped Area

and

N = Number of Crops

cropping diversity may be categorised as high, medium and low according to grades obtained.

Rotation of Crops

Generally rotation of crops is practised with the purpose to maintain the fertility of the soil and for production of yield because fertility of soil is lost due to overcropping, soil erosion, insufficient application of manures and fertilizers. It is apparent that the agricultural land is generally used for growing crops by cultivators without giving due rest. The fertility of land is maintained either by flood water or by the use of manures or by tactful method of cultivation of farmers. Although farmers do not practise scientific method but they certainly consider the rotation of crops for maintaining productivity of the crop. Rotation of crops also controls the incidence of crops diseases. Sometimes rotation of crops moves around year to year.

Demarcation of Crop Combination Region

Crop combination regions are helpful in understanding the crop association patterns and their regional diversification. The study of crop combination has its vital importance in the study of land use. The study of crop combination of the region is fruitful in many ways (Weaver)—

1. It provides adequate understanding of an individual crop geography.
2. Crop combiantion is in itself an integrative reality that demands definitions and distributional analysis; and
3. Such regions are essential for the construction of still more complex structure of valid agricultural regions.

Moreover, crop combination regions may be used to evaluate if a particular combination would lead to dietary adequacy or inadequacy in the essentially agricultural landscape. It is thought to be as a dominant feature of the agricultural land use of a given region. The concept of crop combination regions appear to be valid as it makes possible the establishment of areas differentiated on the basis of several dominance of crops that are specially related and occur together in varying strength (Dayal, 1967).

Jones and Jones (1954) and Weaver has stated that the the generalisation and identification of crop regions on the basis of single crops are far from satisfactory. The concept of crop combiantion regions appears to be valid, as it makes possible the establishment of areas differentiated on the basis of the real dominance of crops, that are spatially related and occur together in varying strength. It may also be pointed here that the delimination of crop combination regions is merely to facilitate descriptions and comprehension of the agricultural complexities of the area. The delimination is not an end in itself but only a tool towards a better understanding of the agricultural situation (Kumar, 1986).

To divide an area into crop combination regions is a difficult task since it involves a question as to what crops should be included and which crops should be dropped. For the categorization of crop-combination regions reputed geographers like Weaver (1954) Thomos (1965), Johnson (1958), Doi (1957) and Athwale (1966) have suggested several techniques. The method of Athawale is less time consuming and simple. Athawale has attempted to associate the value of N (the number of crops to be included in the combination) to determine the crop combination.

To obtain the lower limits, in terms of acreages of crops, Athwale has introduced the following:

Formula:

$$A = \frac{G}{3N}$$

where A = The lower limit in terms of acreage

G = Gross cropped Area

and N = Number of crops having acreage more than or equal to 6/100.

Following the above formula, all crops having acreage more than 'A' will take place in crop-combinations. Athawale has given an example to illustrate the above technique.

Let G = 46464 and crop acreage be 18705 (paddy), 11551 (wheat), 9177 (Potato), 6598 (Maize) 3383 (Khesari), 401 (Gram), 236 (Barley) etc.

Then, $\frac{G}{100} = \frac{46464}{100} = 464.64$

Hence, N = 5 (Five crops have acreage more than 464.64)

The lower limit = $A = \frac{G}{3N} = \frac{46464}{3 \times 6} = 3097.6$

Thus, there are 5 crops above 3097.6 and hence combiantion would be five crops *i.e.* five crop combination regions.

Weavers minimum standard deviation method and the maximum positive deviation method of Refiulla (1972) for the identification of crop combination is notable.

Agricultural Region

Agricultural regions may be explained on the basis of many factors such as crop combination, physiography, landuse etc. because here the individuals are grouped into classes on the basis of similarities using number of statistical procedures. This process of classification is the index method of regionalization (Grigg, 1969). Climatic and physical factors affect the agricultural region on micro and meso level while crop combination determines the agricultural regions on micro level (Sen Gupta and Sadsyuk, 1968).

The integration of crop association, live stock combination and land use combination was invented by Scott (1957) to evolve the agricultural regions. Helbern (1987) refined it with the inclusion of degree of commercialization which was followed by Kawachi (1959) and Thoman in the classification of world agricultural regions. Whittlesey (1936) writing on 'Major Agricultural Regions on the Earth" added the processing and disposal of the products, the tools and the methods used in forming and the complex of structures associated with the farm enterprises, in Melbern's ethodology of agricultural regionalization. Rakitnikov (1962) suggested three indices as composition of commodity production, level of intensity, and volume of production of per unit area for delimiting the agricultural regions. Kostrowicki (1964) made an intensified survey to select an impressive methodology to delimit the agricultural regions and gave a detailed list of indices which may be divided into three principal parts :

(1) Social ownership share of particular form of labour supply and size of farm and their fragmentation.

(2) Organizational and technological teams, and

(3) Economic features.

REFERENCES

1. Athwale, A.G. 1966: Some New Methods of Crop Combination, Geographical Review of India, vol. XXVIII, No. 4, pp. 29-33.
2. Dayal, p. 1967: Crop Combination Region: A Case Study of Punjab Plan, Tejdschrift voor Economist on Social Geography, Vol. VIII, No. 1, p. 39.
3. Doi, K. 1957: The Industrial Structure of Japanese, Prefecture, Proceedings IGU, Regional Conference in Japan, pp. 310-316.
4. Graigg, D. 1969: Agricultural Regions of the World, Review and Reflections, Economic Geography, vol. 45, pt. 2, pp. 101-109.
5. Melbern, M. 1987: The Bases for Classification of World Agriculture, The Professional Geographer, Vol. 9, pp. 207.
6. Johnson B.L.C. 1958: Crop Association Regions of East Pakistan, Geography, Vol. 43, pt. 2, p. 86.
7. Jones P.E. and Jones, C.F.1954: American Geography, Inventory and Prospect, Syracuse University Press, p. 30.
8. Kostrowicki, 1964: Geographical Typology of Agriculture, Principles and Methods, Geographic Polanica, Vol. 1, pp. kkk-146.
9. Kumar, J. 1986: Landuse Analysis; A Case Study of Nalanda District, Bihar, Inter-India Publication, New Delhi, pp. 120-135.
10. Mukherjee, R.K. 1938: Food Planning for Four Hundred Millions.
11. Rafiullah, S.M. 1972: A New Approach to Functional Classification of Towns, Geographer, Vol. XII, pp. 40-43.
12. Rakitmikov, A.K. 1962: Economic Geographic Research in Agriculture, in Harris, C.D.(Ed.) Soviet Geography, Accomplishments and Tasks, New York, p. 230.
13. Scott, 1957: The Agricultural Regions of the Tasmania; A. Statistical Definition, Economic Geography, Vol. 33, pp. 109, 121.
14. Sengupta, P. and Sadasyak, G. 1968: Economic Regionalization of India, Problems and Approaches, Census of India, New Delhi, p. 108.
15. Shafi, M. 1960: Land Utilization in Eastern U.P. Aligarh, p. 48.

16. Street, T.M., 1969, Evaluation of the Concept of the Carrying Capacity, the Professional Geographer, Vol. 21, No. 2, pp. 104-107.
17. Thomas, D. 1965: Agriculture in Wales during the Napobonic War, pp. 80-81.
18. Weaver, J.C.1954: Crop Combination Region in the Middle West, Geographical Review, Vol. 44, pp. 174-200.

CHAPTER

13

Agricultural Development

Anupam Pandey and Vibha Rani Pandey

Introduction of Study Area

Sultanpur is the well known district of Faizabad Division of Uttar Pradesh. Sultanpur (Sadar) and Amethi Constituencies are included in this District in which Amethi constituency is too famous for its contribution in the national politics. The mean length of District from east to west is about 129 kilometres and the extreme width from north to south is about 61 kilometres. It extends between the longitudes of 81°32′ east to 82°41′ east and latitudes of 25°59′ north to 26°40′ north with the total geographical area of 4436 square kilometres (01.82% of the total area of U.P. State). The geographic boundaries of the District is demarcated by Faizabad in north and Pratapgarh in South. Azamgarh, Ambedkar Nagar and Jaunpur Districts make its eastern boundary while Barabanki and Raebareli Districts are located in the west direction of the base District (Gazetter, 1982). The District holds 07 Tehsils and 24 Development Blocks at present (Lal, K., 2007). The whole study region is located in watershed of Gomati river (Aadi Ganga). Only the southern part is drained by Sai river embracing the Pratapgarh District. The climate of study area is semi arid and very hot summer and equally cold winter season. According to the Census report of 2001, the total population of the District exists as 32,14,832 person in which 95.03% is inhabited in rural areas and remaining 04.97% is agglomerated in urban areas. About three-fourth population of the study area is depended on agrobased economy as well as agricultural occupations (District Development Handbook, 2005-06).

Land Use

The trends of land use in the District is being changeable as continuously. During the year of 1863 and 1870, the cultivated area in the region was 52.30% but in 1902 it is marked about 57%. At present (2006-07) it is recorded with increasing upto 64.51% (from 283651 Hectares to 439676 Hectares). The land use pattern (2006-07) shown in **Table 13.1** and **Figure 13.1**.

Table 13.1 : Land use in District Sultanpur 2006-07

Sl.No.	Items	Land use	
		Area (Hectare)	Area (Per Cent)
1.	Net sown area	283651	64.51
2.	Other useful land without agriculture	53087	12.07
3.	Fallow land	47853	10.88
4.	Other fallow land	18973	04.32
5.	Uncultivated waste land	14624	03.33
6.	Cultivable land	9725	02.21
7.	Parks, gardens and trees area	7287	01.66
8.	Pasture land	2419	00.55
9.	Forest area	2057	00.47
	Total Geographical Area	**4,39,976**	**100.00**

Source: Statistical Handbook, District Sultanpur (Hindi) 2008, page no. 46.

The total geographical area as 439676 Hectare registers net shown area as 283651 (64.51%), useful land without agriculture as 53087 (12.07%), fallow land as 47853 (10.88%), other fallow land as 18973 (04.32%), uncultivated waste land as 14624 (03.33%), cultivable land as 9725 (02.21%), parks, gardens and trees area as 7287 (01.66%), pasture land as 2419 (0.55%) and forest area is as 2057 (0.47%) Hectares respectively. Near about two-third net shown area which is densely cropped out have made culturable due to cutting of patches of forest land, using waste land and converting pasture land as permanent agriculture land.

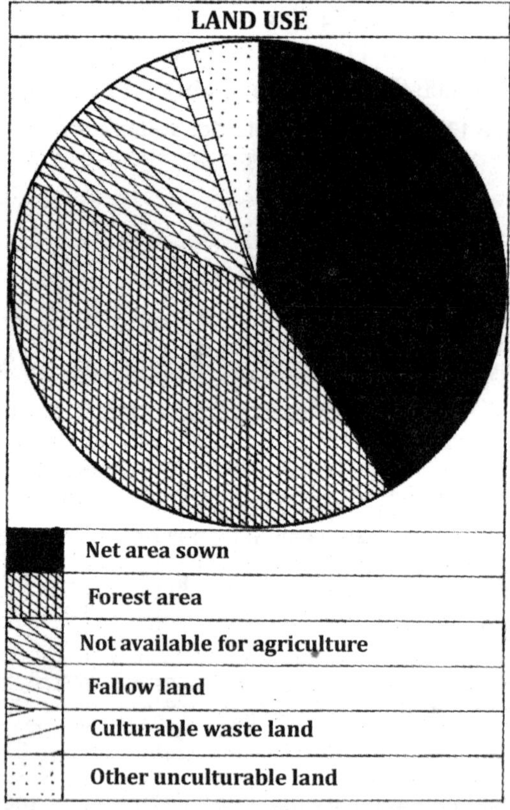

Fig. 13.1. Land use Scenario in the Region 2006-07

Irrigation System

In the beginning of the twentieth century (1901) the total irrigated area of the District was 120239 Hectares. During the session of 2006-07 it has been recorded as 364295 Hectares in which 233309 Hectares area are shown as net irrigated. It represents above the 300% of growth in irrigated area. As regards the means of irrigation, it is depicted through in **Table 13.2** and **Figure 13.2**. The irrigational means wise area

Table 13.2 : Sourcewise Irrigated area in District Sultanpur 2006-07

Sl. No.	Sources of irrigation	Irrigated area	
		Hectare	Per cent
1.	Tubewells	2,52,922	69.42
2.	Canals	1,11,257	30.54
3.	Ponds	75	00.02
4.	Wells	41	00.01
	Total Irrigated Area	**3,64,295**	**100.00**

Source: Statistical Handbook, District Sultanpur (Hindi), 2008, Page Nos. 47-48.

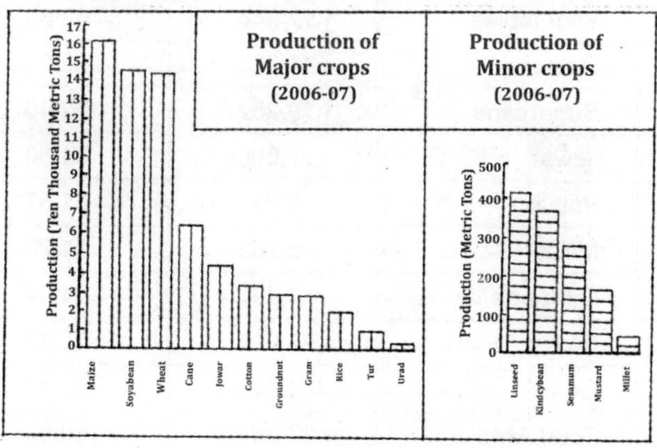

Fig. 13.2. Production of Crops in the Region : 2006-07

and percentage is marked as tubewells 252922 (64.92%), canals 111257 (30.54%), ponds 75 (0.02%) and wells 41 (0.01%) Hectares. The tubewells and canals are the major means of irrigation in the District. Ponds and wells are less effective. There are 132844 private tubewells and pumpsets, 757 public tubewells and 1876 km. length of canals in the study region. The Gomati river is of little use as its bed lies too low so that its waters are only available for the terai lands in which irrigation is usually unnecessary.

Crop Diversity

Crop diversity is the major characteristics of the agricultural development in the region. The wheat, paddy, pulses,

Table 13.3: Area under the Major Crops in District Sultanpur 2006-07

Sl.No.	Name of major crops	Area under the major crops	
		Hectare	Per cent
1.	Wheat	1,68,112	39.36
2.	Paddy	1,56,558	36.65
3.	Pulses	40,738	09.54
4.	Vegetables	12,946	03.03
5.	Pasture	11,264	02.64
6.	Sugarcane	10,252	02.40
7.	Jewar	7,690	01.80
8.	Potato	6,720	01.57
9.	Maize	5,255	01.23
10.	Oilseeds	4,436	01.04
11.	Barley	2,084	00.49
12.	Onion	1,009	00.24
	Total Area	**4,27,064**	**100.00**

Source: Statistical Handbook, District Sultanpur (Hindi), 2008, page nos. 49-50.

vegetables, pasture, sugarcane, jowar, potato, maize, oilseeds, barley and onion are important crops of the area. These crops are cropped out in 427064 Hectares of area. The areal coverage (In Hectares) and percentage of those crops may be indicated as wheat 168112 (39.36%), paddy 156558 (36.65%), pulses 40738 (09.54%), vegetables 12946 (03.03%), pasture 11264 (02.64%),

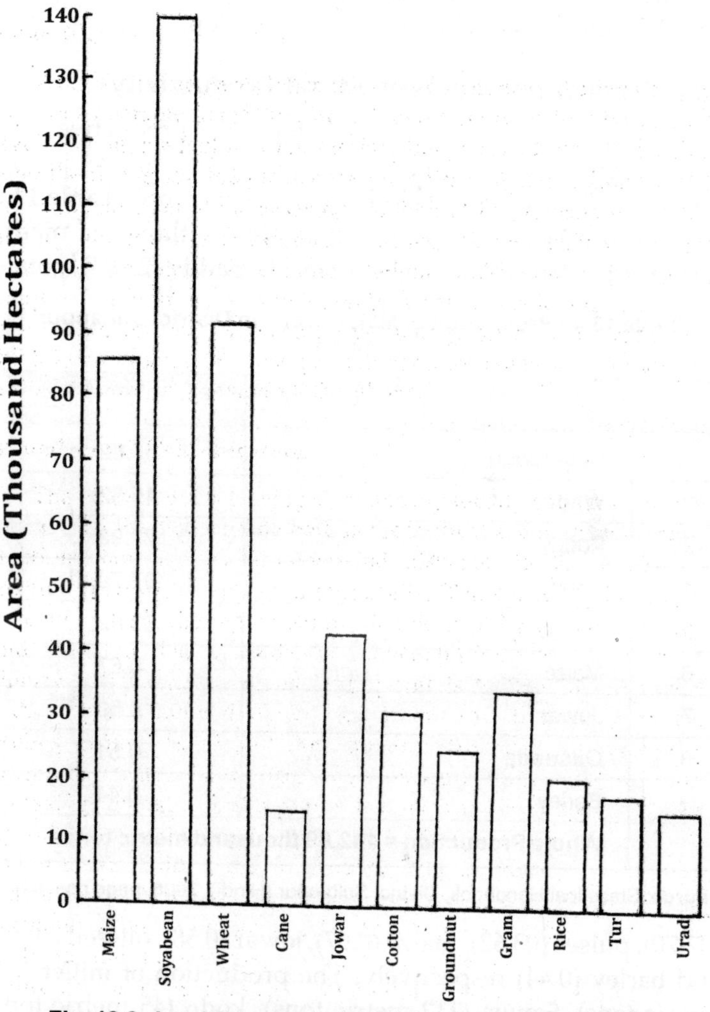

Fig. 13.3. Areal Coverage of Crops in the Region 2006-07

sugarcane 10252 (02.40%), jowar 7690 (01.80%), potato 6720 (01.57%), maize 5255 (01.23%), oilseeds 4436 (01.04%), barley 2084 (0.49%) and onion 1009 (0.24%) respectively (**Table 13.3** and **Figure 13.3**). Wheat denotes the largest area. It is notable that wheat and paddy jointly cover the three-fourth (76.01%) area of the total reported area (427064 Hectares). Millet (248 Hectares), Sanwa (125 Hectares), kodo (72 Hectares) etc. are also the other successive crops of the region.

Crop Production and Agricultural Productivity

According to weight sugarcane is the most productive crop to the region. Wheat paddy, potato, pulses, maize, jowar, oilseeds and barley are the other successive crops. **Table 13.4** and **Figure 13.4** show the production in ten thousand metric tens of sugarcane (55.62), wheat (45.82), paddy (27.93), potato

Table 13.4 : Production of Major Crops in District Sultanpur 2006-07

Sl.No.	Major Crops	Production
1.	Sugarcane	55.62
2.	Wheat	45.82
3.	Paddy	27.93
4.	Potato	07.70
5.	Pulses	03.62
6.	Maize	0.67
7.	Jowar	0.58
8.	Oilseeds	0.51
9.	Barley	0.44
	Whole Production = 142.89 thousand metric tones	

Source: Statistical Handbook, District Sultanpur (Hindi), 2008, page nos. 64-65.

(07.70), pulses (03.62), maize (0.67), jowar (0.58), oilseeds (0.51) and barley (0.44) respectively. The production of millet (376 metric tens), Sanwa (112 metric tons), kodo (45 metric tons)

and sanai (01 metric ton) have been noticed in decreasing order during the year of 2006-07. The sugarcane, wheat and paddy hold 90.54% of production of the total production of all reported crops which is 14289 thousand metric tons. Only sugarcane contributes above one-third production (38.9%).

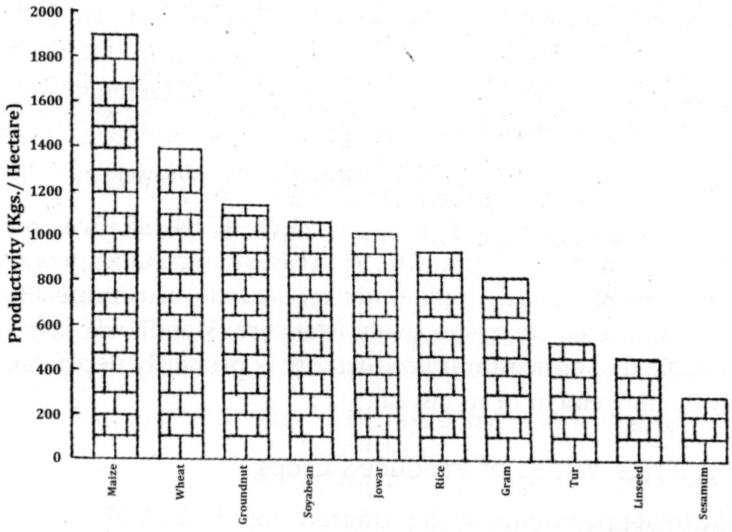

Fig. 13.4. Productivity of Crops in the Region 2006-07

According to **Table 13.5**, the variability in agricultural productivity in all respective ways is recorded. In the year of 2006-07, the mean productivity in quintal per hectare is

Table 13.5 : Mean Productivity of Major Crops in District Sultanpur: 2006-07

Sl.No.	Major Crops	Mean productivity
1	2	3
1.	Sugarcane	542.56
2.	Potato	114.54
3.	Wheat	27.26
4.	Barley	21.05
5.	Paddy	17.84

1	2	3
6.	Millet	15.15
7.	Maize	12.80
8.	Oilseeds	11.51
9.	Sanwa	08.96
10.	Pulses	08.90
11.	Kodo	06.31
12.	Sanai	02.98

Source: Statistical Handbook, District Sultanpur (Hindi), 2008, page no. 62-63.

recorded as 542.56, 114.54, 27.26, 21.05, 17.84, 15.15, 12.80, 11.51, 08.96, 08.90, 06.31 and 02.98 in case of sugarcane, potato, wheat, barley, paddy, millet, maize, oilseeds, sanwa, pulses, kodo and sanai etc. respectively (statistical Handbook, 2008). Notable that agricultural productivity is primarily depended on the movement of monsoon.

The Price Values of Produced Crops

The total price values of all produced crops in 2006-07 is about 9071134 thousand Rupees in which the crops like wheat, paddy, pulses, sugarcane, potato, oilseeds, maize, jowar and barley contribute 3895014, 2625862, 1138483, 695291, 481069, 96520, 51177, 46343 and 37728 thousand Rupees respectively **Table 13.6** and **Figure 13.5**. In this respect the price values of other minor crops like millet, sanwa, kodo and sanai is validated as 2756,627,252 and 12 thousand Rupees in the base year of 2006-07. The wheat is largest price valued crop. Wheat and paddy has returned above to two-third share of whole price value of all produced crops. The price value of pulses, sugarcane and potato in association is marked above to one-fourth of all available crops. During the above base year the minimum supported prices (MSPs) of above crops is follows as wheat 850 Rupees, rice 940 Rupees, Sugarcane 125 Rupees, maize 761 Rupees, jowar 796 Rupees, barley 860 Rupees, millet

733 Rupees, sanwa 560 Rupees, kodo 560 Rupees and sanai 1210 Rupees per quintal.

Table 13.6 : Production values of Major crops in District Sultanpur: 2006-07

Sl.No.	Major crops	Production values (10 crore Rupees)
1.	Wheat	38.95
2.	Paddy	26.26
3.	Pulses	11.38
4.	Sugarcane	05.95
5.	Potato	04.81
6.	Oilseeds	00.97
7.	Maize	00.51
8.	Jowar	00.46
9.	Barley	00.38
	Total Production Values	**89.67 Crore Rupees**

Source: Statistical Handbook, District Sultanpur (Hindi), 2008, page no. 68.

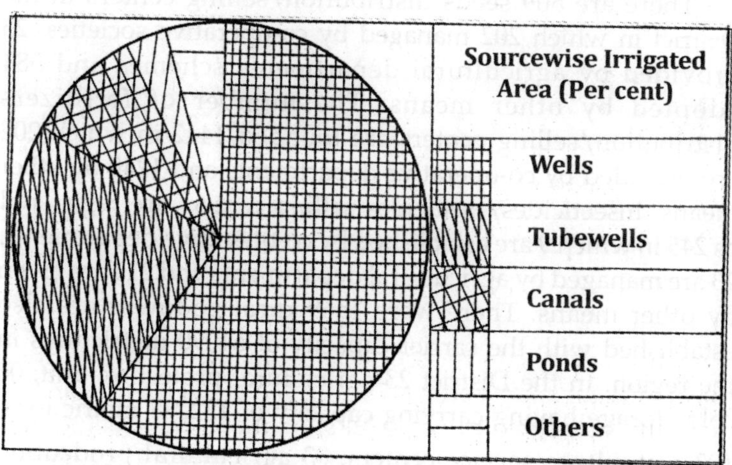

Fig. 13.5. Source-wise Irrigated Area in the Region 2006-07

Facilities for Agricultural Development

Physiographically, the study region is a fertile alluvial plan of Gemati river. The most essential need for agricultural growth as well as development is undoubtedly the advancement of irrigation. In this respect the nets sown area of the region is mostly irrigated by tubewells and canals which is recorded as 82.30% in 2006-07. For the improvement of production about 38279 metric tons nitrogen, 9877 metric tons phosphorus and 2006 metric tons potash has been used as chemical fertilizers in the year of 2006-07. Manures are also used in agricultural yields by rural farmers as well as domestic animals/cattles holder. About 28.7% of the total electrical supply is used by agricultural sectors which elucidates the orientation of agricultural sector in the region. There were 106413 wood cultivators, 17826 iron cultivators, 13949 horrous and advanced cultivators, 28416 threshing machines, 2906 sprayers, 8208 advanced sowing machines and 11207 tractors used in 2006-07 year for the various activities in agriculture. The tractorization is increasing fast day by day in agricultural works here.

There are 809 seeds distribution/selling centers in the District in which 202 managed by co-operative societies, 23 provided by agricultural departments schemes and 584 adopted by other means. The number of fertilizers distribution/selling centers are founded 1442 in which 202 are provided by co-operative departments and 1240 by other means. Insecticides/pesticides selling centers are registered as 245 in which 9 are established by co-operative departments, 23 are managed by agricultural departments and 213 are given by other means. There were 1569 rural godowns are also established with the carrier capacity of 61090 metric tons in the region. In the District 23 agricultural protection unit, 06 cold storage having carrying capacity of 132278 metric tons, 103 agriculture service centers, 03 agricultural prodcution mandi societies are currently accelerating the agricultural processing. Besides the above facilities the 03 foodgrain storage having capacity of 1000 metric tons have been located by IFCI and the state warehouse corporation have also provided 03 cold storage having capacity of 6983 metric tons similarily the state government has also established 15 cold storage having carrying capacity of 2411 metric tons. There are 185 co-operating societies which have agreed agricultural loans for 207168 members. The share money, working money and deposit money of these societies are registered as 20417, 176803 and 13683 thousand Rupees respectively. There are 28 branches of Co-operative Banks which provide initial agriculture loans in the region.

Conclusion

The study region shows an unique scenario of agro-diversity in which wheat, paddy, sugarcane have played dominant role. The pulses, oilseeds and pasturage have also contributed the role in agro-diversity. About two-third land use under the cultivated area, 82.3% net area as irrigated, 1428.9 thousand metric tons whole prodcution of all crops, 907 million Indian Rupees of yield values in the assessment year of 2006-07 is the indicative of agro-based economy of the study area. The facilities for agricultural development by Public and Private sectors are satisfactory. The banking facilities are remarkable in view of providing agricultural loans for agro-advancement and its modern development. In all respective ways the physiography of the concerned region has harvested on excellent crop land in the lap of Aadi Ganga Gomati's alluvial blanketing but the governmental and non-governmental assistance are not satisfied and beneficial in practice when surveyed critically. Banking facilities more generally richer land and the poorer farmers are seen still in tribal conditions. Thus the contradiction of facilities cause normal agro-development. The traditions must be changed in technical and the backwardness of agriculture must be minimised by using technique Scientific awareness and by providing easy economical increments.

REFERENCES

1. Census Abstract, 2001: Directorate of Census Operations, U.P.
2. District Development Handbook (Hindi), 2005-06: Information and Public Relation Department, Sultanpur, p. 11.
3. Gazetteer of India, 1982: Sultanpur District, U.P., Department of District Gazetteers, U.P., Lucknow, pp. 78-82.
4. Lal, K.; 2007: The Role of Population Resource in the Areal Development, Edited by Prasad, G., Pandey, A. and Kislaya, S. in 'Population and Environment (Hindi), Discovery Publishing House, 4831/24, Ansari Road, Daryaganj, New Delhi, pp. 16-17.
5. Statistical Handbook (Hindi) District Sultanpur, 2008: Statistical Office, Sultanpur, State Planning Institution, U.P., pp. 46-50, 62-65 and 68.

CHAPTER

14

Development of Rice Agriculture

Introduction

Rice is the most important foodcrop of India. The plant of rice or paddy (Oryza Sativa) was germinated first of all in India. The country takes second place in production and first place in area of rice as worldwide stage. About one-fourth share of total sown area of the nation is occupied under the crop of rice. More than half of human population belong to the nation is dependent on rice foodcrop. The rice is an monsoony crop so India is an ideal country for this crop. This paper highlights the geographical conditions, area and production, productivity, availability, export, minimum support prices, problems and preparation of rice agriculture with governmental efforts. The secondary data obtained through various surveys and Governmental/Non-governmental journals/books have taken with consideration for analysis. The cartographical techniques as map and diagrams are also used for marvellous visual presentation.

Geographical Conditions

The Ecographical conditions for optimum growth of rice views as temperature rainfall, soil nature of terrain and sufficient labourers. About 25° centigrade mean temperature and 125 to 200 centimetre mean annual rainfall for rice is suitable and comfortable climatic conditions (Sharma S.K., 2003). The soil which contains be mixture of deep clay and sand with fertility, is suitable to the rice. Rich alluvial plain and sufficient labourers should be necessary for the easily harvesting of rice. The implementation of technology is also accepted for high production of rice.

Area and Production

According to Economic Survey 2004-05 there were 44.7 million hectares area and 85.0 million tons production of rice in the entire country is 2000-01. **Figure 14.1** presents the major and

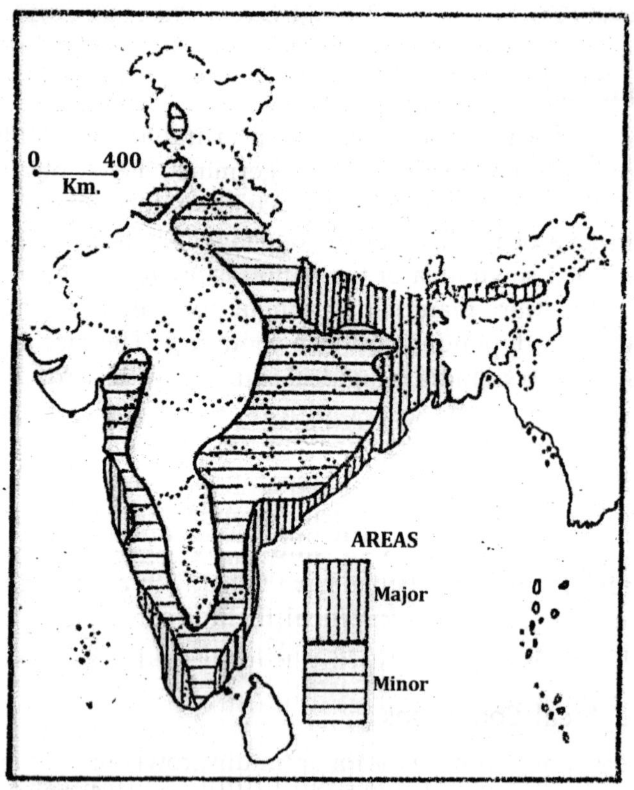

Fig. 14.1. India Areas of Rice Production

minor areas of rice production in India in which U.P., West Bengal, Odisha, Andhra Pradesh, Bihar, Chhattisgarh, Assam, Punjab, Haryana, Tamil Nadu, Karnataka, Kerala, Maharashtra, M.P., Jharkhand, Jammu and Kashmir etc. states area included. **Table 14.1** and **Figure 14.2** represents the areas and production of rice in India driving the period of 1950-51

Table 14.1 : Areas and Production of Rice in India: 1950-51—2000-01

Years	Area (Million Hectares)	Production (Million Tons)
1950-51	30.8	20.6
1960-61	34.1	34.6
1970-71	37.6	42.2
1980-81	40.2	53.6
1990-91	42.7	74.3
2000-01	44.7	85.0

Source: Economic Survey, 2004-05, and Gautam, A., Bharat ka Brihad Bhoogol, 2007, p. 304.

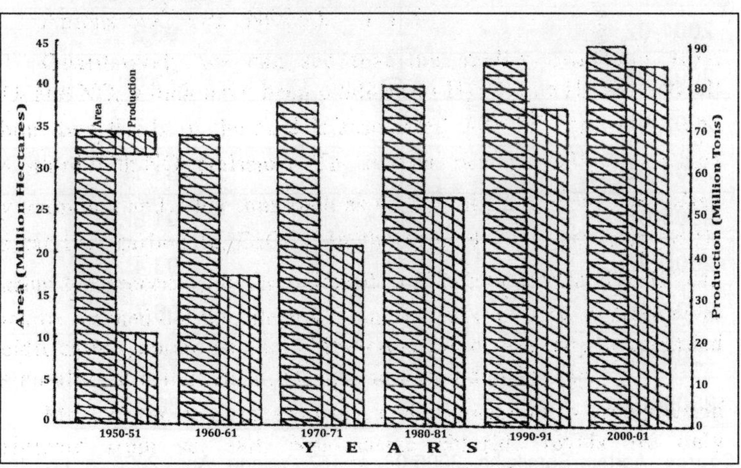

Fig. 14.2. Areas and Production of Rice in India 1950-51—2000-01

and 2000-01. Area (million hectares) and production (million tons) of rice is recorded a 30.8 and 20.6 in 1950-51, 34.1 and 39.6 in 1960-51, 37.6 and 42.2 in 1970-71, 40.2 and 53.6 in 1980-81, 42.7 and 74.3 in 1990-91 and 44.7 and 85.0 in 2000-01. In this duration of half century the area and production has been increased as 13.9 million hectares (45.1%) and 64.4 million tons (312.6%) respectively. In the mean time, the highest area and highest production of rice has been recorded in between 1960-61 to 1970-71 and 1980-81 to 1990-91 respectively. The major cause of area increasement was beginning of 'Green revolution' and further production increasement was highly use of chemical fertilizers and modern technology. **Table 14.2** and **Figure 14.3** highlights the yearwise current rice production in India between 2001-02 and 2009-10. The production (million tons) as 93.3 in 2001-02, 71.8 in 2002-03, 88.3 in 2003-04, 83.1 in 2004-05, 91.8 in 2005-06, 93.4 in 2006-07, 96.7 in 2007-08, 99.2 in 2008-09 and 80.9 in 2009-10 (Planning Commission, 2008, and Chand, R. and

Table 14.2 : Current Rice Production in India: 2001-02—2009-10

Years	Production
2001-02	93.3
2002-03	71.8
2003-04	88.3
2004-05	83.1
2005-06	91.8
2006-07	93.4
2007-08	96.7
2008-09	99.2
2009-10	80.0

Source: Aarthik Samiksha, 2005-06, p. 157, Yojana, April 2008, p. 06, and Yojana August 2010, p. 16.

Shinoj, p., 2010). The low production in 2003-04 (71.8 million tons) and in 2009-10 (80.0 million tons) has been recorded due to below average rainfall of the season. Writable that the country received around 25% less rainfall in the Kharif season in 2009 with respect to average of a long term. The reduction in rice production was about 20% with comparison to the previous year. 99.2 million tons production of rice in 2008-09 is the highest record in the history of rice agriculture in India.

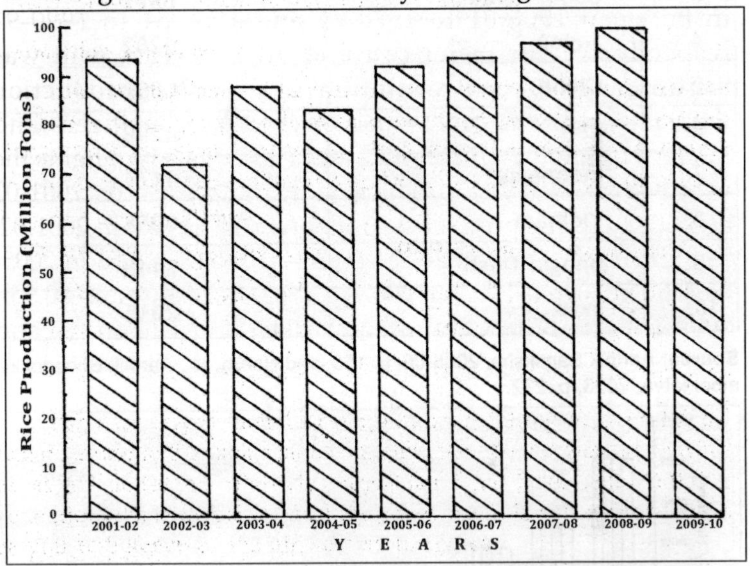

Fig. 14.3. Current Rice Production in India 2001-02—2009-10

Productivity

Although India has the largest area under the rice and second largest production of the rice worldwide yet productivity is very low in an average. There is only 2915 kgs./hectare yield of rice is the mean productivity of rice in the country. **Table 14.3** and **Figure 14.4** has presented the comparison of rice productivity of India at worldwide. Following table and figure presents the mean productivity in kgs per hectare area is marked as 9135 in Egypt, 7372 in U.S.A. 6997 in South Korea, 6282 in Japan, 6069 in China, 4298 in Iran, 4174 in

Table 14.3 : International Comparison of Rice Productivity of India

Sl.No.	The Nations	Mean Productivity (Kg./Hectare)
1.	Egypt	9135
2.	U.S.A.	7372
3.	South Korea	6997
4.	Japan	6282
5.	China	6059
6.	Iran	4298
7.	Indonesia	4174
8.	Vietnam	3958
9.	Bangla Desh	3448
10.	India	2915

Source: Aarthik Samiksha, 2005-06, p. 156, and Harun, M., Aarthik Bhoogol ke mool tatva, 2003, p. 232.

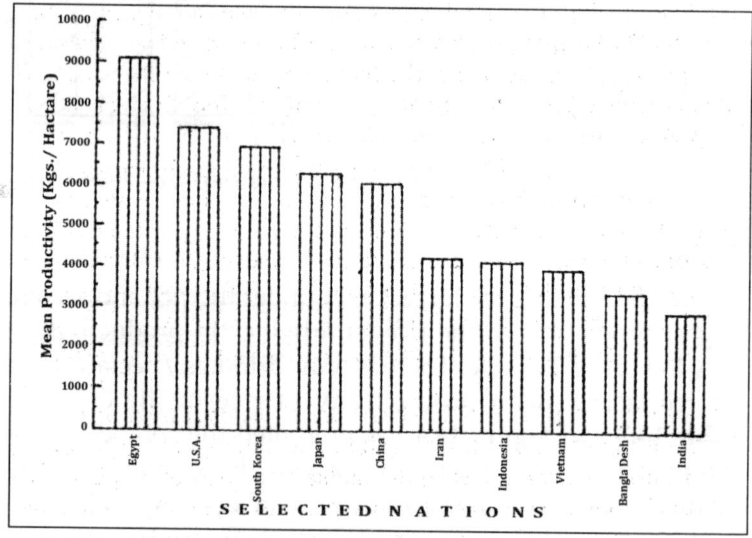

Fig. 14.4. International Comparison of Rice Productivity of India

Indonesia, 3958 in Vietnam and 3448 in Bangladesh (Harun, M., 2003, and Economic Survey 2005-06). The mean productivity of Egypt is highest which is above to triple than India. Beside it South Korea, Japan and China hold above to double productivity and remaining countries like Iran, Indonesia, Vietnam and Bangladesh country are also shown high productivity as 1383, 1259, 1043 and 533 kgs./hectare. The main causes of low productivity are as illiteracy and poverty of Indian farmers, dependency of monsoon, lack of irrigation, low grade of seeds, indiscriminated use of fertilizers and pesticides and minor use of recent technological aspects.

Availability

Table 14.4 and **Figure 14.5** has shown per capita rice availability of all foodgrains in India between 1951 and 2005. The share of rice availability in all foodgrains is about half in all base years. All foodgrains and rice availability in Grams per capita per day is registered as 394.9 and 158.9 in 1951, 468.7 and

Table 14.4 : Per Capita Rice Availability in All Foodgrains Availability in India 1951-2005

Years	Rice availability (Gram Per Capital Per Day)	All foodgrains availability (Gram Per Capital Per Day)
1951	158.9	394.9
1961	201.1	468.7
1971	192.6	468.8
1981	197.8	454.8
1991	221.7	510.1
2001	190.5	416.2
2005	177.3	422.4

Source: Ministry of Agriculture, Dubey, B.K., Kurukshetra, July 2008, p. 16.

201.1 in 1961, 468.8 and 192.6 in 1971, 454.8 and 197.8 in 1981, 510.1 and 221.7 in 1991, 1 416.2 and 190.5 in 2001 and 422.4 and 177.3 in 2005 respectively. During the base year of 1991, the availability of 221.7 Gram per capita per day stands highest due to high production of rice in the corresponding year of 1990-91.

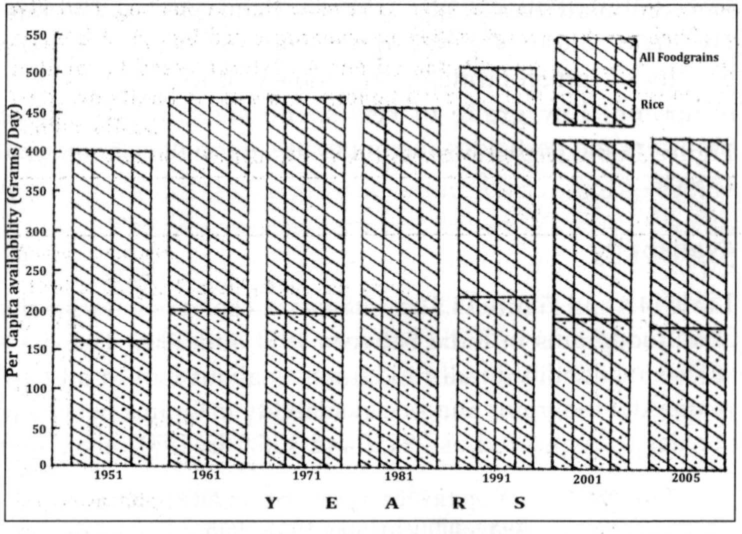

Fig. 14.5. Availability of Rice with All Foodgrains in India 1951-2005

The current human population of India is about 120 crore person (Pandey, A., 2007) and this is increasing day by day so the balanced availability of all foodgrains including rice is a challenge for country. The projected domestic demand of rice is as 94.5 million tons for 2011, 96.9 million tons for 2021 and 102.2 million tons for 2026 at the rate of 8% G.D.P. per annum (Kumar, V.S., 2010). The hybrid rice cultivars have given us new hopes for boosting of rice production. The potential area for the hybrid rice in India has been projected between 8-15 million hectares and adoption of the hybrid cultivars in such a large area, could increase the rice production by 10-20 million tons of more rice (Rai, B., 2006). Beside the above declaration, the recent technology for high production of rice is the prime need for food security as well as balanced rice availability.

Export

India is the second largest producer (9.2 million tons) of rice which accounts for nearly one-fourth global rice production. It is largest producer of world's best 'Basmati ' rice, but the trends of export is comparatively below because there is high domestic demands of that kinds of rice in the country. Notwithstanding the export of rice (mainly Basmati) is possible at present and now India is the second largest exporter of rice after Thailand (Rai, B., 2006). **Table 14.5** and **Figure 14.6** has presented the rice export with quantity and values of India between the years of 1990-91 to 2008-09. The quantity (thousand tons) and values (crore Indian Rupees) of exported rice have been shown as 505.0 and 462 in 1990-91, 1534.4 and 2943 in 2000-01, 6449.0 and 11755 in 2007-08, and 2488.2 and 11164 in 2008-09 (Subbaiah, S.V. 2006, and DGCI & S, Kolkata). In these years the highest export has been possible in 2007-08 in quantity and values both. The growth of rice exported quantity and values has been recorded as 1181% and 2444% between the duration of 1990-91 and 2007-08 respectively. During the year of 2007-08 and 2008-09 degradation is recorded in quantity and values of rice due to some affecting causes. If the quantity and quality of rice is being improved, the export will be fortified.

Table 14.5 : Rice Export from India: 1990-91—2008-09

Years	Quantity (Thousand Ton)	Value (Crore Rs.)
1990-91	505.0	462
2000-01	1534.4	2943
2007-08	6469.0	11755
2008-09	2488.2	11164

Source: DGSI & S, Kolkata, The Hindu Survey of Indian Industry, 2010, p. 272-273.

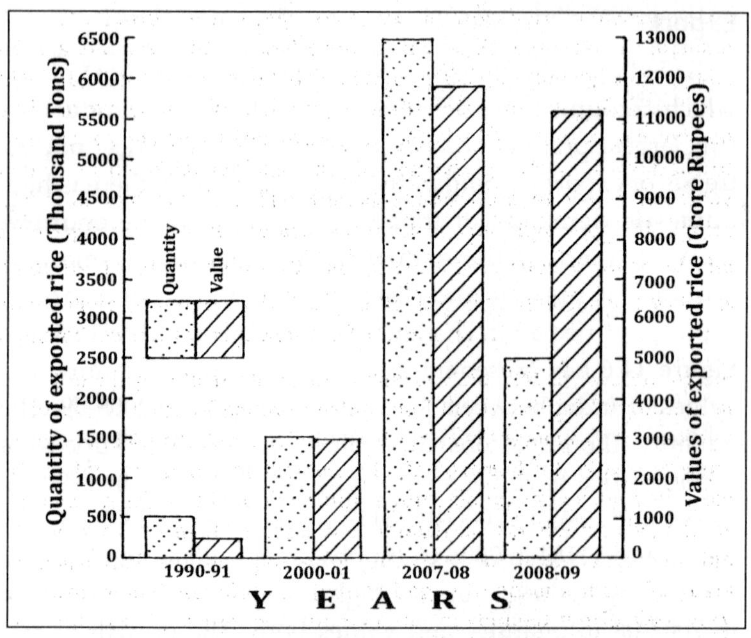

Fig. 14.6. Rice Export from India 1990-91—2008-09

Minimum Support Prices (MSPs)

The MSPs of paddy is essential for better trade and economy. According to the Ministry of Agriculture the present MSPs of paddy in Indian Rupees per quintal is as 950 in February 2010 and 1000-1030 for February 2011. It was registered as 360-380 in 1994-95, 395-415 in 1996-97, 470 in 1998-99, 540 in 2000-01, 560 in 2002-03, 590 in 2004-05 and 650 in February 2006. MSPs has been increased as 178% between 1994-95 and February 2011 (Ministry of Agriculture, and Sabnavis, M., 2010) which indicated high increasement of prices in short-term of 15 years. The increasement in MSPs is the result of expansion of rice agriculture.

Some Problems of Rice Agriculture

The problems of rice agriculture may be followed as given:

(i) Small and marginal land holding

(ii) Dependency of monsoon
(iii) Environmental hazards
(iv) Incapabilities of farmers
(v) Low productivity
(vi) Lack of agricultural inputs
(vii) Deficient infrastructure
(viii) Downfall of irrigational growth rate
(ix) Unscientific landforms systems
(x) Expensive agriculture
(xi) Stagnation in agriculture
(xii) Economic insecurity
(xiii) Imbalanced MSPs
(xiv) Miserable investment in agro-research and development.

Pre-Solutions of Problems of Rice Agriculture

The solutions of problems of rice agriculture are as follows:

(i) Land use
(ii) Development of permanent irrigation
(iii) Minimizing the environmental hazards
(iv) Encouragement of farmers activities
(v) Increasing the productivity
(vi) Management of agricultural inputs
(vii) Development of well infrastructure
(viii) Rising the irrigational capacity and techniques
(ix) Stimulation to land reforms
(x) Changing the traditional patterns of agriculture
(xi) Economical enrichment
(xii) Improving MSPs.
(xiii) Optimum use of hybrid seeds
(xiv) Constituting importance to agriculture

(xv) Inhancing the management of banking facilities
(xvi) Adopting the trends of organic farming
(xvii) Development of agricultural research and programmes
(xviii) Supporting national policy for farmer centre
(xix) Encouragement to the agricultural publications
(xx) Advertisement of agricultural informations and awareness to farmers.

Governmental Efforts for Development of Rice Agriculture

There is not a single special scheme for the development of rice agriculture in the country but the combined schemes launched by Government are numerous in this connection. National Agriculture Development Scheme (NADS, 2007), Accelerated Irrigation Benefit Programme (AIBP, 1996-97), National Seed Corporation (BSC, 1969), Integrated Pest Management Programme (IPMP), National Bank for Agricultural and Rural Development (NABARD, 1982), Kisan Credit Card (K.C.C., 1998-99), National Agricultural Insurance scheme (NAIS, 1999-2000). Agricultural Insurance Company of India Limited (AIC, 2002), Kisan call center (toll free no. 1551) (2004) and Kisan Channel Scheme (2004) etc. have been implemented by Government of India to the farmers. Banking loans is being provided by Co-operative banks, Regional rural banks and various commercial banks in which commercial banks is top of one. During the 11th Plan (five yearly) soil conservation, water conservation and water bodies renewation, reforms in loans, insurances, marketing, technology and inputs are seriously undertaken by Government of India (Pandey, B., 2009).

Conclusion

The fertile crop-cultured land of India associates the top favourable circumstances of rich production of rice unit now. Undoubtedly, production of rice on an average satisfactory but the productivity is not found sufficient. The trends of per capita availability of rice is continuously improving in last few years. The MSPs should be increased timely for making balance between farmers and consumers. The solution of various types of problem of rice agriculture is one of the challenging chapter before policy makers and it will be removed paying lift to public sector because Governmental efforts in all respect is not sufficient and satisfactory. Human resource development is the fruitful application for modern agriculture of rice in highly developing India. The second green revolution with organic forming thought is highly necessary today. Use of organic farming system, developing bio-technological efforts and by implementation the rice agriculture must be highlightened in vibrating and developing India on globe. Green Plants growing culture must be obtained and the quality maintenance should be taken on priority basis.

REFERENCES

1. Aarthik Samiksha, 2005-06: Economic Division, Ministry of Finance, Government of India, pp. 156-157.
2. Chand, R. and Shinoj, p., 2010: 'Food Inflation in India: Causes and Remedies' Published Paper in Yojana: A Development Monthly, August, 2010, Ministry of Information and Broadcasting, Yojana Bhawan Sansad Marg, New Delhi, p. 16.
3. Centre for Monitoring Indian Economy, Planning Commission, 2008; Economic Indicators, Yojana A. Development Monthly, April, 2008, Ministry of Information and Broadcasting, Yojana Bhawan, Sansad Marg, New Delhi, p. 6.
4. DGCI & S. Kolkata, 2010: Principal Exports. The Hindu Survey of Indian Industry, 2010, N. Ram, Kasturi Buildings, 859 & 860, Anna Salai, Chennai-600002, pp. 272-273.
5. Dubey, B.K., 2008: 'Harit Kranti Mein Bhubhmari' Published Paper in Kurukshetra, July, 2008, Publication Division, Ministry of Information and Broadcasting, Government of India, Soochna Bhawan, New Delhi, p. 15.
6. Gautam, A., 2007: Bharat Ka Brihad Bhoogol, Sharda Pustak Bhawan, 11, University Road, Allahabad-2, P. 304.
7. Harun, M., 2003: Aarthik Bhugol ke Mool Tatva, Vasundhara Prakashan 236, Daudpur, Gorakhpur, p. 232.

8. Kumar, V.S. 2010: 'Securing food for all', Published Paper in Yojana: A Development Monthly, October, 2010, Ministry of Information and Broadcasting, Yojana Bhawan, Sansad Marg, New Delhi, p. 38.

9. Pandey, A., 2007: 'Waya Pradushan evam Amlavarsha, Published Paper in Manav Evam Paryawaran, 2007, Edited by Prasad, G., Pandey, A. and Kislaya, S., Discovery Publishing House, 4831/ 24, Ansari Road, Darya Ganj, New Delhi-110 002, p. 85.

10. Pandey, B., 2009: 'Mauzuda Krishi Vikas Yojana ka Mulyankan' Published Paper in Kurukshetra, February, 2009, Publication Division, Ministry of Information and Broadcasting, Government of India, Soochna Bhawan, New Delhi, pp. 9-10.

11. Rai, B. 2006: 'Agricultural exports' Published Paper in Yojana: A Development Monthly, September, 2006, Ministry of Information and Broadcasting, Yojana Bhawan, Sansad Marg, New Delhi, p. 33.

12. Sabnavis, M., 2010: 'Revamping Food Procurement and Pricing Policies', Published Paper in Yojana: a Development Monthly, October, 2010, Ministry of Information and Broadcasting, Yojana Bhawan, Sansad Marg, New Delhi, p. 11.

13. Sharma, S.K., 2003; Bharat-Log aur Arthvyawastha, Publishing Division, NCERT, Sri Arvind Marg, New Delhi-110 016, p. 86.

14. Subbaiah, S.V., 2006: 'Several Options being Tapped', Published Paper in the Hindu Survey of Indian Agriculture, 2006. N. Ram on Behalf of M/s. Kasturi & Sons. Ltd. at the National Press, Kasturi Building, Chennai-600002, p. 50-52.

CHAPTER

15

Progressive Agriculture of Sugarcane

Gitanjali and Madhavi Gutpa

Introduction

India is the largest sugar consumer country of the world. The nation has recorded more than hundred crore population, and 13 million tons sugar consumption per annum. It is also the second largest producer of sugar with the largest area of the world. Sugarcane is originated in India. The country receives more than one fifth area and production of sugarcane of the world. Sugar is the second largest agro-processing industry of India. It is established under 4.5 million hectares area associating 5 crore farmers of sugarcane producers along with investment estimates of 40 thousand crore rupees (2009). The sugar industry consists of 625 large mills corresponding 7.5 per cent of the total rural population as active and passive. At present time per capita availability of sugar is estimated as 23 kilograms per annum. Export of sugar is very irregular because Indian agriculture is totally depended on the mood of monsoon. Productivity of sugarcane is medium in comparison of some high producing countries.

About the Sugar and Sugarcane

Sugar is the sweet products of sugarcane. The sugar beet maple and date palm trees are the other sources of sugar. The majority of production of sugar in India is based on sugarcane crops. Sugarcane belongs to grass family of tropical climate. It becomes tall, hard including thick stem which grows to a height of 3.5 metres (12 feet) or more. Sugar is stored in the stem of cane (Leons, G.C. and Morgon, G.C., 1982). Bagasse and molasses are the by products of sugarcane.

Responsible Geographic Atmosphere for Sugarcane

The sugarcane is a tropical and subtropical crop which requires the most suitable temperature between 20° and 30° centigrade and precipitation between 150 and 200 centimetre. High humidity and irrigational facilities are also thought to be responsible geographical atmosphere. The deep rich loamy and black soils are most useful for its agriculture. The sufficient labourers are also needed for the cropping of sugarcane.

Areas of Production of Sugarcane

The sugarcane is being cultivated in all over India from latitudes between 8° North and 33° North except cold hilly nominated areas as Kashmir valley, Himachal Pradesh and Arunachal Pradesh. There are two several zones of tropical and subtropical climates for sugarcane production in the national scenario. Maharashtra, Karnataka, Tamil Nadu, Andhra Pradesh, Gujarat, Kerala and Odisha states are included in tropical climatic zone and Uttar Pradesh, Bihar, Haryana, Punjab, Uttarakhand, Madhya Pradesh, Rajasthan, West Bengal and Assom states are consisted in sub tropical climatic zone. In the total area under the sugarcane about one third is connected with tropical and hugely two third belongs to sub tropical climatic zone (Yadav, R.L. and Verma, R.S., 2006).

The entire area under sugarcane agriculture in India was noted as 17.07 lakh hectares in 1950-51 which is increased upto 40 lakh hectares in 2003-04 (**Figure 15.1**). It was recorded in 2000-01 as 43.16 lakh hectares which was more than

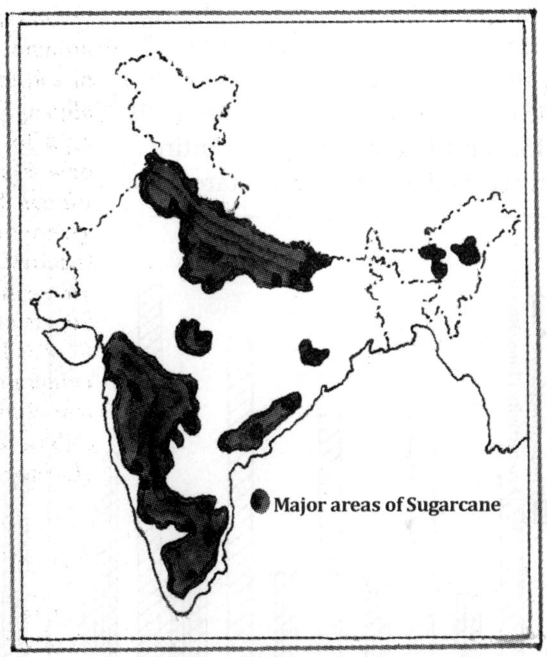

Fig. 15.1. India—Areas of Sugarcane

Table 15.1 : Area, Production and Productivity of Sugarcane in India: 1950-51—2003-04

Years	Area (Lakh Hectares)	Production (Crore Tons)	Productivity Tons/Hectare)
1950-51	17.07	05.71	33.4
1960-61	24.15	11.00	45.5
1970-71	26.15	12.64	48.3
1980-81	26.67	15.42	57.8
1990-91	36.86	24.10	65.4
2000-01	43.16	29.60	68.6
2003-04	40.00	23.73	59.0

Sources: India, 2002, and Economic Survey, 2004-05.

153 per cent of last fifty years (1950-51 to 2000-01). It was decadal recorded as 24.15 in 1960-61, 26.15 in 1970-71, 26.67 in 1980-81 and 36.86 lakh hectares in 1990-91 respectively (**Table 15.1** and **Figure 15.2**). The entire area under this crop has been reached 4.5 million hectares in 2009 in the nation.

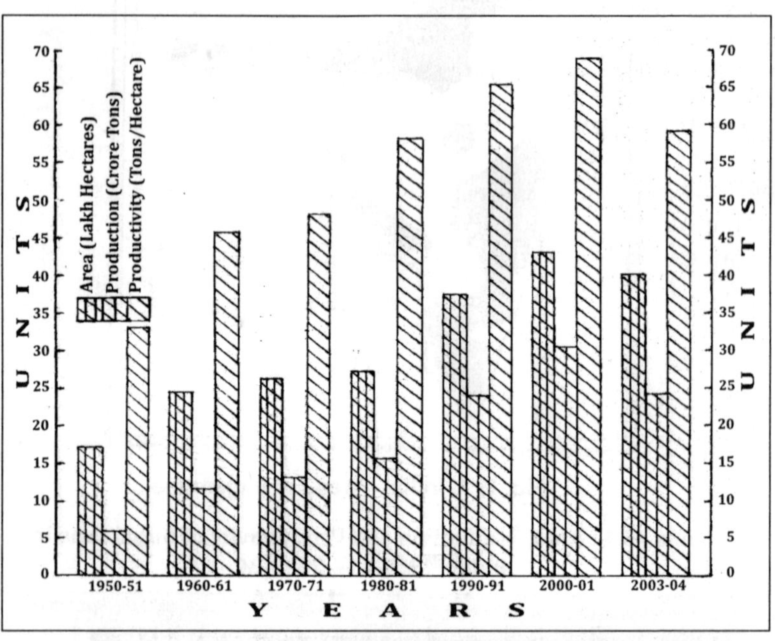

Fig. 15.2. Area, Production and Productivity of Sugarcane in India 1950-51—2003-04

Production of Sugarcane

India has noted a large growth of sugarcane until now. About 418 per cent growth has been registered between fifty years of 1950-51 and 2000-01. **Table 15.1** and **Figure 15.2** has shown the successive growth of sugarcane production. It is estimated as 5.71 in 1950-51, 11 in 1960-61, 12.64 in 1970-71, 15.42 in 1980-81, 24.10 in 1990-91, 29.60 in 2000-01 and 23.73 crore tons in 2003-04 respectively (Economic Survey, 2004-05). The lower production of the evaluation year of 2003-04 is too much lower than that of the year of 2000-01 because of lesser the precipitation coming drought conditions in the sugarcane producing region (Rajagopal, v., 2010). Although about 34.53 crore tons production in 2006-07 is presented the increasing phenomena (Yojana, April, 2008).

Productivity of Sugarcane

The productivity of sugarcane in tons/hectare was founded as 33.4 in 1950-51, 45.5 in 1960-61, 48.3 in 1970-71, 57.8 in 1980-81, 65.4 in 1990-91, 68.6 in 2000-01 and 59.0 in 2003-04. More than double growth in productivity of sugarcane has been gained between 1950-51 and 2000-01 (**Table 15.1** and **Figure 15.2**). **Table 15.2** and **Figure 15.3** has presented the comparative chart of sugarcane productivity of India and abroad. According to Table and figure shown above the productivity of sugar in India (68.6 tons/hectare) is below than that of

Table 15.2 : Comparative Chart of Sugarcane Productivity in India and Abroad

Sl. No.	Country	Productivity (Tons/Hectare)
1.	Egypt	110.8
2.	Australia	100.4
3.	U.S.A.	80.2
4.	South Africa	76.4
5.	China	71.3
6.	India	68.6
7.	Brazil	68.4
8.	Vietnam	50.6
9.	Pakistan	50.3
10.	Thailand	49.5

Sources: F.A.O. Production Year Book, 1999, and Statistical abstract of India, 2003.

Egypt (110.8 tons/hectare), Australia (100.4 tons/hectare), U.S.A. (80.2 tons/hectare), South Africa (76.4 tons/hectare) and China (71.3 tons/hectare). It is measured above to Brazil (68.4 tons/hectare), Vietnam (50.6 tons/hectare), Pakistan (50.3 tons/ hectare) and Thailand (49.5 tons/hectare) respectively (F.A.O. Yearbook, 1999 and Statistical abstract of India, 2003). The productivity of India is below to Egypt and Australia as 61.5% and 46.4%. It is found above to Pakistan and Thailand as 36.4% and 38.6% respectively. Notable that the productivity of India and Brazil is similar.

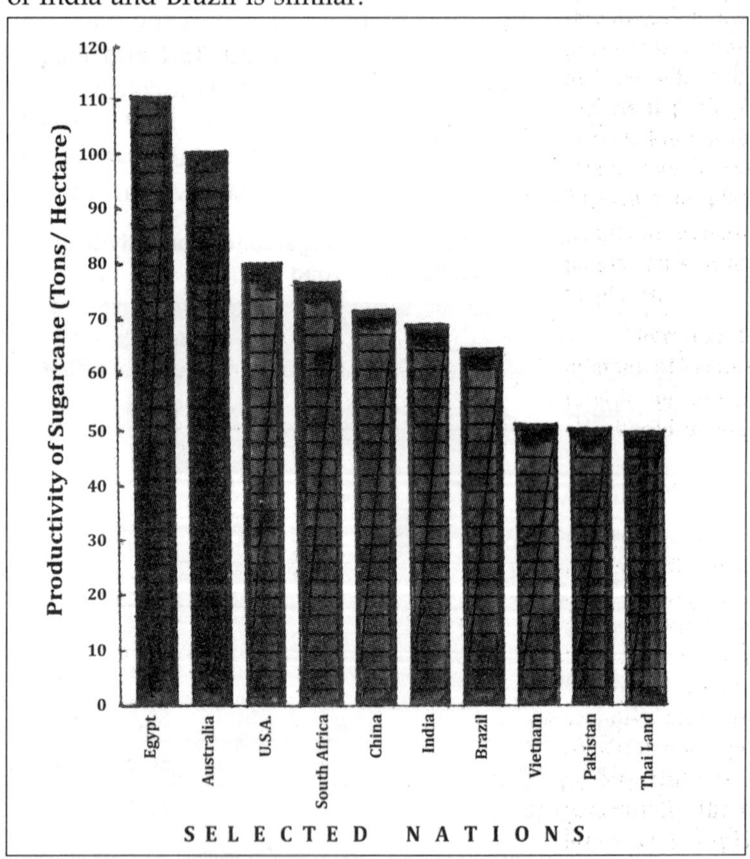

Fig. 15.3. Comparative Chart of Sugarcane Productivity of India and Abroad

Statewise Area, Production and Productivity of Sugarcane

The 11 states (U.P., Maharashtra, Karnataka, Tamil Nadu, Andhra Pradesh, Gujarat, Bihar, Haryana, Punjab, Uttarakhand and M.P.) of India have shown the maximum impact of area, production and productivity of sugarcane in the assessment year of 2002-03. **Table 15.3** and **Figure 15.4** show the area (in 10 thousand hectares), production (in million tons) and Productivity (in tons/hectare) of Sugarcane namely as 185.2, 116.3 and 62.8 in U.P., 59.9, 37.0 and 61.8 in Maharashtra, 38.5, 32.5 and 84.4 in Karnataka, 28.4, 30.3 and 106.6 in Tamil Nadu, 23.4, 15.4 and 65.8 in Andhra Pradesh, 20.3, 14.1 and 69.3 in Gujarat, 18.7, 04.6 and 24.6 in Bihar, 18.0, 08.0 and 44.4 in Haryana, 15.4, 09.3 and 60.3 in Punjab, 13.0, 07.7 and 59.3 in Uttarakhand and 05.3, 02.1 and 39.3

Table 15.3 : State-wise Area, Production and Productivity of Sugarcane in India: 2002-03

Sl.No.	States of India	Area (Ten Thousand Hectares)	Production (Million Tons)	Productivity (Tons/ Hectare)
1.	Uttar Pradesh	185.2	116.3	62.8
2.	Maharashtra	59.9	37.0	61.8
3.	Karnataka	38.5	32.5	84.4
4.	Tamil Nadu	28.4	30.3	106.6
5.	Andhra Pradesh	23.4	15.4	65.8
6.	Gujarat	20.3	14.1	69.3
7.	Bihar	18.7	04.6	24.6
8.	Haryana	18.0	08.0	44.4
9.	Punjab	15.4	09.3	60.3
10.	Uttarakhand	13.0	07.7	59.3
11.	Madhya Pradesh	05.3	02.1	39.3
	All India	43.61	281.6	68.6

Source: Statistical abstract of India, 2003.

M.P. states respectively. The highest area (1852 Thousand hectares) and production (116.3 million tons) is recorded in U.P. which is as 42.47% and 41.31% of the entire national area and production of sugarcane respectively. But the highest productivity of sugarcane was gained in Tamil Nadu who was about 106.6 Tons per hectare. It is notable that the productivity of U.P. is measured below than Tamil Nadu about 70% in per hectare.

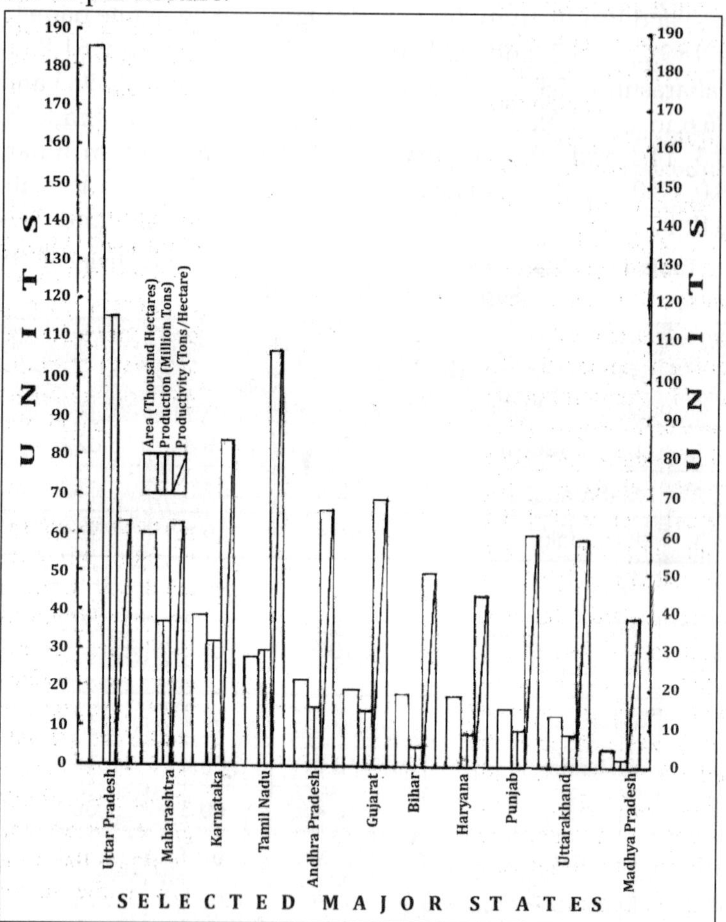

Fig. 15.4. Area, Production and Productivity of Sugarcane in Selected States of India 2002-03

Production of Sugar

Sugar is the principal product of sugarcane which is sweet in the taste. India has been the second largest producer of sugar

Table 15.4 : Production of Sugar in India: 1950-51—2007-08

Years	Production (Million Tons)
1950-51	01.13
1960-61	03.03
1970-71	03.74
1980-81	05.15
1990-91	12.05
2000-01	18.51
2003-04	13.96
2007-08	26.30

Sources: Department of Food and Public Distribution, Directorate of Sugar, The Hindu Survey of Indian Industry, 2010.

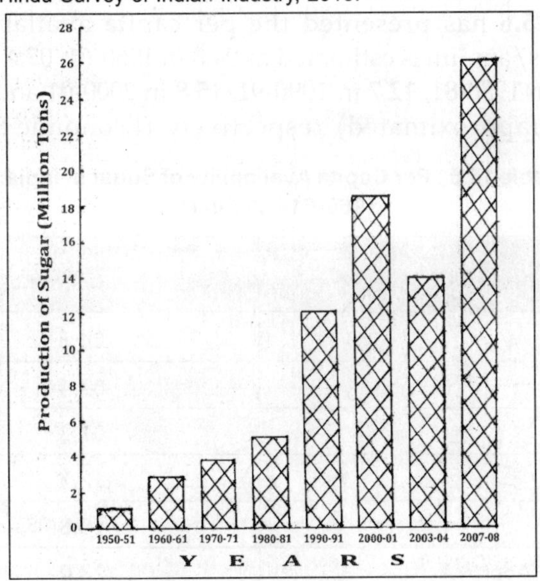

Fig. 15.5. Production of Sugar in India 1950-51—2007-08

after Brazil for a long time and accounts for around 11% of global, production (Subbu, R., 2010). **Table 15.4** and **Figure 15.5** has presented the production of sugar in India between 1950-51 and 2007-08. Production of sugar (in million tons) was estimated as 01.13 in 1950-51, 03.03 in 1960-61, 03.74 in 1970-71, 05.15 in 1980-81, 12.05 in 1990-91, 18.51 in 2000-01, 13.96 in 2003-04 and 26.30 in 2007-08 respectively. The production of sugar is progressed above to 23 times since 1950-51. The decrease (negative growth) in production is found in the session of 2003-04.

Availability of Sugar

The population of India is expected to be 116 crore by 2010 at the annual growth rate of 01.6% and thus the corresponding estimated requirement of sugar will be 24.3 Million Tons. Based on the existing trend of per capita availability of sugar in the country, it is estimated to be 23 kilograms per annum by 2010-11 (Yadav, R.L. and Verma, R.S., 2006. **Table 15.5** and **Figure 15.6** has presented the per capita availability in kilograms/annum is estimated as 04.8 in 1960-61, 07.4 in 1970-71, 07.3 in 1980-81, 12.7 in 1990-91, 15.8 in 2000-01 and 23.0 in 2010-11 (approximated) respectively (Economic Survey,

Table 15.5 : Per Capita Availability of Sugar in India: 1960-61—2010-11

Years	Per Capita availability (Kgs./Annum)
1960-61	04.8
1970-71	07.4
1980-81	07.3
1990-91	12.7
2000-01	15.8
2010-11 (Approx.)	23.0

Source: Economic Survey, 2005-06.

2005-06). Between the year of 1960-61 and 2000-01, the availability percentage of sugar is estimated as 229.17%. In the present content production of sugarcane and sugar consumption must be improved.

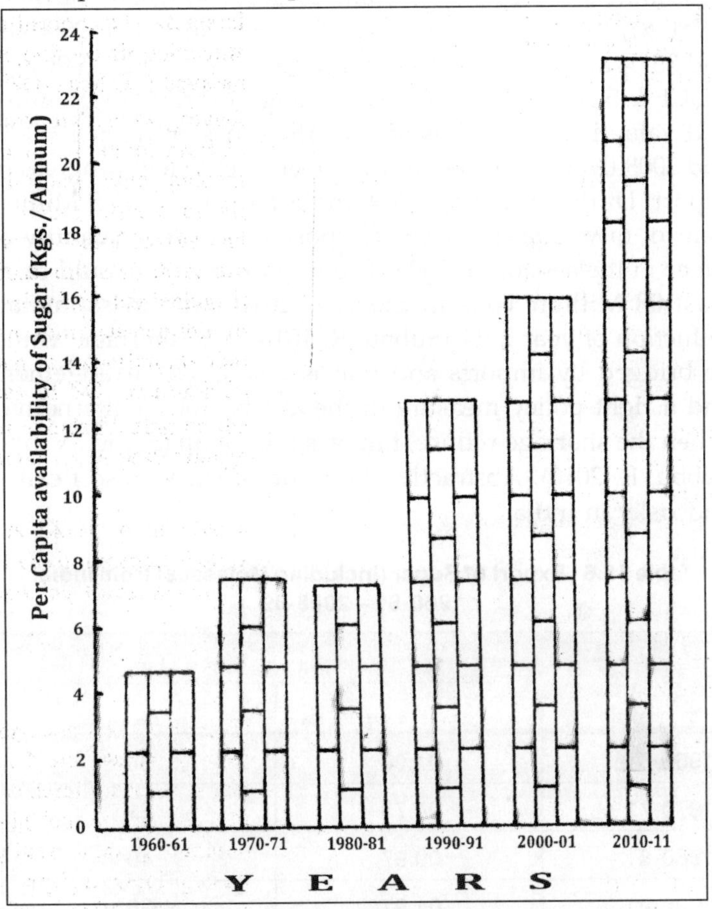

Fig. 15.6. Per Capita Availability of Sugar in India 1960-61—2010-11

Trade of Sugar

The trade of sugar is based on export and import circumstances which is found plus and minus of average trade.

Table 15.6 and **Figure 15.7** indicate the export of sugar (including molasses) from India between the duration of 1960-61 and 2008-09. The export in quantity and value is given in Lakh Tons and Crore Rupees respectively. It was found as 01.00 and 30 in 1960-61, 04.73 and 29 in 1970-71, 0.97 and 40 in 19780-81, 01.91 and 38 in 1990-91, 07.69 and 511 in 2000-01, and 35.04 and 45.32 in 2008-09 (Economic Survey 2005-06 and DGCI & S. Kolkata, 2010). The change in trade in quantity and value is validated as 35 and 151 times between 1960-61 and 2008-09 which is the indicative of an excellent progress in export. During the year 2009, India has imported 5 Million Tons of raw sugar in place of exporting a similar quantity of sugar in the session of 2008. The import of sugar could be at least 08 Million Tons in the year 2010 with an estimated reduction of year 2011 (Subbu, R. 1010). The shortage would be bridged by imports and that is a stop-gap arrangement and a right policy measure in the absence of an alternative. When the shortage reduce, imports must stop (Sarogi, V. and Subbu, R. 2010). Abstractly, the trade of sugar is so flexible and risky in India.

Table 15.6 : Export of Sugar (Including Molasses) from India: 1960-61—2008-09

Years	Export	
	Lakh Tons	Crore Rs.
1960-61	01.00	30
1970-71	04.73	29
1980-81	00.97	40
1990-91	01.91	38
2000-01	07.69	511
2008-09	35.04	4532

Sources: Economic Survey, 2005-06 and DGCI & S. Kolkata, The Hindu Survey of Indian Industry, 2010.

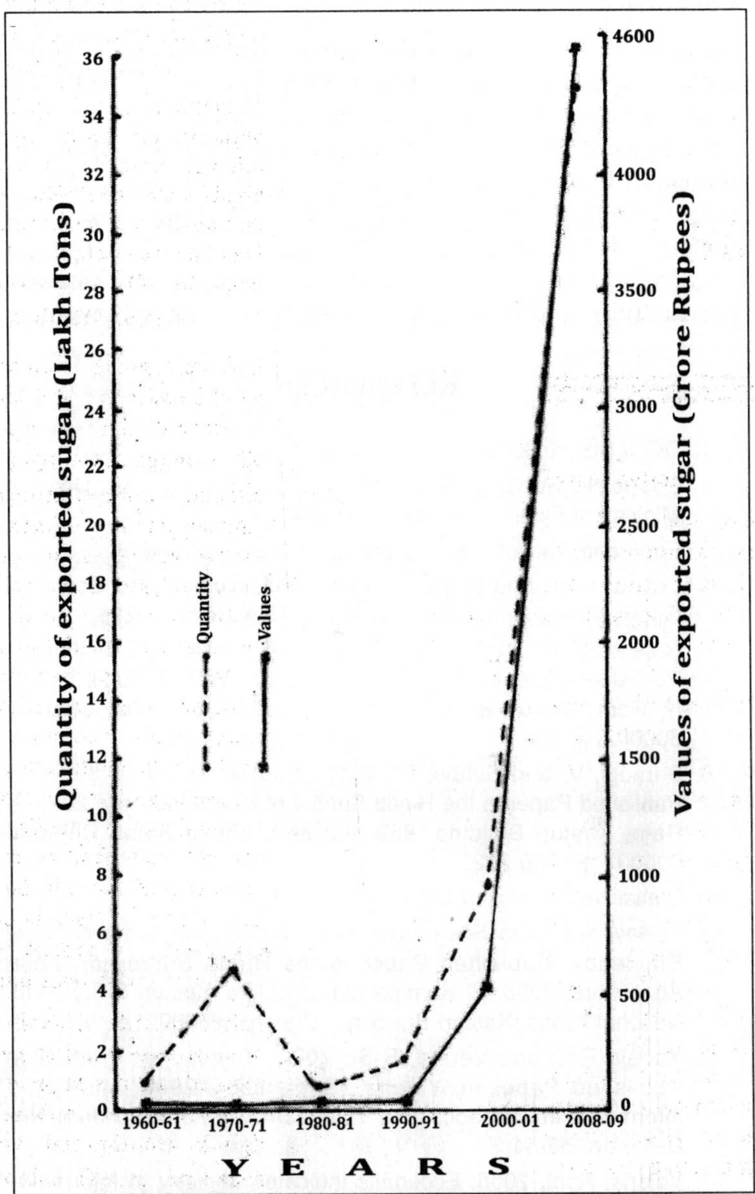

Fig. 15.7. Export of Sugar (Including Molasses) from India 1960-61—2008-09

Conclusion

India leads as the largest consumer, largest area holder and second largest producer country of sugar in the world. The tropical and sub tropical climatic zones of the country have provided an optimum condition for sugarcane agriculture but monsoon is the dominant factor of determine the climax of crop. The application of recent agro-technology is made possible in all respective ways but the productivity of sugarcane is not sufficient in quantity and quality. Growing productivity, India will stand on the top of the achievement.

REFERENCES

1. DGCI & S, Kolkata.
2. Economic Survey, 2004-05 and 2005-06: Economic Division, Ministry of Finance, Government of India.
3. Food and Agricultural Organisation, Year Book, 1999.
4. Leong, G.C. and Morgan, G.C., 1982: Human and Economic Geography, Oxford University Press, New Delhi, p. 216.
5. Rajagopal, V., 2010: 'Preparedness to Face Drought Challenges' Published Paper in The Hindu Survey of Indian Agriculture, 2010, N. Ram, Kasturi Building, 859 and 860, Anna Salai, Chennai-600002, p. 13.
6. Saraogi, V. and Subbu, R., 2010: 'Supply Tightness to Persist' Published Paper in the Hindu Survey of Indian Industry, 2010, N. Ram, Kasturi Building, 859 and 860, Amma Salai, Chennai-600002, p. 260-262.
7. Statistical Abstract of India, 2003.
8. Yadav, R.L. and Srivastava, A.K., 2006: 'Improving Nitrogen Efficiency, Published Paper in the Hindu Survey of Indian Agriculture, 2006, N. Ram on Behalf of M/s. Kasturi & Sons Ltd., National Press, Kasturi Buildings, Chennai-600002, p. 108.
9. Yadav, R.L. and Verma, R.S., 2006: 'Canesugar Production' Published Paper in 'Yojana', September, 2006, Ministry of Information and Broadcasting, Yojana Bhawan, Sansad Marg, New Delhi, pp. 53-54.
10. Yojana, April, 2008: Economic Indicator, Ministry of Information and Broadcasting, Yojana Bhawan, Sansad Marg, New Delhi, p. 6.

CHAPTER

16

Expansion of Tea Cultivation

Gitanjali and Amita Pandey

Introduction

Tea is the best beverage crop of India. Which is made from leaves of a tropical shrub of the 'Camellia family'. Chang Jiang or Yangtze valley is noted as early birth place of tea during the 6th century of Christ. 'Assam' and 'Chinese' are the two principal varieties of this plant in which Assam Variety (Indian) is tasted as taller and longer leaves with excellent quality. At present, the use of tea have taken its global position as a permanent drink. Although China is the early origin country of this beverage crop yet India is the largest consumer at worldwide context. India is also the second largest producer occupying the second largest geographical area, fourth largest exporter and fifth largest productivity gainer country of tea at present time.

Geographical Conditions for the Tea Cultivation

The temperature, precipitation, soil, topology etc. are the major geographical conditions suitable for tea cultivation. The monthly temperature between 22°C and 34°C is created the optimum heat for growth of plant and leaves (Memoria, C.B., 2002). Mean annual precipitation should be about 200 cm. to 250 cm. The shaded environment is very adoptive for plants but hail and cold waves are harmful. Continue and equal distribution of precipitation is too much suitable to plant growth. The forest soil with richness of humus and iron content is best suited. The well drained, deep and friable loamy soil is also useful. The sloping ground (vertilinear slope) on mountains/plateaus hills is better to them. Beside its phosphorus and potash based manures and fertilizers and cheap labourers are also important for tea cultivation.

Cultivation and Processing

On a large scale the cultivation of tea in the country is occupied in Assam (The Brahmaputra Valley and Surma Valley), West Bengal (Darjeeling and the Doars), Tamil Nadu, and Kerala (Kollam and Kottayam District) states and moderately it is cropped out in Tripura, Uttarakhand, Himachal Pradesh and Karnataka states. For the best cultivation of tea, the land, preferably sloping terrain is firstly acceptable. Tea cuttings are raised in a nursery (plant height about 18 cm.) and transplanted into the desirable fields in October-November month. April to June, July to August and September to October the best periods of picking or plucking of tea leaves in the year. Tea plucking it the skillful work in which women labourers are better because women can be employed relatively cheaply to man and quickly picker also. India is mainly black tea producer country which is taken with milk and sugar. In processing black tea the collected or gathered leaves are first dried in the sunlight for one or two days to extract any humidity or moisture environment. After its, mechanically rolling between steel rollers in used to break up the presented fibres. The leaves are dried again or baked lightly over charcoal fires, until they become raddish brown in colour. Further colouring the formation and packing processes are come (Leong, G.C. and Morgan, G.C., 1982).

Areal Distribution and Production

There were 567 thousand hectares of area consumed under the tea cultivation in 2008 of the country. It was 436 thousand hectares in the 2001 in which about 97% of areas was under only four states as Assam, West Bengal, Tamil Nadu and Kerala (**Table 16.1** and **Figure 16.1, 16.2**). The area under the crop in thousand hectares and its per cent in above states were as 232 (53.21, in Assam, 103 (13.62) in West Bengal, 51 (11.70) in Tamil Nadu, 37 (08.49) in Kerala. Remaining 13 (02.98) as other scattered area. The production of tea in thousand Tons and per cent of above states were as 414 (51.43) in Assam, 180 (22.36) in West Bengal, 108 (15.90) in Tamil Nadu, 68 (08.45) in Kerala and remaining 35 (01.86) as others in the base year of 2001. The total production of the tea in whole country was 805 thousand Tons in this year (**Table 16.1** and **Figure 16.2**). It is worthy of quotation that Assam is the largest area holder and producer state of tea in the nation. It occupies more than half of the total area and production of the country.

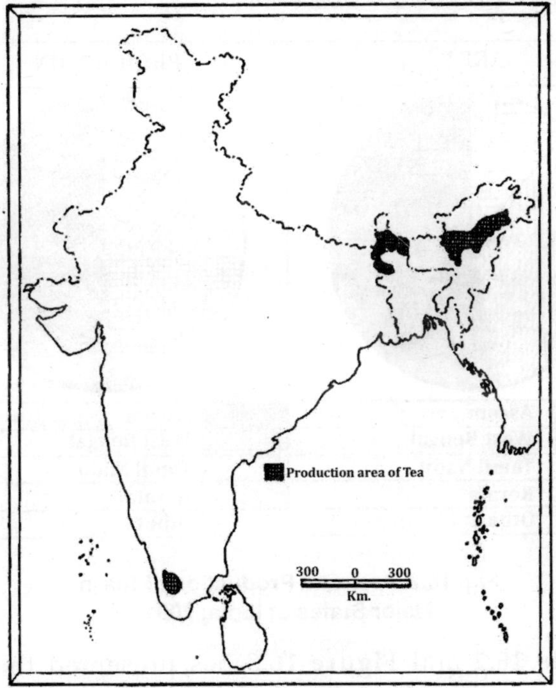

Fig. 16.1. India—Production Area of Tea

Table 16.1 : Area and Production of Tea in Major States of India: 2001

Major States	Area		Production	
	Thousand Hectares	In per cent	In Thousand Tons	In per cent
Assam	232	53.21	414	51.43
West Bengal	103	23.62	180	22.36
Tamil Nadu	51	11.70	108	15.90
Kerala	37	08.49	68	08.45
Others	13	02.98	35	01.86
Totals	436	100.00	805	100.00

Source: Statistical Abstract of India, 2001.

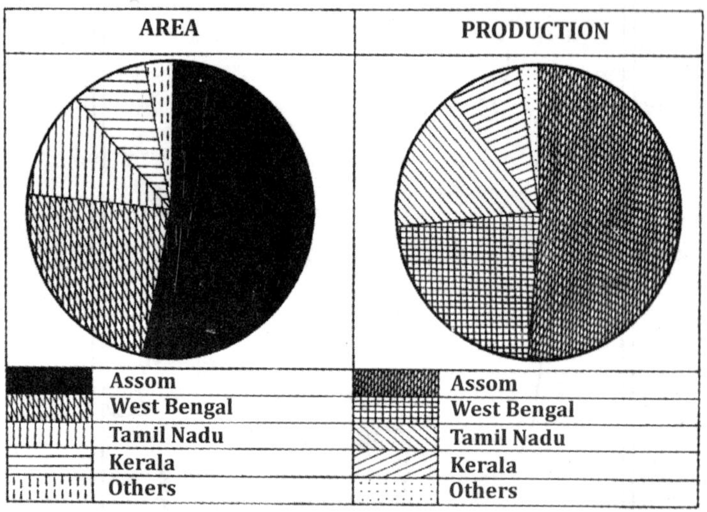

Fig. 16.2. Area and Production of Tea in Major States of India: 2001

Table 16.2 and **Figure 16.3** has presented the area, production and productivity of tea in India between 1950-51 and 2008-09. Area (in thousand hectares), production (in thousand tons) and productivity (in kgs/hectare) of the aforesaid years is marked as 316,178 and 879 in 1950-51, 331, 321 and 971 in 1960-61, 354, 419 and 1182 in 1970-71, 382, 570 and 1491 in 1980-81, 421, 720 and 1794 in 1990-91, 436, 805 and 1846 in 2000-01 and 567, 981 and 1732 in 2008-09 respectively. The area, production and productivity has been increased as 79.43%, 252.88% and 97.04% during the last 58 years. Notable that the highest productivity (1846 kgs./ hectare) was recorded in 2000-01 which shows more than 110.01% productivity with respect to the year of 1950-51. The highest decadal growth of area, production and productivity were recorded between 2000-01 and 2008-09 (in eight years), 1980-81 and 1990-91 and 1970-71 and 1980-81 as 30.04%, 26.32% and 26.14% respectively. Negative change in productivity is also recorded between 2000-01 and 2008-09 as 06.58%. It is stated in world tea statistics 2008 that India the second largest area of 17% of the world after China. It is also the second nation of the world after China contain 26% of tea production of the world. After Malawi, Kenya, Argentina and Uganda,

Table 16.2 : Area, Production and Productivity of Tea in India: 1950-51—2008-09

Years	Area (Thousand Hectares)	Production (Thousand Tons)	Productivity (Kgs./ Hectare)
1950-51	316	278	879
1960-61	331	321	971
1970-71	354	419	1182
1980-81	382	570	1491
1990-91	421	720	1794
2000-01	436	805	1846
2008-09	567	981	1732

Source: Statistical Abstract of India, 2003, Economic Survey, 2004-05, Gautam, A, 2007 and The Hindu Survey of India Industry, 2010.

India stands as fifth nation of the world in view of tea productivity which is stated as 1732 kgs/hectare. The tea industry provides direct employment to more than one million labourers of whom a sizeable number are female belonging to the weaker class of society (Baraih, G., 2006).

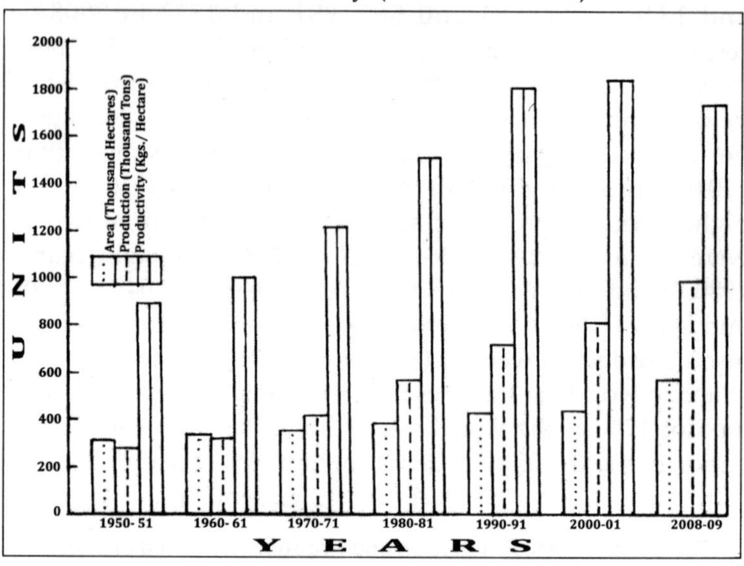

Fig. 16.3. Area, Production and Productivity of Tea in India, 1950-51—2008-09

Comparative Analysis of Tea Productivity

Although India has better position in tea production but demerit in tea productivity which is not a good sign of tea cultivation. **Table 16.3** and **Figure 16.4** has shown the comparison of tea productivity between India and some major countries during the base year 2008. In productivity the position of India comes after Malawi (2333 kgs./H), Kenya (2184 Kgs/H), Argentina (1895 kgs/H) and Uganda (1870 Kgs/H). The productivity of tea in India is as 1732 Kgs/Hectare which is below to Malawi 34.70%, Kenya 26.10%, Argentina 09.41% and Uganda 07.97%. In another words the productivity of India is less than Malawi 601 Kgs/H, Kenya 452 Kgs./H,

Table 16.3 : Comparison of Tea Productivity between India and some Major Countries: 2008

Sl. No.	Country	Productivity (Kg./Hectare)
1.	Malawi	2333
2.	Kenya	2184
3.	Argentina	1895
4.	Uganda	1870
5.	India	1732
6.	Sri Lanka	1697
7.	Rwanda	1417
8.	Bangladesh	1093
9.	Indonesia	1045
10.	China	718

Source: The Hindu Survey of Indian Industry, 2010.

Argentina 163 Kgs./H and Uganda 138 Kgs/H. Beside the above the productivity of Sri Lanka (1697 Kgs/H), Rwanda (1417 Kgs/H). Bangla Desh (1093 Kgs/H), Indonesia (1045 Kgs/H) and China (718 Kgs/H) is below to India. The productivity of India is more than Sri Lanka 35 Kgs/H (02.06%), Rwanda 315 Kgs/H (22.23%), Bangla Desh 639 Kgs/H (58.46%), Indonesia 687 Kgs/H (65.74%) and China 1014 (141.23%). It is remarkable that the production of tea in the country (India) is more than China about 141.23% but it is unworthy less than that of Malawi as 34.70%. The major cause of low productivity in India (in comparison) is higher average age of tea bush. Acknowledging the need for accelerated replantation and rejuventation activity, the Tea Board has implemented a special purpose Tea Fund (SPTF) Scheme. The objective is to cover above 2 lakh hectares area over a 15 year of period (Patra, S., 2010).

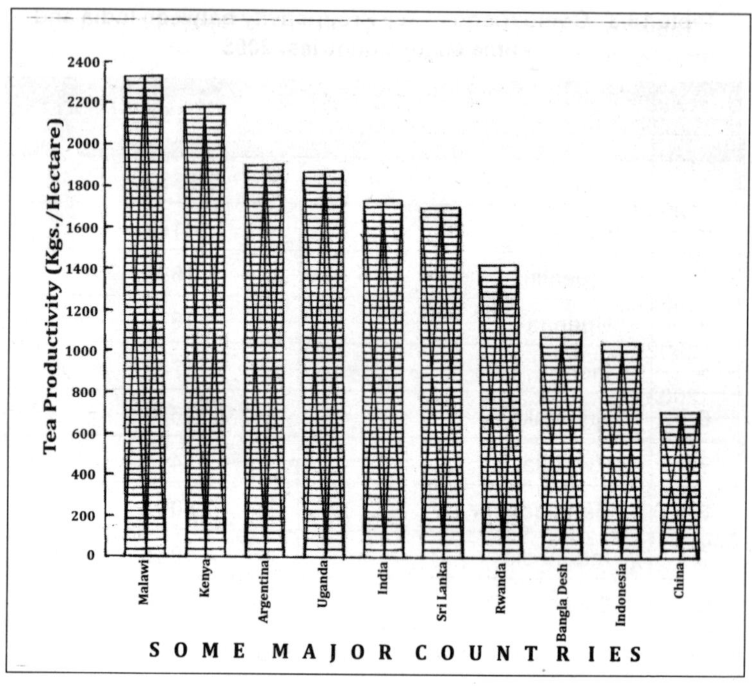

Fig. 16.4. Comparison of Tea Productivity of India with Some Major Countries—2008

Level of Consumption of Tea

The tea is a most wanted and popular beverage of not only in India but also world. At present the level of tea consumption in India is less than U.K., Ireland, Turkey (above to 2 Kgs. per capita annnually each), Afghanistan, Pakistan and CIS (above to 1 kg per capita annually each) countries (Patra, S., 2010). There is only 730 grams per capita annually tea consumption in India. **Table 16.4** and **Figure 16.5** has indicated about consumption of tea in India between 1998-99 and 2008-09 year which register the continue growth of consumption. The consumption of Tea in thousand Tons is mentioned as 615 in 1998-99, 633 in 1999-2000, 653 in 2000-01, 673 in 2001-02, 693 in 2002-03, 714 in 2003-04, 735 in 2004-05 and 830 in

Table 16.4 : Consumption of Tea in India: 1998-99—2008-09

Years	Consumption (Thousand Tons)
1998-99	615
1999-00	633
2000-01	653
2001-02	673
2002-03	693
2003-04	714
2004-05	735
2008-09	830

Source: Economic Survey, 2005-06 and The Hindu Survey of Indian Industry, 2010.

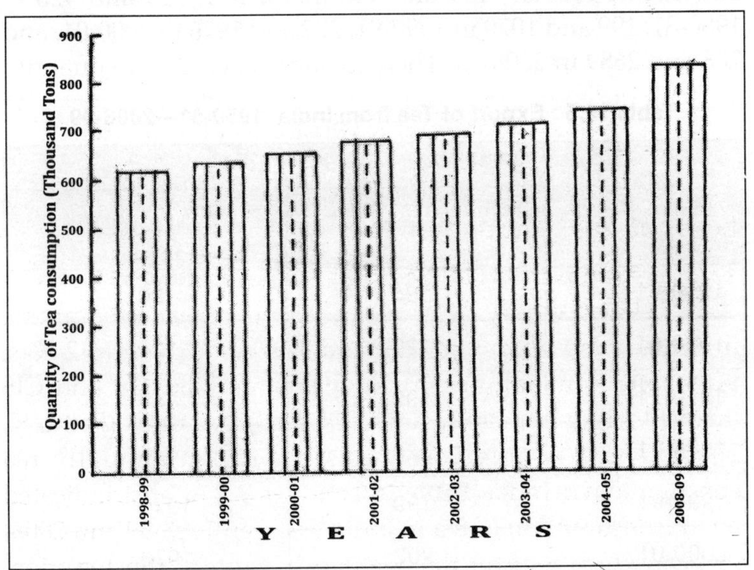

Fig. 16.5. Consumption of Tea in India, 1998-99—2008-09

2008-09 years. India has shown 215 thousand Tons (34.96%) growth in consumption of tea during past 10 years (1998-99 to 2008-09). It is cleared by Biological research that the tea is a medicinal beverage of antioxidents so the level of consumption should be balanced.

International Trade

The international trade of tea in India including export and import is given as follows:

(a) Export: India is the fourth largest exporter country of tea with 12% share of the world export. The total tea exported quantity is 21.20% (208 thousand Tons in 981 thousand tons) of the whole production of the nation (2008-09) which is only one-fourth of gross domestic consumption. But it is the larger quantity than that of import. **Table 16.5** and **Figure 16.6** has interpreted about the export of tea from India between 1950-51 and 2008-09. The exported quantity (thousand Tons) and value (crore Rupees) is reported as 195 and 80 in 1950-51, 199 and 124 in 1960-61, 199 and 148 in 1970-71, 229 and 426 in 1980-81, 199 and 1070 in 1990-91, 202 and 1976 in 2000-01, and 208 and 2689 in 2008-09. There is nominal change in quantity

Table 16.5 : Export of Tea from India: 1950-51—2008-09

Years	Export	
	In Quantity (Thousand Tons)	In Value (Crore Rupees)
1950-51	195	80
1960-61	199	124
1970-71	199	148
1980-81	229	426
1990-91	199	1070
2000-01	202	1976
2008-09	208	2689

Source: Economic Survey, 2004-05, Gautam, A., 2007 and the Hindu Survey of Indian Industry, 2010.

of export but about 34 times growth in export value have been accounted during the last 58 years of time. The growth in export quantity is compulsory for gaining to foreign currencies.

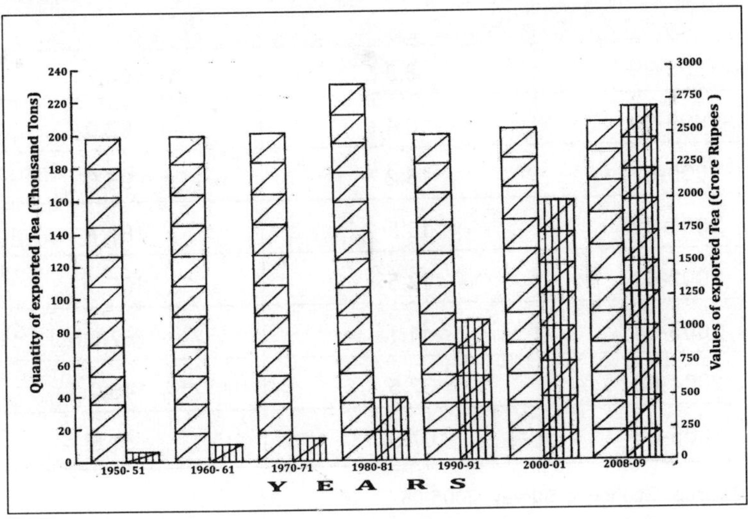

Fig. 16.6. Export of Tea from India 1950-51—2008-09

Import: In special case nominal import of tea is highlighted in comparison of the export of tea. **Table 16.6** and **Figure 16.7** represents the import of tea in India between the years of 1998-99 and 2005-06. The quantity (thousand Tons) and value (Crore Rupees) of import with in the above base years were obtained as 8.9 and 64.7 in 1998-99, 10.4 and 62.0 in 1999-2000, 15.2 and 95.5 in 2000-01, 16.8 and 86.7 in 2001-02, 22.5 and 105.3 in 2002-03, 11.1 and 67.0 in 2003-04, 32.5 and 145.0 in 2004-05, and 07.9 and 51.5 in 2005-06 respectively. The highest quantity and value of imported tea had recorded in 2004-05 as 32.5 thousand Tons and 145.0 crore Rupees. The quantity of imported tea in India is found as 24, 16 and 20 thousand Tons in the respective years of 2006-2007 and 2008 (Patra, S. 2010) It is fact that the yearwise series of tea import is not regular because it is depended on production and demand.

Table 16.6 : Import of Tea in India: 1998-99—2005-06

Years	Import	
	In Quantity (Thousand Tons)	In Value (Crore Rupees)
1998-99	8.9	64.7
1999-00	10.4	62.0
2000-01	15.2	95.5
2001-02	16.8	86.7
2002-03	22.5	105.3
2003-04	11.1	67.0
2004-05	32.5	145.0
2005-06	07.9	51.5

Source: Economic Survey, 2005-06.

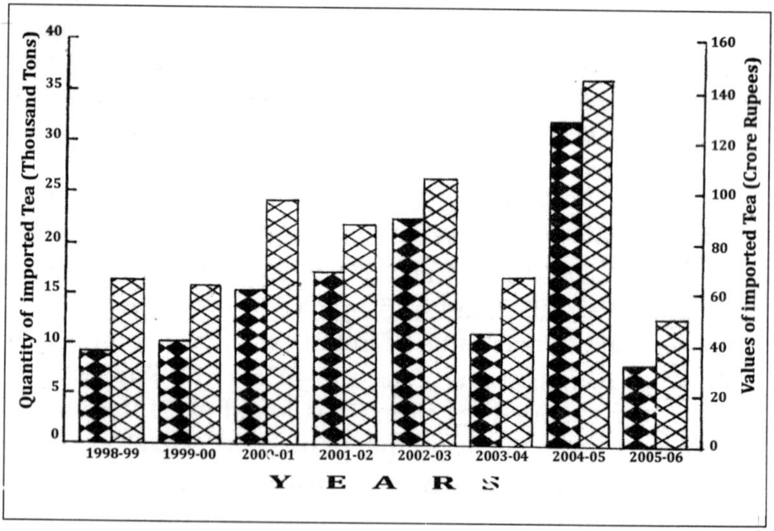

Fig. 16.7. Import of Tea in India 1998-99—2005-06

Conclusion

It is clear that the tea is a most significant beverage of India. As surveyed in now a days localities 'any time is tea time' in the nation. India has a pioneer role along with 17% area, 26% production, 12% export and 23% consumption in tea cultivation. India has one-third area under the tea cultivation in comparison of China but the production of these two countries are equivalent. The modern technology and innovative trends of cultivation are so necessary for India's first rank in tea production. With the increasement of productivity, availability and exports foreign current in turn may be obtained in the country which is analysing the interested story of expansion of tea cultivation.

REFERENCES

1. Bariah, G., 2006: 'Substantial Forex Earnings', Paper Published in The Hindu Survey of Indian Agriculture 2006, N. Ram on Behalf of M/s Kasturi and Sons Ltd. National Press, Kasturi Buildings, Chennai-600002, p. 213.
2. Economic Survey, 2004-05 and 2005-06: Economic Division, Finance Ministry, Government of India.
3. Gautam, A., 2007: Advanced Geography of India, Sharda Pustak Bhawan, 11, University Road, Allahabad-2, p. 334-336.
4. Leong, G.C. and Morgan, G.C., 1982: Human and Economic Geography, Oxford University Press, New Delhi, pp. 191-194.
5. Memorial, C.B., 2002: Advanced Geography of India, Sahitya Bhawan Publications, Hospital Road, Agra-282003, pp. 288-291.
6. Patra, S., 2010: 'Cost Reduction for Future Growth', Paper Published in the Hindu Survey of Indian Industry, N. Ram, Kasturi Buildings, 859 and 860, Anna Salai, Chennai-600002, p. 234-238.
7. Statistical Abstract of India, 2001 to 2003.
8. The Hindu Survey of Indian Industry, 2010: Production of Selected Industries and Principal Exports, N. Ram, Kasturi Buildings, 859 & 860, Anna Salai, Chennai-600002, pp. 271-273.

CHAPTER

17

Unexpected Bloom of Dairy Farming

Aditya Narain Pandey and Mahendra Kumar

Introduction

India is the well known country of the global world. It extends geographically between parallels of latitudes 08°04′ to 37°06′ north and longitudes 68°07′ to 97°25′ east covering 32,87,263 square km. of area. It is the seventh largest country of the world with 02.4 per cent of landed area of globe. Pakistan, Afghanistan, China, Nepal, Bhutan, Bangladesh and Myanmar are the neighbouring country of it. The country is situated on the western fringe of the Indian ocean. The tropic of cancer runs almost through the central point of the country and divides it into two halves as tropical and sub tropical zones. The nation holds 28 states, 06 union territories and 01 national capital region. It is divided into three geological divisions as northern mountainous region, middle Indus-Ganga plain and Southern peninsular region. The Ganga river makes the largest drainage system. Alluvial and black soils are the major soil types of this. The climate of the nation is like tropical monsoony in which four seasons are registered as winter, summer, rainy and post monsoony.

The population of the country is 1,02,70,15,247 person according to census abstract of 2001 and at present (in the last of year 2010) it is estimated as about 120 crore persons which is settled in 5,93,616 villages and 5,161 urban centres (2001). The total working population occupies 38.5 per cent cultivators, 26.4 per cent agricultural labourers and 02.5 per cent engaged in mining and forestry, 12.1 per cent population are settled in industrial, constructional and other as secondary sector and 20.5 per cent are marked in trade, commerce, transport, storage and communications as tertiary sector (Statistical outline of India, 2003-04).

Importance of Dairy Products

Dairy farming is one of the most important agro-based occupation of India which makes to it as world's largest producer country of milk. The milk may be used in its original form or changed into cheese, curd, butter and ghee. It is an important food for nomadic herdsman, for urban and rural population. According to Leong, G.C. and Morean, G.C. 1982 "Milk is a highly nutritions food containing all the essential minerals and vitamins for human growth, hence its importance for feeding babies."

Optimum Geographical Conditions for Dairy Farming

'Money, material, market, men motive power, machinery, management momentum of an early start trade, transport techniques and governing' may be thought as the major anthropogenic factors for dairy farming as well as highly milk production. The optimum geographical conditions for dairy farming are given as follows:

(i) Climate
(ii) Fodder
(iii) Water
(iv) Labourer
(v) Capital
(vi) Transportation
(vii) Market
(viii) Scientific research and development programmes

(i) Climate: An adaptive climate for dairy cattles is essential for dairy farming. In India, there are four cattle rearing areas climatically treated suitable as Himalaya's mountainous region, northern semi arid region, east and west humid region, and sub humid region in which second and fourth regions are rich in dairy farming having high milky cattles. It is proved that semi arid and sub humid climate is the highly adaptive for dairy cattles. In these areas Punjab, Haryana, Delhi, Rajasthan, U.P., M.P., Maharashtra, Gujarat, Karnataka, Andhra Pradesh, Tamil Nadu etc. States/N.C.R. are jointed.

(ii) Fodder: Availability of fodder is one of the most basic necessity for dairy cattles. The homogeneous physiography of Great plain of the country has provided an unique condition for food of dairy cattles. It is the major agricultural belt of wheat, paddy and jowar. Besides it mountainous-plateaux and other regions have provided the grazing conditions. The production of forage crops is being highly in Punjab, Haryana, U.P. etc. states where milk production is very high. Dry foods for dairy cattles is also available in several states.

(iii) Water: The need for fresh water for healthy dairy cattles as cow should be 150 to 200 litres per day to drink and bath. An enough quantity of fresh water for drinking maintains the digestion and temperature of body of dairy cattles. Daily bathing of dairy cattles is so useful because it prevents to various types of bacteria, virus predator and diseases of body-skin. In view of water availability, India is an ideal country in the world.

(iv) Labourer: Dairy farming is the labour based industry in the motion so it needs enough and cheap but skilful labourers. In the densed populous areas, dairy farming is highly upgraded in the country. Male and female both labourers are similarly suitable for it. Intensive subsistence tillage, subsistence crop and livestock farming and commercial crops and livestock farming regions are the major agricultural belt of dairy farming where labourers are available in huge numbers.

(v) Capital: Capital is the most important economic basement for dairy farming as well as industry. For the extensive land, infrastructural background, buying of dairy cattles and dairy related machines there should be a lot of capital. The insurance of dairy cattles is must for circumstances of diseases and deaths. Buying of advanced breeds of dairy cattles need too much pocket money for dairy former.

(vi) Transportation: The accessibility and connectivity of roads and streets have provided on excellent occasion to growth and development of dairy farming. The rapid accessibility from station to destination of milk and dairy products is must for successful development of it. Low living services of transportation are desirable.

(vii) Market: The suitable place, where milk and other dairy products are bought and sold is the necessary for dairy farming. Megalopolises and metropolises centre of India provide a large and extensive market for it where high demand is notable Mumbai, Delhi, Kolkata, Chennai, Bangalore, Hyderabad, Ahmedabad, Pune, Kanpur, Jaipur, Lucknow etc. urban centres generally present the good market centres.

(viii) Scientific Research and Development Programmes: The various types of scientific research and development programme are desirable for the growth of dairy farming and for high milk production. Scientific researches as hybreedation of dairy cattles, dairy related modern technology and storage are acceptable. The development programmes concerned with public awareness for high milk production is also adoptable and implementable at present.

Background of Dairy Farming Development

The well known that dairy farming is one of the oldest occupation of the country. Milk production is an important uniform part of our agriculture system. Description of dairy cattle as cow and milk production on a large quantity is available in 'vedas' and other Indian tomes. The modern development of dairy farming is started in 1964-65 when 'Intensive Cattle Development Programme (ICDP) came in the existence. This programme was the backbone of 'white revolution' whose target was highly production of milk. The famous personality Dr. Kuryan, V was the founder of 'white revolution' who started 'Operation flood programme' in the whole country. The three phases of operation flood programme has been successfully completed from July 1970 to April 1996. At present 'National Dairy Development Board (NDDB), Anand (Gujarat), National Dairy Research Institute (NDRI), Karnal (Haryana) and Indian Council of Agricultural Research (ICAR), New Delhi are working in the field of dairy development and research and abroad which are giving an unexpected bloom of dairy farming.

Major Dairy Cattles

According to Data of 1992, the composition of cattles is as cows 44 per cent, buffaloes 18 per cent, sheeps 11 per cent, goats 24 per cent and remain others 3 per cent in the country. The nation holds largest population of dairy cattles of the world. The major milk breeds of cows are found as Giri, Sahiwal, Tharparkar, Deoni, Sindhi, Dangi and Nili, and in the case of buffaloes it is counted as Murra, Zafarabadi, Mahisana, Bhadawari, Surati, Nagpuri, Malawi, Nimari, Tonda, Elichpuri etc. The Jamunapari, Barbari, Surati and Bengali goats and the Marwari, Magra, Karakul, Lohi and Kutchi sheeps are also important dairy cattle breeds for the nation. Now a time hybrid of Sahwal, Red Sindhi, Friesiar, Jersy, Murra etc. are the advanced dairy cattles provided by national institutions.

Milk Production

India is the largest milk producer country in the world. The place of U.S.A. and China comes after this. Before some times Indian cows were called as 'tea cup cow' but today Indian goats are also not threated as 'tea cup goat'. At present with

15 per cent of the world production (100.2 Million Tons), India is the largest milk producer.

In 2005-06 the nation has 185.2 lakh cows and 97.1 lakh buffaloes which was the largest cattle population of the world. About 14 per cent of national income is collected by dairy industry. **Table 17.1** and **Figure 17.1** highlights the milk production in 1950-51 and 2006-07 was 17.0 and 100.1 Million Tons has registered as about 6 times fold in the last 56 years. The production in other years was as 20.0 Million Tons in 1960-61, 22.0 Million tons in 1970-71, 31.6 Million Tons in 1980-81, 53.9 Million tons in 1990-91 and 80.6 Million Tons in 2000-01 respectively. This production may be to increase upto 2020 approximately 235.0 Million Tons. It indicates upwarding graph of milk production of the nation. Out of total milk production near about 80 per cent output is concerned with non-organised sectors and remaining 20 per cent outcome correlate with co-operative and private dairy sectors. About 1.2 lakh village level co-operative dairy committees associating 1.24 crore members as well as farmers collect 2.1 crore litre milk daily in an average. The contribution of dairy sector in gross domestic products was 5.3 per cent in the year of

Table 17.1 : Milk Production in India:1950-51 to 2006-07

Year	Production (Million Tons)
1950-51	17.0
1960-61	20.0
1970-71	22.0
1980-81	31.6
1990-91	53.9
2000-01	80.6
2006-07	100.1
2020	235.0 (Approx)

Source: Economic Review (Hindi)-2005-06, p. 159 and Kurukshetra (Hindi), November 2008, p. 22.

2006-07 (Livestock and Dairy Department, New Delhi). There were 16 crore dairy cattles with 110 crore engaged population of the country was registered during the year 2006-07 (Kumar, R., 2008).

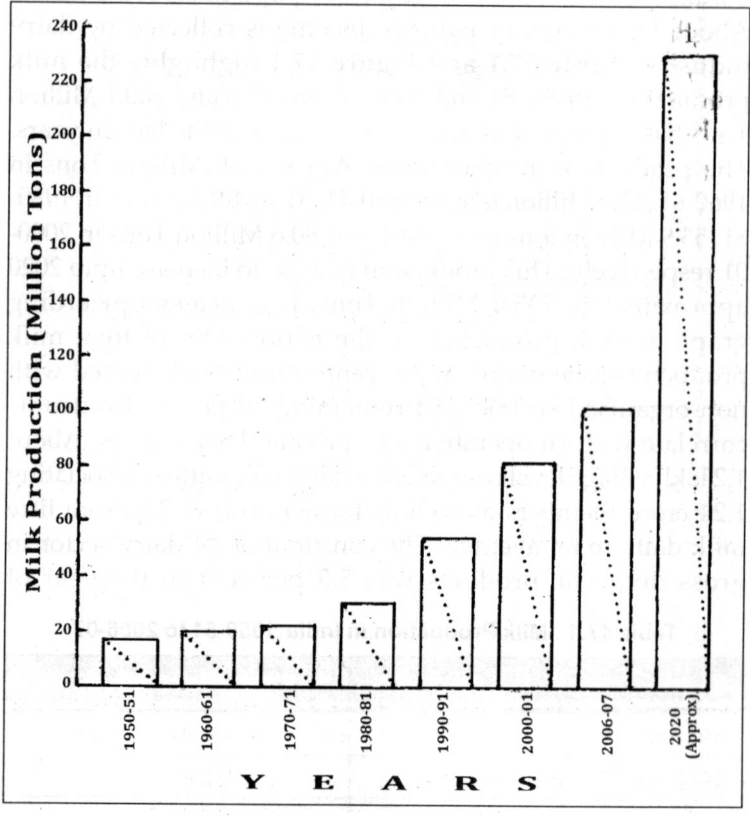

Fig. 17.1. Milk Production in India, 1950-51—2020

The cows and buffaloes are major, and sheeps and goats are minor dairy cattles of the country. Areal distribution of these dairy cattles are in adequate nature. **Figure 17.2** shows the distribution of cows in India. The dark shade shows the major areas and liner shade shows minor areas respectively, U.P., M.P., Bihar, Maharashtra, Rajasthan, Andhra Pradesh, West Bengal and Tamil Nadu are the major states and

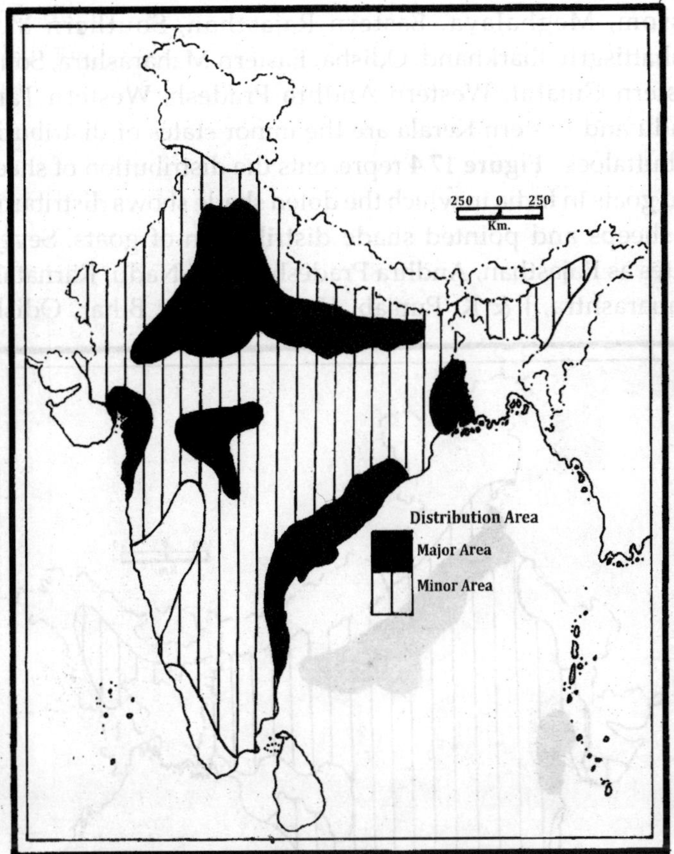

Fig. 17.2. India—Distribution of Cows

Karnataka, Gujarat, Assom, Meghalaya, Punjab, Haryana, Delhi, Uttarakhand, Himachal Pradesh, Odisha, Chhattisgarh, Jharkhand etc. are the miner states of distribution of cows. **Figure 17.3** indicates the distribution of buffaloes in major and minor areas in which dark shade is the indicator of major areas and linear shade depicts minor areas. Punjab, Haryana, Delhi, U.P., Northern, M.P., Western Maharashtra, North-Western Karnataka, Eastern Andhra Pradesh and Northern Tamil Nadu are the major states and Bihar, West Bengal,

Assom, Meghalaya, Eastern Rajasthan, Southern M.P., Chhattisgrh, Jharkhand, Odisha, Eastern Maharashtra, South-eastern Gujarat, Western Andhra Pradesh, Western Tamil Nadu and Eastern Kerala are the minor states of distribution of buffaloes. **Figure 17.4** represents the distribution of sheeps and goats in India in which the doted shade shows distribution of sheeps and pointed shade distribution of goats. Several states as Rajasthan, Andhra Pradesh, Tamil Nadu, Karnataka, Maharashtra, J & K, Punjab, Haryana, U.P., Bihar, Odisha,

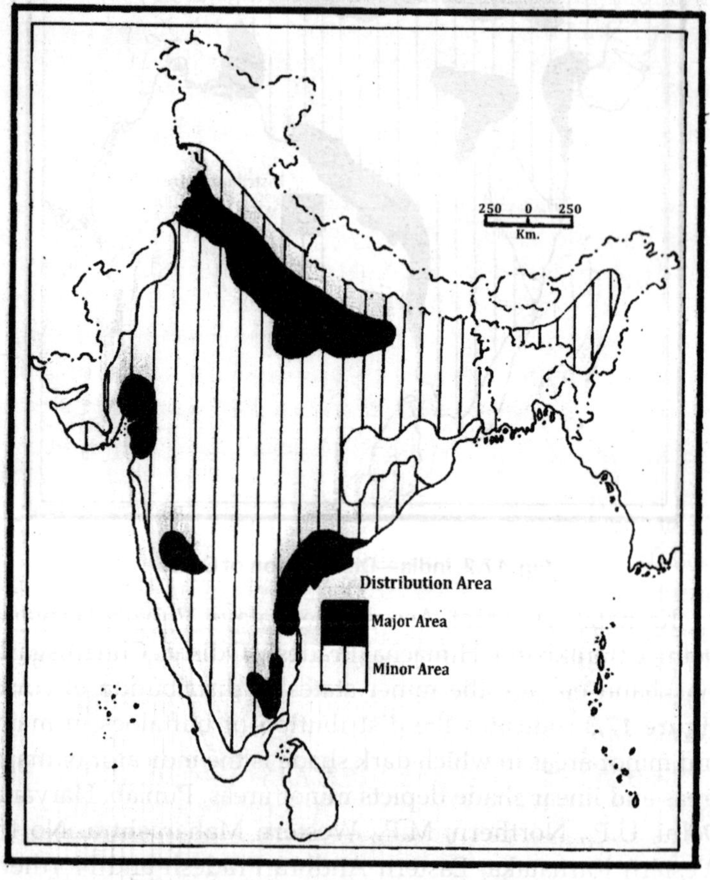

Fig. 17.3. India—Distribution of Buffaloes

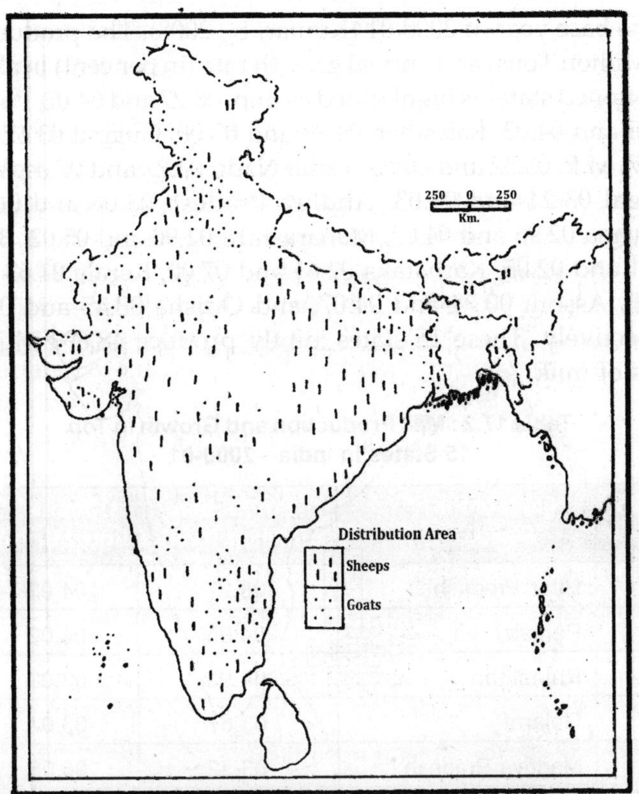

Fig. 17.4. India—Distribution of Sheeps and Goats

Jharkhand, Chhattisgarh, West Bengal, M.P., Gujarat, Kerala, Assom, Tripura etc. are major sheep raising states. The distribution of goats are mainly occupied in Bihar, Eastern U.P., West Bengal, J. & K., Punjab, Haryana, Eastern Rajasthan, Gujarat, M.P., Maharashtra, Andhra Pradesh, Karnataka, Kerala and Tamil Nadu states.

Table 17.2 and **Figure 17.5** have illustrated the milk production and growth in top 15 states of India during the year of 2000-01. According to above illustrations the highest production coasted in U.P. (08.27 million Tons) and the highest annual growth rate is recorded in West Bengal (09.03 per cent) in the base year of 2000-01 (Kumar, L., 2008). The production (in Million Tons) and annual growth rate (in per cent) in above mentioned states is highlighted as m.p. 08.27 and 04.02, Punjab 04.95 and 04.02, Rajasthan 04.93 and 03.00, Gujarat 03.67 and 03.07, M.P. 03.32 and 06.08, Tamil Nadu 03.27 and 07.04, West Bengal 03.24 and 09.03, Andhra Pradesh 03.06 and 06.04, Haryana 02.96 and 04.02, Maharashtra 02.90 and 05.02, Bihar 02.71 and 02.05, Karnataka 02.61 and 07.00, Kerala 01.63 and 08.05, Assom 00.74 and 04.07, and Odisha 00.45 and 01.05 respectively. These 15 states jointly produce 48.692 Million Tons of milk.

Table 17.2 : Milk Production and Growth in Top 15 States in India—2000-01

Sl.No.	Name of the States	Production (Million Tons)	Annual growth (%)
1.	Uttar Pradesh	08.27	04.02
2.	Punjab	04.95	04.02
3.	Rajasthan	04.93	03.00
4.	Gujarat	03.67	03.07
5.	Madhya Pradesh	03.32	06.08
6.	Tamil Nadu	03.27	07.04
7.	West Bengal	03.24	09.03
8.	Andhra Pradesh	03.06	06.04
9.	Haryana	02.96	04.02
10.	Maharashtra	02.90	05.02
11.	Bihar	02.7	02.05
12.	Karnataka	02.61	07.00
13.	Kerala	01.63	08.05
14.	Assam	00.74	04.07
15.	Odisha	00.45	01.05

Source: Kurukshetra (Hindi), November, 2008, p. 22.

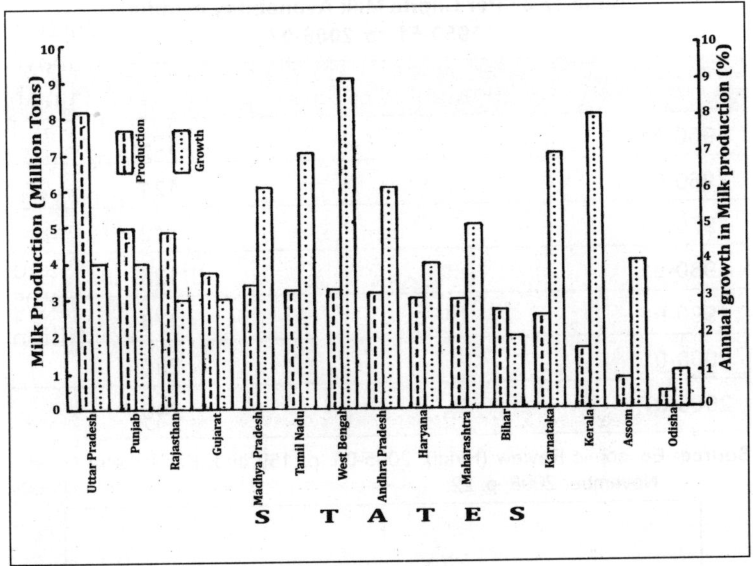

Fig. 17.5. Milk Production and Growth in Top 15 States of India: 2000-2001

Milk Availability

The per capita milk availability is changeable in India. During the successive decades as 1950-51, 1960-61, 1970-71, 1980-81, 1990-91 and 2000-01 and in the year 2006-07 per capita milk availability have traced out as 124 Gram, 124 Gram, 112 Gram, 128 Gam, 176 Gram, 220 Gram and 246 Gram per day respectively. The per capita availability have increased just double in the above duration (Economic Review, 2005-06 and Kurukshetra, November 2008). As regards the population growth between 1950-51 (36.10 crore) and 2006-07 (115 crores) it has increased triple times with respect to positive growth of per capita milk availability in India. Perhaps it is a challenging episode of milk production. **Table 17.3** and **Figure 17.6** represent per capita milk availability in India during 1950-51 to 2006-07.

Table 17.3 : Per Capita Milk Availability in India: 1950-51 to 2006-07

Year	Availability (Gram per day)
1950-51	124
1960-61	124
1970-71	112
1980-81	128
1990-91	176
2000-01	220
2006-07	246

Source: Economic Review (Hindi), 2005-06, p. 159 and, Kurukshetra (Hindi), November 2008, p. 22.

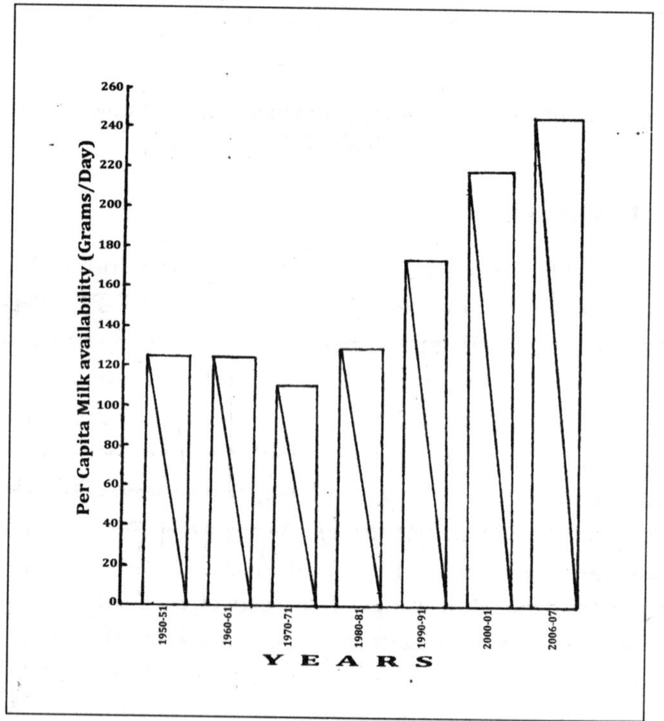

Fig. 17.6. Per Capita Milk Availability in India, 1950-51—2006-07

The comparative response of per capita milk availability between India and U.S.A. for the assessment year of 1950-51 to 2006-07 is given in **Table 17.4** and **Figure 17.7**. Per capita milk availability as per day between India and U.S.A. is obtained as 124 and 512 Gram in 1950-51, 124 and 617 Gram in 1960-61, 112 and 550 Gram in 1970-71, 128 and 741 Gram in 1980-81, 176 and 860 Gram in 1990-91, 220 and 856 Gram in 2000-01 and 246 and 900 Gram is 2006-07 respectively (Kurukshetra, November, 2008). Milk availability in U.S.A. in the comparison of India is found more than 413% in 1950-51, 498% in 1960-61, 491% in 1970-71, 579% (Highest) in 1980-81, 489% in 1990-91, 389% in 2000-01 and 366% in 2006-07. The rising gap of milk availability between India and U.S.A. as losing in the successive years (as 579% in 1980-81 and 366% in 2006-07) is the positive indicator for the bright future of India in milk availability as well as production. In India recently, 'Dairy scenario 2010' determines the target of fourfold growth in milk production and triple growth in milk marketing.

Table 17.4 : Per Capita Milk Availability: Comparison between India and U.S.A. 1950-51 to 2006-07

Year	Per capita milk availability (Gram per day)	
	India	U.S.A.
1950-51	124	512
1960-61	124	617
1970-71	112	550
1980-81	128	741
1990-91	176	860
2000-01	220	856
2006-07	246	900

Source: Kurukshetra (Hindi), November, 2008, p. 21.

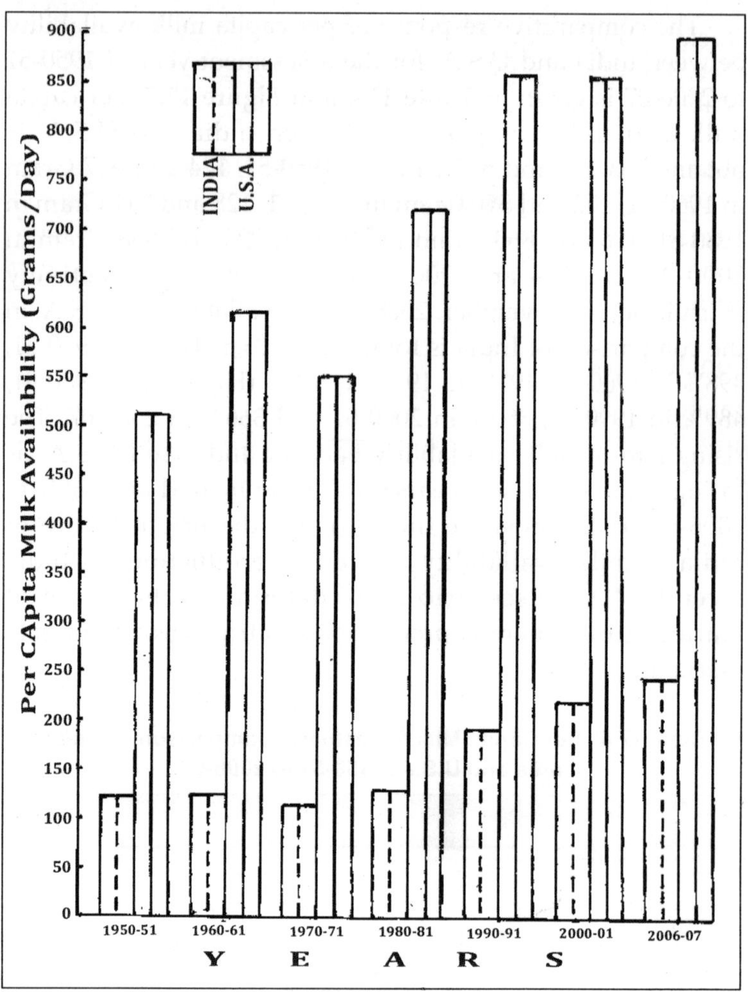

Fig. 17.7. Comparison of Per Capita Milk Availability between India and U.S.A. 1950-51—2006-07

Export of Dairy Products

India, not only ranks first in the milk production with 100 Million tons per annum but is also growing at a compound annual growth rate (CAGR) of above to 4 per cent with 15 per cent share of total milk production of the world. But illuckily, our export in dairy products is limited to butter, ghee, skim milk powder and whole milk powder only. The established players to complete with India in the international markets are European Union Nations, Australia, New Zealand and U.S.A. however, the developed countries provide heavily trade distorting export subsidies on their dairy products and rule the market (Rai, B., 2006). The export of mozafella, cheese, casein, whey and instant energy beverage may be possible in future.

Conclusion

Taking an image of world's largest producer country of the milk, India holds the largest population of dairy cattles, above to one hundred Million Tons milk production annually, more than four per cent CAGR, fifteen per cent share of whole milk production of the world and above five per cent share in GDP of the country. About 235 Million Tons milk production in 2020 may be possible which is an happiness index for country future. But in view of progress of export of dairy products, it should be highly increased in the future for the strong economy of the dairy farmers. The needs of massive education, knowledge, training, tools and equipments, hybreed dairy cattles must be provided for the dairy farmers.

REFERENCES

1. Chandramogan, R.G. 2006: Dairy Development—Lack of Technology and Awareness, the Hindu Survey of the Indian Agriculture, 2006 (Annual), Kasturi Building, Chennai, 600002, p. 129.
2. Economic Review, 2005-06: Agriculture, Government of India, Finance Ministry, Economic Division, p. 159 (Hindi).
3. Gautam, A., 2007: *Advanced Geography of India*, Sharda Pustak Bhawan Publishers and Distributors, 11, University Road, Allahabad-2, pp. 363-366 (Hindi).
4. Harun, M., 2003: *Major Elements of Economic Geography*, Vasundhara Prakashan, 236, Daudpur, Gorakhpur, pp. 220-221 (Hindi).

5. India, 2007: *Agriculture, Research, Reference and Training Division*, Publishing Department, Information and Broadcasting Ministry, Government of India, pp. 105-107 (Hindi).
6. Kaushik, S.D. and Gautam, A., 2000: *Resource Geography*, Rastogi Publications Shivaji Road, Meerut-250002, pp. 175-177 (Hindi).
7. Kumar, L., 2008: India on the Mouth of Second White Revolution, Kurukshetra, November, 2008, Room no. 655, 'A' Wing, Gate no. 5, Nirman Bhawan, Rural Development Ministry, New Delhi-110 011, pp. 21-22 (Hindi).
8. Kumar, R., 2008: Milk production—Resource of Income and Employment, Kurukshetra, November, 2008, Room no. 655, 'A', Wing, Gate No. 5, Nirman Bhawan, Rural Development Ministry, New Delhi-110 011, pp. 27-30 (Hindi).
9. Leong, G.C. and Morgan, G.C., 1982L Human and Economic Geography, Second Edition, Oxford University Press, Oxford New York, p. 295.
10. Mameria, C.B., 2002: Advanced Geography of India, Sahitya Bhawan publications, Agra-282003, p. 344-357 (Hindi).
11. Pandey, A., 2007: *Population Geography of India*, Discovery Publishing House 4831/24, Ansari Road, Daryaganj, New Delhi-110 002, pp. 8-9 (Hindi).
12. Rai, B., 2006: Agricultural Exports, Yojana, September, 2006, Yojana Bhawan, Sansad Marg, New Delhi (Published by the Ministry of Information and Broadcasting) p. 34.

CHAPTER

18

Development of Land Use Studies

Govind Prasad and Gitanjali

Introduction

Land is the expression of a variety of topo-ecofeatures. Land use is the surface utilization of all developed and vacant land on a specific point at a given time and space. The present work is deeply related to land use expression where in scope and objectives of land use studies, review of researches of land use studies and land use classification presented by various scholars and associations have been arranged systematically. The land use classification is cartographically shown in the last of the text. The theme mirrored in the text is reviewed from previous pioneer works done from time to time.

Concept of Land use

Land is the expression of a variety of topo-litho and dimo features, water bodies and natural drainage basins together with everygreen, deciduous and mixed sod cover and soft carpet of tall, small, wet and dry grasses. Man as the maker of cultural landscape, in graves his agricultural farms and fields, constructs his home ranging from hamlet to sky high buildings and ultimately nets his rural and urban inhabitations jointing with continued lines of communication. Over the basement of physical landscapes man has emerges cultural landscapes depleting forests and tapping so many underground resources. The relationship between earth and man has portrayed a variety of land problems which differs through spatio-temporal context.

Land is expressed as mirror of out appearance of earth surface. Face of the earth is defined and distributed in two parts nominated as land and water which is geographically termed by continents and Ocean basins. These turn topographical features are thought to be as first order relief features of the earth surface. Ocean basins cover about 2/3 area of the globe. The solid portion of the surface of the globe is defined as land. It may be also known as dry and solid portion of earth. It includes farming ground/arable land fit for cultivation. The word 'use' means the act of using or putting to a purpose.

The word 'Land use' may be expressed as **(Figure 18.1)**. On the basis of the above discussion. It may be said that land use in the surface utilization of all developed and vacant land on a specific point at a given time and space. This leads one back to the village farm and the farmer to the fields, gardens, pastures, fallow land, forests and to the isolated farmstead. The role of geographers becomes to analyse the relationship between various uses of land and planning (Foreman, 1968). This analysis enable people to use land more properly and obtain high yields to solve the problems of mankind.

According to Nanawati (1957) "Landuse is also related to conservation of land from one major use to another general use. The primary uses of land may be arranged as in form of crops, forest, pasture, mining, transportation, garden, residential, recreational, industrial, commercial and uncultivable waste, barren and fallow land etc. Land use category depends upon the changing needs of human society in a given spatio-temporal context. Stamp (1948) has classified the needs of man into six major categories *viz.*, the need of work, home, food, transportation, communication, defence

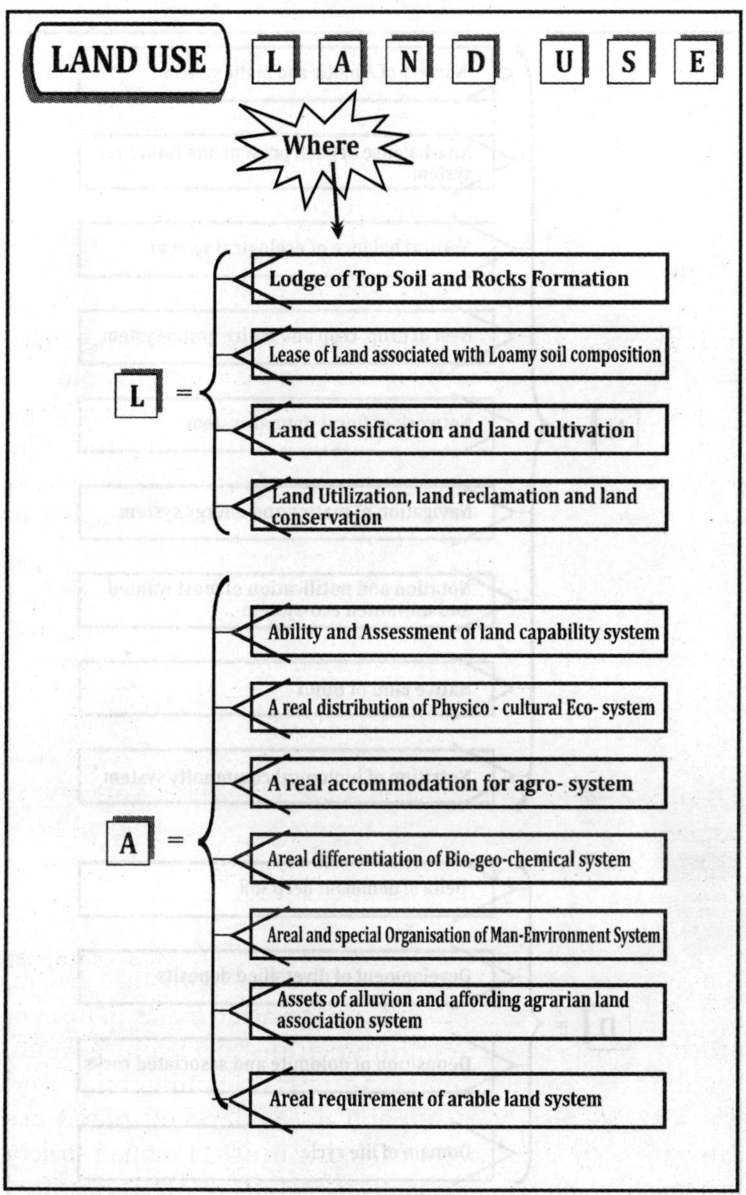
LAND USE
L
A
N
D
U
S
E
Where
L =
Lodge of Top Soil and Rocks Formation
Lease of Land associated with Loamy soil composition
Land classification and land cultivation
Land Utilization, land reclamation and land conservation
A =
Ability and Assessment of land capability system
A real distribution of Physico - cultural Eco- system
A real accommodation for agro- system
Areal differentiation of Bio-geo-chemical system
Areal and special Organisation of Man-Environment System
Assets of alluvion and affording agrarian land association system
Areal requirement of arable land system

Fig. 18.1. ......

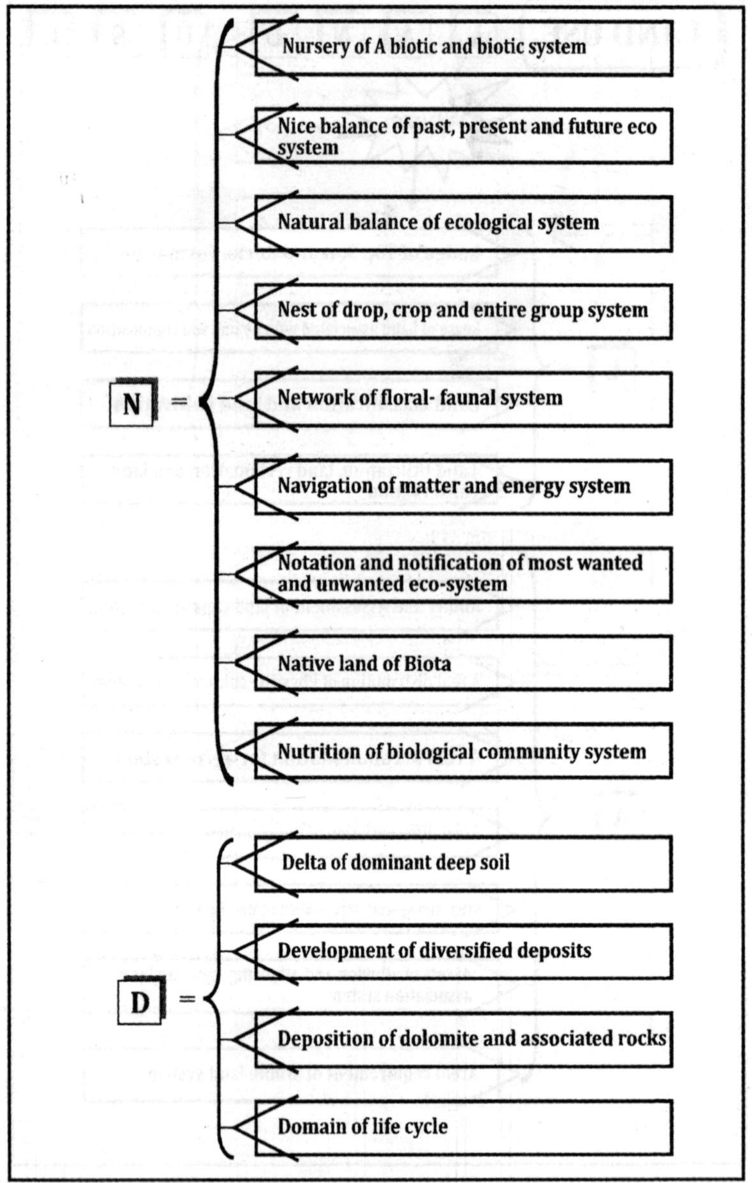
Nursery of A biotic and biotic system
Nice balance of past, present and future eco system
Natural balance of ecological system
Nest of drop, crop and entire group system
N =
Network of floral- faunal system
Navigation of matter and energy system
Notation and notification of most wanted and unwanted eco-system
Native land of Biota
Nutrition of biological community system
Delta of dominant deep soil
Development of diversified deposits
D =
Deposition of dolomite and associated rocks
Domain of life cycle

Fig. 18.1. ......

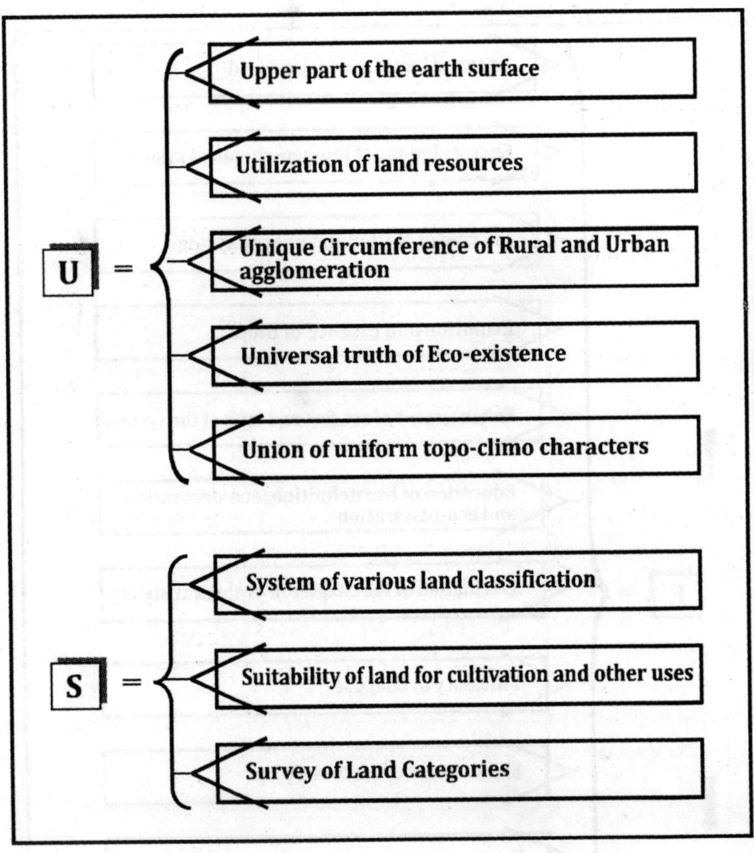
U =
Upper part of the earth surface
Utilization of land resources
Unique Circumference of Rural and Urban agglomeration
Universal truth of Eco-existence
Union of uniform topo-climo characters
S =
System of various land classification
Suitability of land for cultivation and other uses
Survey of Land Categories

Fig. 18.1. ...

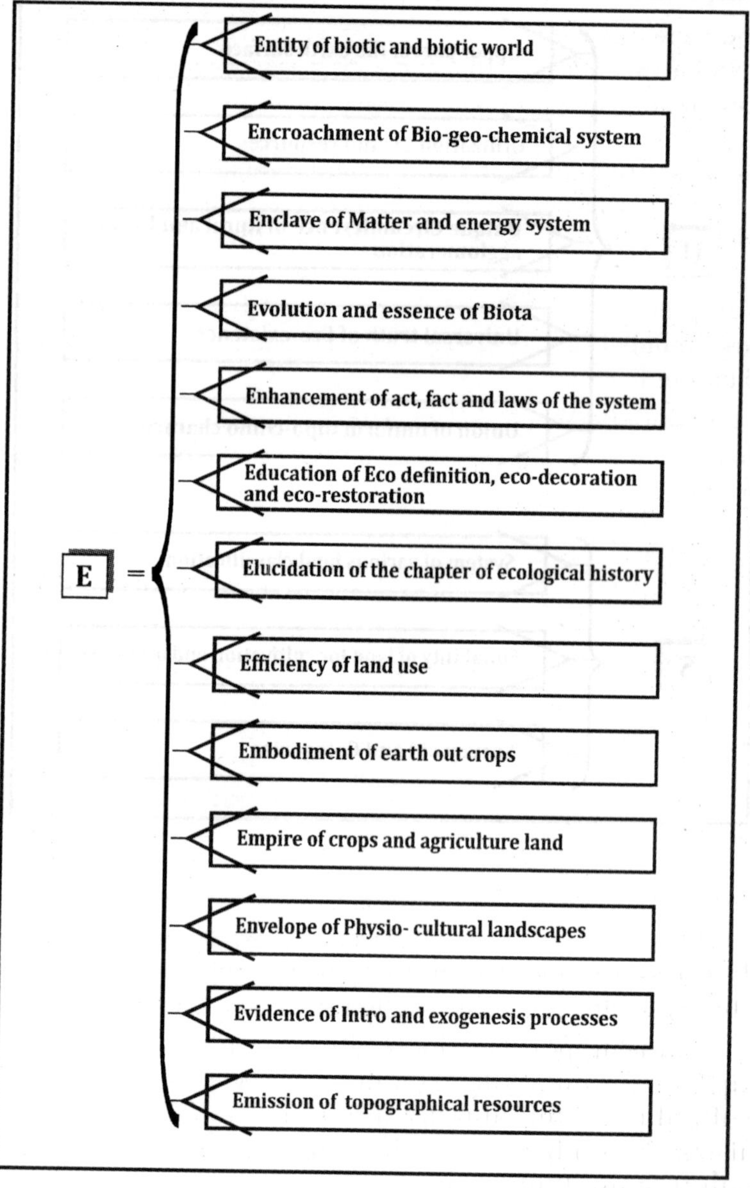
E =
Entity of biotic and biotic world
Encroachment of Bio-geo-chemical system
Enclave of Matter and energy system
Evolution and essence of Biota
Enhancement of act, fact and laws of the system
Education of Eco definition, eco-decoration and eco-restoration
Elucidation of the chapter of ecological history
Efficiency of land use
Embodiment of earth out crops
Empire of crops and agriculture land
Envelope of Physio- cultural landscapes
Evidence of Intro and exogenesis processes
Emission of topographical resources

Fig. 18.1.

and recreation. For the accomplishment of his essential needs man has to look towards land. The need of food means the conservation of fertile agricultural land for production as well as the development of poorer land for prodcution of food and cash crops. The land of the similar quality may be used to satisfy the needs of developing transportation and communication by means of railways, highways and airways. Land is also consumed for recreational usage in shape of parks, play grounds, gardens, clubs etc. Apart from the above, a large number of uses of land may be classified according to choice of man.

History denotes the fact that man has made proper uses, misuses, underuses and overuses of land. The growth of population and the resultant needs make the conflicts of landuse more serious, the concept of landuse capacity refers to the ability of any given unit of land resources to produce a net return above the production cost associated with its use. The amount of this net return provides an index of use capacity. Land areas with high use capacities normally have higher market values than those of lower used capacities. Farmers tend to use their land resources for those purpose which promise them the highest return. In fact a land use study should find measures to provide optimum return to land utilizers. A land utilization projects aim and striking balance between added mouths and landuse capacity. The concept of landuse, therefore, revolves round the man's accomplishments in conversion of land: major use to another general use. Each stage of such change may involve many problems to pave the path for attaining equalibrium in use of land (Singh, 1967).

Increasing population and changing needs of the time requires revision of land utilization. The revision is done by trial and error method which leaves its trace of success and failure. The study of land utilization makes it imperative to present an excellent opportunity to rectify past errors and to overrule further errors through scientific methods. The successs of national planning is dependent upon the proper utilization of land. Some day in our country a planned programme will determine the pattern of land use and there not only crops and tamed animals but indirectly things will be determined by man's conscious planning and use of land (Klages, 1947).

Scope and Objectives of Land Use Studies

The study of land use has recently developed and it has become one of the most important branches of economic geography. Majority of peoples of global earth have its close relationship with the primary activities which concern with land. Scientists much closer to earth's study can present a clearer view of the potentials of land use, conductive to fruitful planning for a massive agricultural turnover. A plan for the utmost utilization of land asset should essentially include the requirements of land for location of industries, site for houses, schools, public buildings roads and railways, irrigational channels etc. Land use differs in rural and urban areas. Most of the land in rural areas is used for agricultural purposes while in urban areas it is used mostly under residential, commercial, industrial and other uses.

The study of land use is not only concerned with land use classification, use and misuse of land, land capability, land use planning but it also includes several socio-economic aspects like man-land ratio, changing pressure of man on land, land use changes due to dynamism of socio-political conditions and scientific innovations etc. The study of land use in closely related with rural settlements, population, agriculture science, geomorphology, urban geography and so many branches of humanities and social sciences. Rural and Urban land use are the two major part of study. Land use study principally requires basic information about topo-litho and pedocharacter is of the global earth. Population geography and demographers is deeply related with land studies.

The techniques of land use study include field investigation, preparation of field maps, design of sampling and the presentation of data by different cartographical techniques suggested by reputed scholars in diverse fields of land use study.

Review of Researches of Land use Studies

Man environmental relationships expose the importance of land use study on world wide scale. Population pressure has given a new dimension of land use. Land is decreasing as well as the population is increasing. The decreasing mainland ratio has raised the value of land and its uses in various forms. Geographers, planners and other scholars have realised the importance of the subject and they have paying more attention to the problem.

During the year of 1930 stamp has established an independent research organisation called 'Land Utilization Survey of Britain'. On the basis of extensive survey and maps he published a voluminous book entitled "The Land of Britain" in 1962. The work of stamp was praised on world-wide scale. The work of Baber in United States entitled 'Land utilization in the US; Geographical Aspects of the Problem" was emphasised on the need of land classification and survey. But the American contribution was less than that of the work done in Britain. According to Stamp (1964) land use survey has been given the highest priority in Japan.

Land use surveys are progressed in various countries like Pakistan, Cyprus, Bangladesh, China, Poland etc. Several geographers have paid attention in India on different's aspects of land use studies under the guidelines of Stamp. Chatterjee (1945, 1952), Shafi (1952, 1961, 1966, 1969 & 1972) Dayal and Sharan (1972), Sinha (1968), Amani (1968), Mishra (1969), Ayyar (1968), Sharma (1972), Singh (1920), Das (1969), Roy (1976), Rao (1976), Lahiri (1950), Karimi (1949-50), Bharadwaj (1960), Roy (1668), Tripathi (1968) Garg (1968), Jha (1980), Das (1979), Prasad (1977) Singh (1980), Mandal (1982), Bhatia (1981), Vidya (1992, 1996) Sanjay Kumar (2006), Singh (1985), Suneel Kumar (1992) etc. have done scientific researches on land use analysis in India.

Different Government agencies have also contributed to the knowledge of land use studies. The 'Agriculture Atlas of India, the 'National Atlas' and the 'Census Atlases' of different states contain chloroplast and dot maps related to landuse and crops.

Since the ultimate goal of landuse study is to suggest the planning for better utilization of available land of the society and land use planning is not in practice in most areas. Scholars should influence the implementing agencies for its practice so that proper use of land and improved technique of cultivation would not only solve the food problems of the nation but it would may provide surplus products for export purposes (Kumar, 1986).

Land use Pattern/Classification of Land

The purpose of land use classification is to maximise the productivity and to conserve the land for prosperity. A classification of land requires considerable time and expense. It is necessary for better land use. The primary aim of the general pattern of land use study is to portray the plan and distribution of land to various uses ranging from field to factory, forest to foundry, pasture to pond, sandy stretch to settlement, courtyard to country and heal to hills top. The pattern of landuse is too much influenced by physical and human response factors of the country concerned.

Land classification is the expression of division of land into different categories as causative factors involved. The land classification relates to climatic factors, soil characteristics, slope of the land, degree of dissection, water supply, drainage and various environmental conditions. Thel and use capability classification/portrays the physical capabilities of land to produce over a long period of time under stated conditions of uses and which can provide land operations with a basis for actual practice on scientific units of land (Graham). Any classification of land in any part of the world is guided primarily by the classification of Stamp. Land classification may be presented as given in **Fig. 18.2** to **Fig. 18.15**.

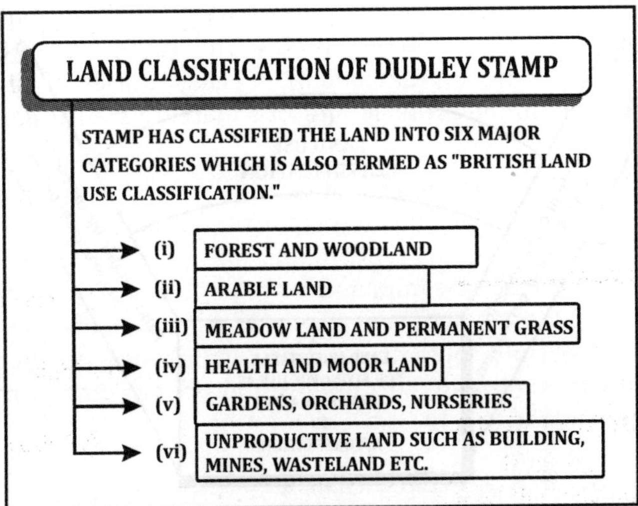

Fig. 18.2.

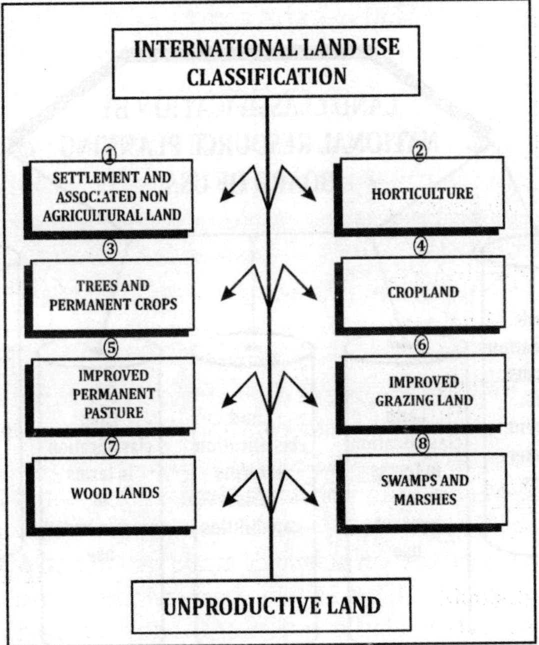

Fig. 18.3.

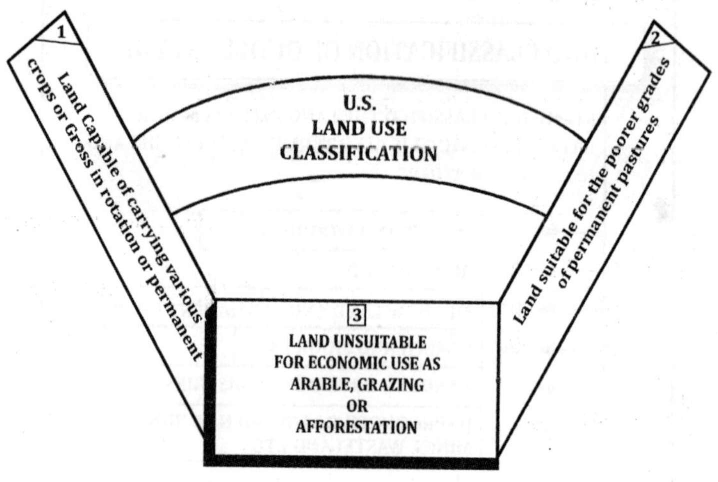

Fig. 18.4.

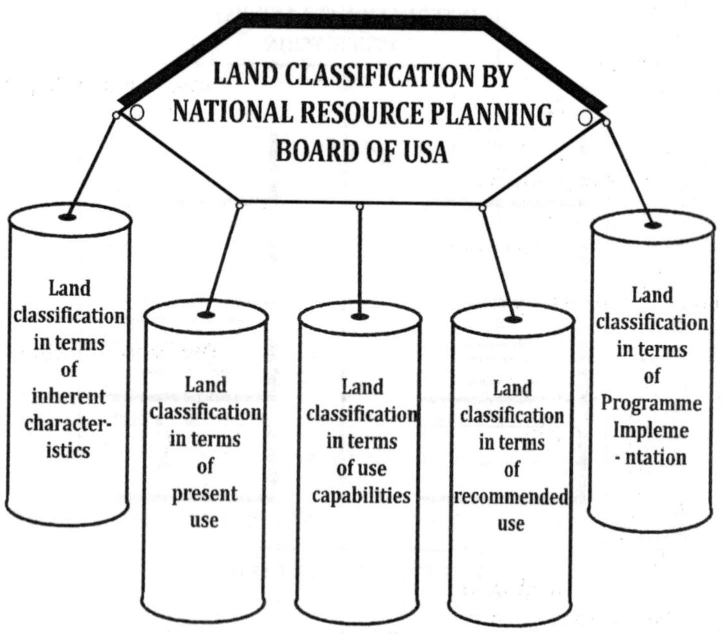

Fig. 18.5.

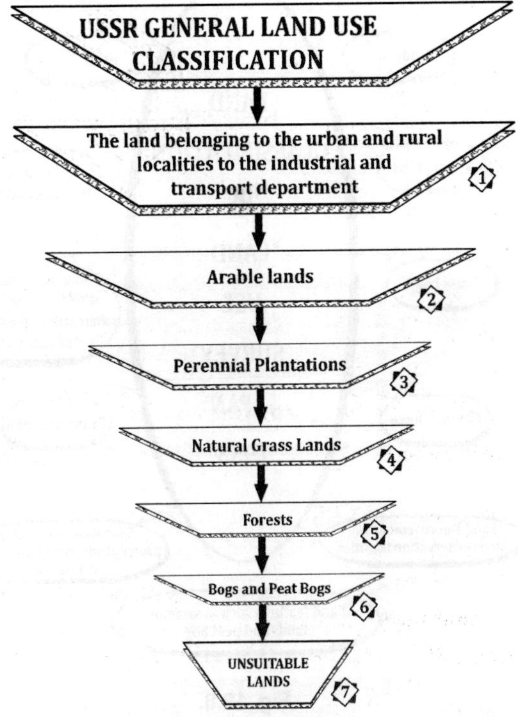

Fig. 18.6.

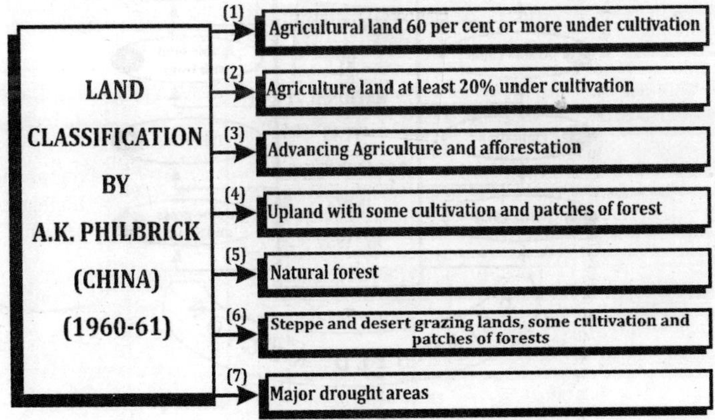

Fig. 18.7.

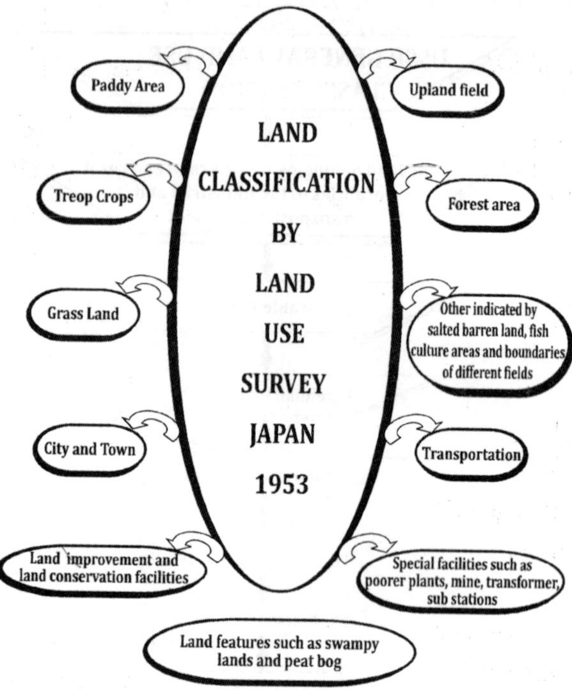

Fig. 18.8.

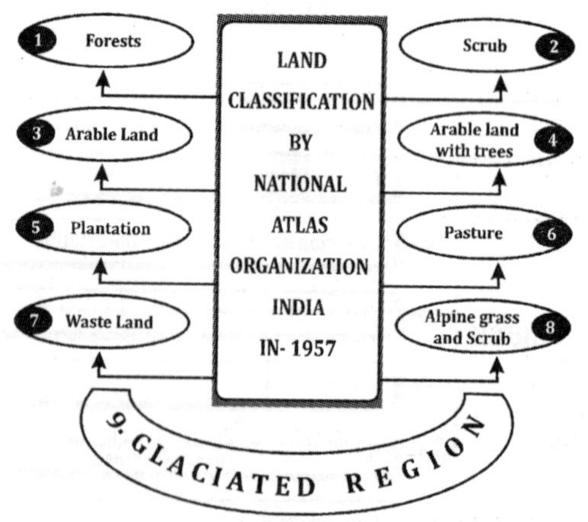

Fig. 18.9.

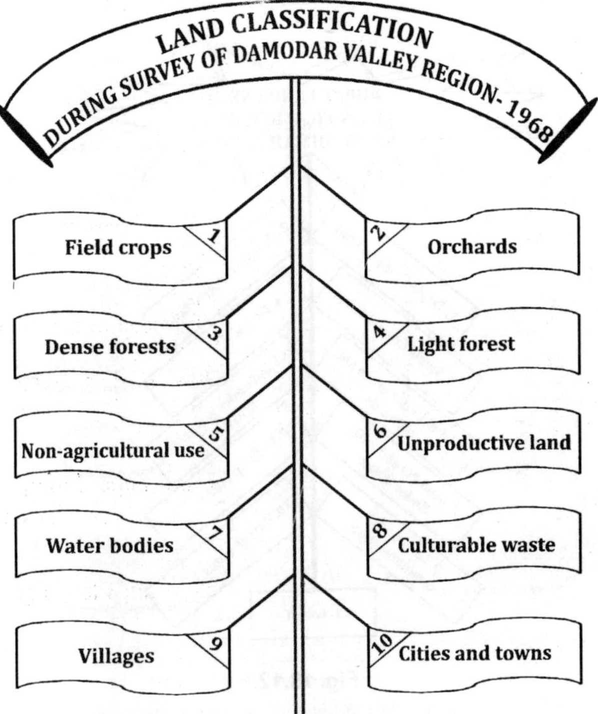

Fig. 18.10.

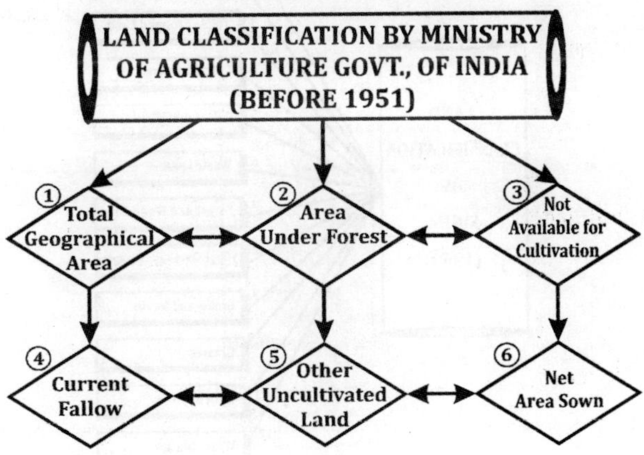

Fig. 18.11.

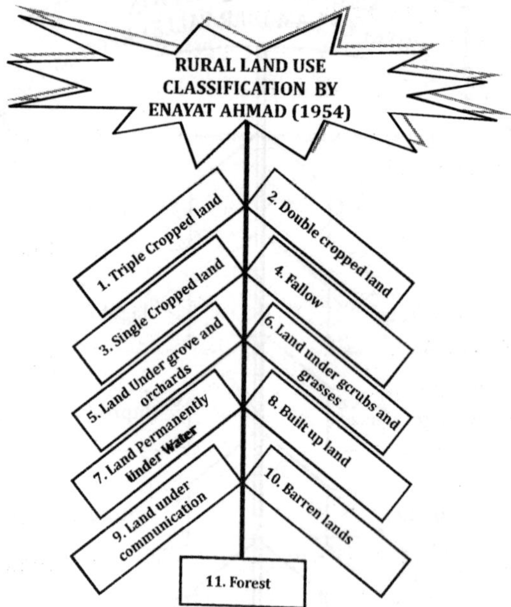

Fig. 18.12.

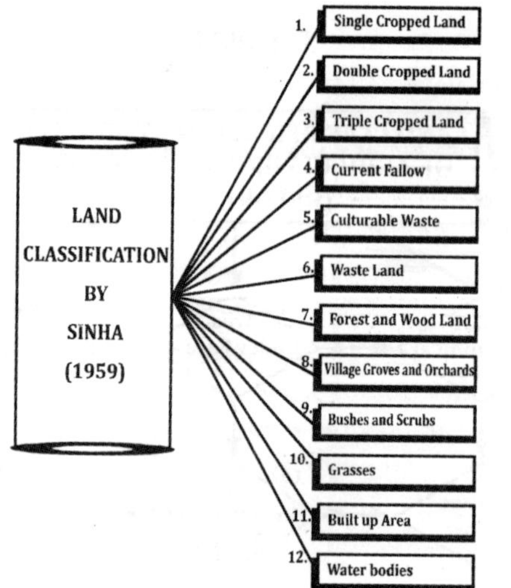

Fig. 18.13.

Fig. 18.14.

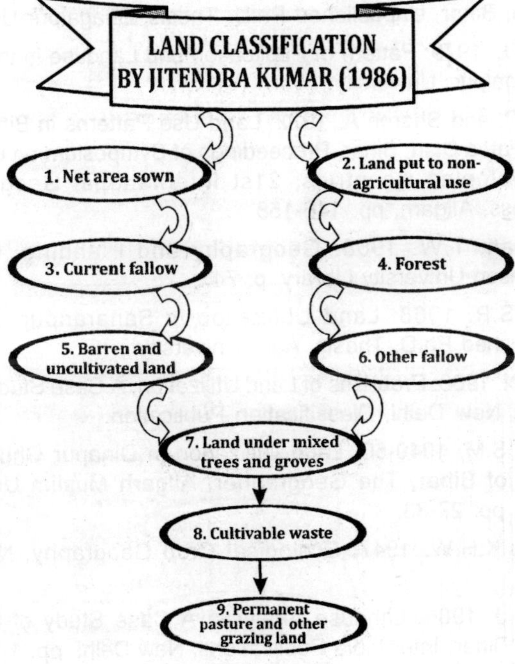

Fig. 18.15.

REFERENCES

1. Ahmad, E. 1954: Geographical Essays on India, Patna pp. 15-16.
2. Amani, K.Z. 1968: Land Utilization in village Golagarhi, Geographer, Special Number, Land Use, Vol. 15.
3. Ayyar, N.P. 1968: Crop Regions of Madhya Pradesh: A Study in Methodology, Geographical Review of India, Vol. XXXI, No. 1, pp. 4-5.
4. Bharadwaj, D.P. 1960: Land Use in Bist-Jullundur Doab, National Geographical Journal of India, vol. 7, pt. 4.
5. Chatterjee, S.P. 1945: Land Utilization in District of 24 Parganas Bengal B.C. Law.
6. Chatterjee, S.P. 1952: Land Utilization Survey of Howrah Districts, Geographical Review of India, Vol. 14, No. 3.
7. Das, K.N. 1969: Population and Landuse Changes in the Kosi Region, Bihar, Unpublished Ph.D. Thesis, Bhagalpur University.
8. Das, S.L. 1979: Pattern of Publication and Landuse in the District of Bhagalpur, University.
9. Dayal P. and Sharon A. 1972: Land Use Patterns in Bihar Sharif Area, Patna Distt. Bihar, Proceedings of Symposium on Land Use in Developing Countries, 21st International Geographical Congress, Aligarh, pp. 146-158.
10. Foreman, T.W. 1968: Geography and Planning, London, Hutchinson University Library, p. 74.
11. Garg, S.P. 1968: Land Utilization in Saharanpur Districts, Unpublished Ph.D. Thesis, Agra University.
12. Jha, B.N. 1980: Problems of Land Utilization, A Case Study of Kosi Region, New Delhi, Classification Publication.
13. Karimi, S.M. 1949-50: Land Utilization in Dinapur Ghurahra, A Village of Bihar, The Geographer, Aligarh Muslim University Aligarh, pp. 27-33.
14. Klages, K.H.W. 1947: Ecological Crop Geography, Newyork, p. 10.
15. Kumar, J. 1986: Landuse Analysis: A Case Study of Nalanda District, Bihar, Inter India Publications, New Delhi, pp. 1-15.
16. Lahiri, R. 1950: Land Utilization in Some Villages near Jasidih, Calcutta Geographical Review, Vol. 12, No. 1.

17. Mandal, R.B. 1982: Land Utilization Theory and Practice' Published Ph.D. Thesis, Patna University, Concept Publishing Company, New Delhi.
18. Mishra, S.N. 1969: Land Use in Khadar and Ravine Tract of the Lower Middle Gomati Valley, National Geographical Journal of India, Vol. XV, Part II, pp. 125-137.
19. Nanawati, M.B.: 1957: Readings in Land Utilization, The Indian Society of Agricultural Economics, Bombay, p. 2.
20. Prasad, M. 1997: The Changing Pattern of Landuse in Bodh Gaya Block, Unpublished Ph.D. thesis, Magadh University.
21. Rao, V.L.S.P. 1947: Soil Survey and Land Use Analysis, Indian Geographical Journal, Vol. 22, No. 3.
22. Roy, B.K. 1968: Measurement of Rural Land Use in Azamgarh Middle Ganga Valley, The Geographer, Special No. Land Use, Vol. XVI.
23. Roy, S.R. 1976: Land Use and Settlements in the Districts of Bhojpur and Rohtas, Bihar, Unpublished Ph.D. Thesis, Bhagalpur University.
24. Sanjay Kumar, 2006: Agricultural Landuse and Crop Productivity; A Case Study of Shahganj Tahsil, Jaunpur Distt., Ph.D. Thesis Submitted to Allahabad University.
25. Sharma, H.S. 1972: Land Capability Classification of the Lower Chambal Valley, Proceedings of Symposium on Landuse in Developing Countries, 21st International Geographical Congress, Aligarh.
26. Shafi, M. 1961: Land Utilization in Eastern Uttar Pradesh, Aligarh Muslim University, Aligarh.
27. Shafi, M. 1966: Techniques of Rural Land Use Planning with Reference to India, Geographer, Vol. 13.
28. Shafi, M. 1972: Land Use Studies; A Trend Report; A Survey of Research in Geography, Bombay; Popular Prakashan, p. 19.
29. Singh, R.P.1967: Concept of Land Use, Patna University Journal, Vol. 22, No. 1, pp. 52-62.
30. Singh, V.R. 1970; Land Use Pattern in Mirzapur and Environs, Unpublished Ph.D. Thesis, B.H.U. Varanasi.
31. Singh, H., 1980: Land Utilization in Koilwar Block, Bhojpur, Unpublished Ph.D. thesis, Magadh University.
32. Singh, B.N. 1985: Agricultural Land Use in Deoria Tahsil of Deoria Distt. U.P. Unpublished Ph.D. Thesis, Allahabad University.

33. Singh, S.K. 2006: Agricultural Land Use and Crop Pproductivity: A Case Study of Shahganj Tahsil, Jaunpur Distt., Unpublished Ph.D. Thesis, Allahabad University.

34. Sinha, B.N. 1968: Crop Combination Techniques: A Search for an Ideal Tool, Deccan Geographer Vol. 6, No. 2.

35. Stamp, J.D. 1948: The Land of Britain and How it is Used, London Longman, pp. 74-77.

36. Stamp, J.D. 1962: Thel and of Britain; its Use and Misuse, London.

37. Tripathi, S.K., 1992: Changing Agricultural Landuse Pattern of Saraon Tahsil of Allahabad Distt., Unpublished Ph.D. Thesis, Submitted to Allahabad University.

38. Vaidya, B.C.1996: Impact of Physical Environment on Agricultural Land Use Pattern in Mula Basin, Maharastra, U.P. Geographical Journal, Vol. 1, pp. 1-8.

CHAPTER

19

Land Use Change and Agricultural Progress

Introduction

Land use change is the most important phenomena of present time of varying topo-litho-climo and pedo-features of M.P. State, India. Population increaseness and environmental unstability is the major causative factor for land use change. Agricultural progress in the present auspicious need of human's socio-economic activities. It is also plays vital role to survive human health and agro-cyclic system.

About the Study Area

The study area, Chhindwara District is one of the largest District of M.P. State which is located along Satpura Range of Vindhyachal-Baghelkhand region and politically in Jabalpur commissioner's Division. It extends between latitudes of 21°27′30″ and 22°47′45″ North and longitudes of 78°15′10″ and 79°24′30″ East. The shape of region is like equilateral elongated from South to North (Prasad, G. and Pandey, A., 2009). The District of Hoshangabad and Narsimhapur make the Northern boundary of the area, and Nagpur and Amrawati Districts of Maharashtra State mark the southern boundary of the study area. Beside its Seoni and Betul Denmark the East and West boundary respectively. The total geographical area of the region is estimated as 11815 square kilometres. There are 08 Tahsils *e.g.* Tamia, Amanwara, Chaurai, Jamai, Parasia, Chhindwara, Sausar and Pandhurna, and 11 Development Blocks as Tamia, Amarwara, Chaurai, Jamai, Parasia, Chhindwara, Sausar and Pandhurna, and 11 Development Blocks as Tamia, Amarwara, Chaurai, Jamai, Parasia, Chhindwara, Sansar, Bichhua, Pandhurna, Mohkher and Harrai in the study area (Gazetteer, 1995).

Geo-Cultural Aspects of the Region

The general height of the district to sea level is about 650 metres which presents a plateau shaped terrain in a large extent. The Northern part of the region is marked by the high Ranges of hills and mountains till 1250 metres height who is called by 'Backbone of Satpura Range' and dissected but extended plateau running from West to East. The District is occupied mostly by the Archaean rocks (250 Million years of old) comprising granite gnisses, green schist, intrusive granite, basic rocks, quartz veins etc. The soil nature of area is in various types and different quality appear as black clay, brown loamy, stony, deep black, yellow and also in the poorest characteristics. According to Kopen's climatic classification the region is marked under the 'AW' class where mean annual temperature and mean annual rainfall were recorded as 25.97°C and 103.04 cm. respectively in the year of 2007. The region is well drained by dense drainage system of Narmada and Godawari rivers with its tributaries (Pandey, A., 2010).

Based on Census data of 2001 the total number of villages in the District are 1984 in which 81 villages are uninhabited. According to Census of 2001, the total population of District is as 1849283 persons in which 31.65% of population belong to Scheduled Tribes and 11.58% of Scheduled Castes. The urbanisation rate as 24.45% is marked in the area (Pandey, A., 2007). Above 50% population of the total population as working is connected with cultivation in which 36.5% share belongs to females.

Land use Change

In the year of 1973-74, the total geographical area of the District was occupied under the cultivated land, forest area and others when 43.41%, 38.10% and 18.49% share of total area was under the cultivation, forest and others respectively. The 'others' shows to the permanent pastures and grazing lands. The three, between themselves, made the District rich in forest, well cultivated and with plenty of grazing area available for animal husbandry. During this year land use as for net area sown was 477798 hectares, forest area was 452531 hectares, other unculturable land was 80203 hectares, not available for agriculture was 68371 hectares, fallow land was 67776 hectares and culturable waste land was 38239 hectares. The position of land use in about 33 years later (1973-74 to 2006-07) did not show any substantial change in the region. In the year of 2006-07, the land use had been recorded as for net area sown was 484373 hectares, forest area was 479502 hectares, other unculturable land was 52043 hectares, not available for agriculture was 80290 hectares, fallow land was

Table 19.1 : Land use Scenario in Chhindwara, M.P.: 2006-07

Sl. No.	Land use categories	Area under the land use categories	
		In Hectares	In Percentage
1.	Net area sown	484373	40.878
2.	Forest area	479502	40.467
3.	Area not available for agriculture	80290	06.776
4.	Fallow land	71103	06.001
5.	Culturable waste land	17612	01.486
6.	Other unculturable land	52043	04.392
	Total geographical area	1184923	100.000

Source: District Statistical Handbook, 2007, Table no. 3.1, pp. 24-25.

71103 hectares and culturable waste land was 17612 hectares respectively. During this span of time net area sown, forest area, area not available for agriculture and follow land were increased minutely but other unculturable land and culturable waste land comparatively have been decreased (**Table 19.1** and **Figure 19.1**).

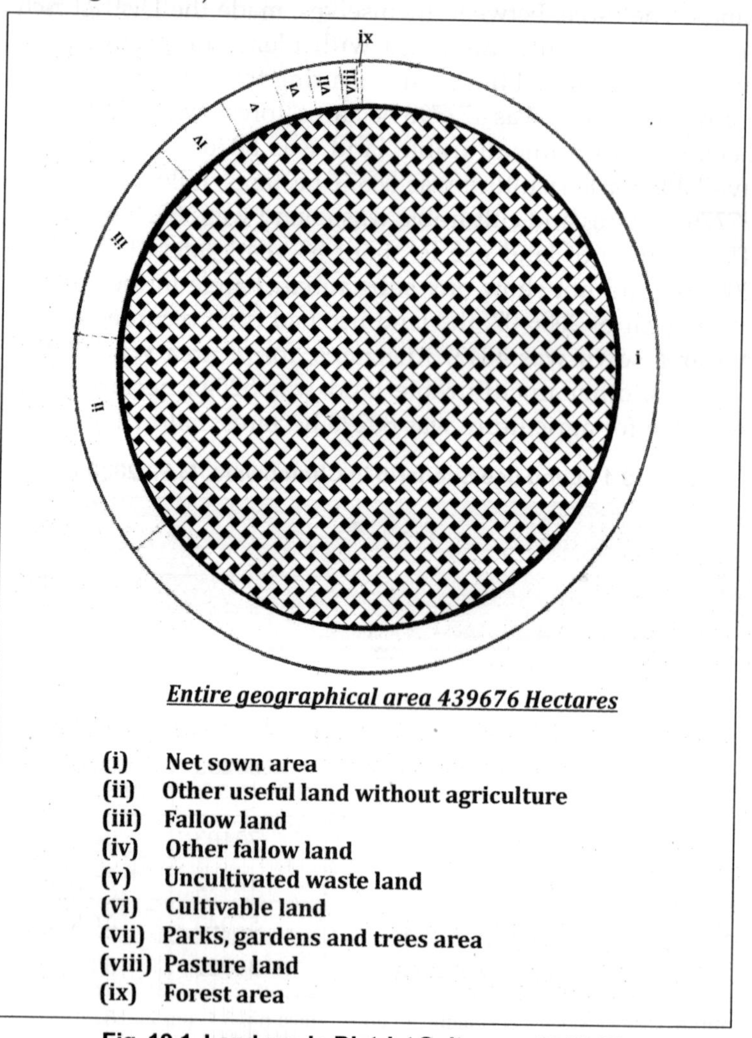

Fig. 19.1. Land use in District Sultanpur, 2006-07

Agricultural Progress

It has been cleared that there is 40.878 per cent area of the total geographical area is exposed as net area sown in the session of 2006-07 in the study region. In the all sown crops, maize is the main productive crop. Other major crops are noted as soyabean, wheat, sugarcane, Jowar, cotton, groundnut, gram, rice, tur, urad etc. and minor crops are

Table 19.2 : Production of Major and Minor Crops in Chhindwara, M.P., 2006-07

Sl.No.	Major/Minor Crops	Production (Metric Tons)
1.	Maize	161070
2.	Soyabean	147487
3.	Wheat	146417
4.	Sugarcane	84626
5.	Jowar	43502
6.	Cotton	31389* (thousand bels)
7.	Groundnut	28237
8.	Gram	27786
9.	Rice/Paddy	19097
10.	Tur	9491
11.	Urad	3119
12.	Linseed	416
13.	Kidney bean	368
14.	Sesamum	272
15.	Mustard	159
16.	Millet	38

*1 bel = 170 kg.

Source: District Statistical Handbook, 2007, Table no. 3.5, pp. 33-34.

listed as linseed, kindcybean, sesamum, mustard and millet. The diversified nature of agriculture has determined the agro-diversity. The production of aforesaid crops (in Metric tons) were found as maize 161070, soyabean, 147487, wheat 146417, sugarcane 84626, jowar 43502, cotton 31389 bales (1 bale = 170 kg.), groundnut 28237, gram 27786, rice 19097, tur 9491, urad 3119, linseed 416, kindcybean 368, Sesamum 272, mustard 159 and millet 38 during the year of 2006-07 (**Table 19.2** and **Figure 19.2**).

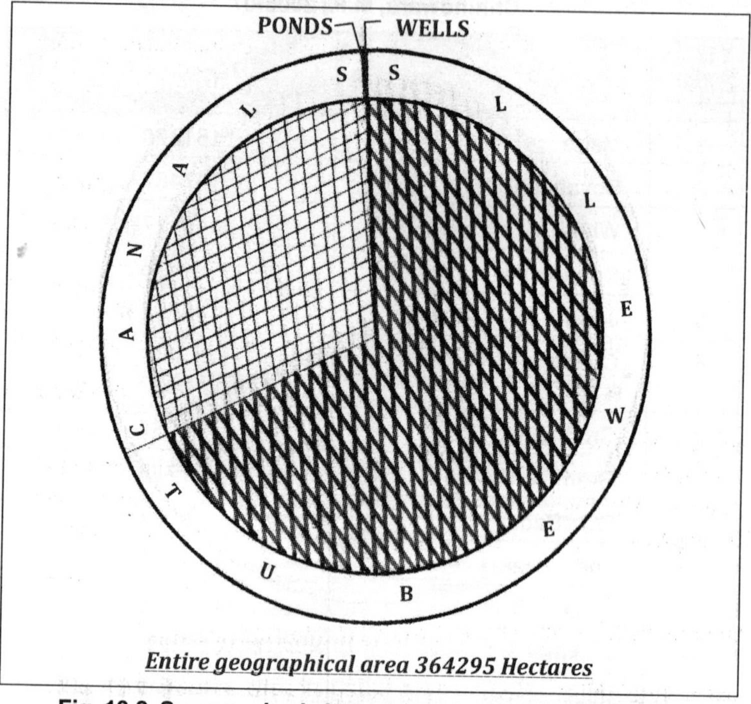

Fig. 19.2. Source-wise Irrigated Area in District Sultanpur: 2006-07

Areal coverage of various crops (in Hectares) existed as 85132 (maize), 139798 (soyabean), 91326 (wheat), 14692 (Sugarcane), 43989 (Jowar) 31096 (Cotton), 24813 (Groundnut), 34732 (Gram), 20557 (Rice), 18322 (Tur), 15441 (Urad), 915 (Linseed), 948 (Sesamum) and 517 (Mustard) in the Base Year of 2006-07 (**Table 19.3** and **Figure 19.3**). Descending Order of Crops in Areal coverage is Given as soyabean, wheat, maize, jowar, gram, cotton, groundnut, rice, tur, urad, sugarcane, sesamum, linseed and mustard.

Table 19.3 : Area under the various Crops in Chhindwara, M.P.—2006-07

Sl.No.	The Crops	Area (Thousand Hectares)
1.	Maize	85.132
2.	Soyabean	139.798
3.	Wheat	91.326
4.	Sugarcane	14.692
5.	Jowar	43.989
6.	Cotton	31.096
7.	Groundnut	24.813
8.	Gram	34.732
9.	Rice/Paddy	20.557
10.	Tur	18.322
11.	Urad	15.441
12.	Linseed	00.915
13.	Kindcybean	D.N.A.*
14.	Sesamum	00.948
15.	Mustard	00.517
16.	Millet	D.N.A.*

*D.N.A. = Data not available.

Source: District Statistical Handbook, 2007, Table no. 3.2, pp. 26-29.

The productivity of maize in per Hectare area is the highest as 1892 kg. in the year of 2006-07. In this year the productivity of other crops like wheat, groundnut, soyabean, jowar, rice, gram, tur, linseed and sesamum have been tabulated as 1382,

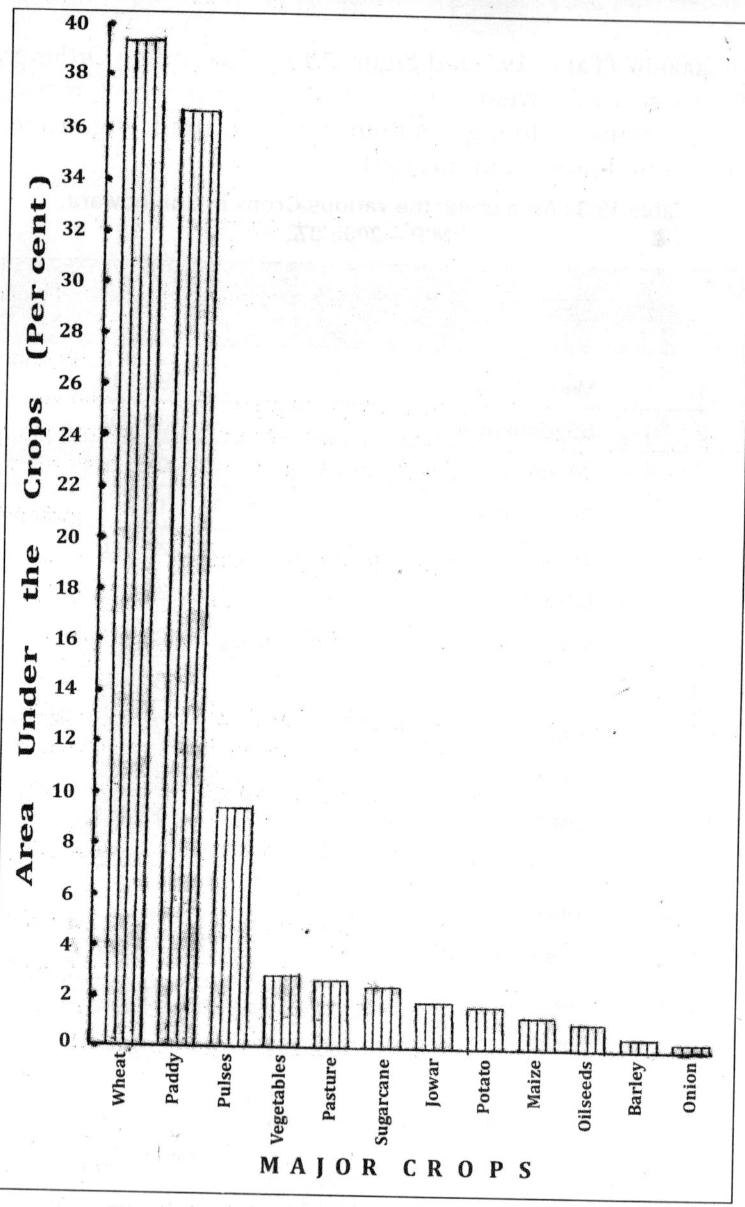

Fig. 19.3. Area under the Major Crops in District Sultanpur: 2006-07

1138, 1055, 991, 929, 800, 518, 455 and 287 respectively in descending order. The maize, wheat, groundnut and soyabean are marked above 1000 kg. per Hectare productivity in the region (**Table 19.4** and **Figure 19.4**).

Table 19.4 : The Productivity of various Crops in Chhindwara, M.P.: 2006-07

Sl.No.	The Crops	Productivity (kg. per Hectare)
1.	Maize	1892
2.	Wheat	1382
3.	Groundnut	1138
4.	Soyabean	1055
5.	Jowar	991
6.	Rice/Paddy	929
7.	Gram	800
8.	Tur	518
9.	Linseed	455
10.	Sesamum	287

Source: District Statistical Handbook, 2007, Table no. 3.4, p. 32.

Irrigation is the backbone and lifeline of agriculture. Before the independence of nation, it is quoted in Mr. Mantgomerie's Settlement report existed in Gazetteer "The water is lifted in a circular leather bag (mot) attached by a rope running over a pully to the yoke of a pair of oxen, which lift the water-bag as they pace down an inclined run and return backwards up the slope when the water has been discharged."

At present, wells are the major source of irrigation which have provided 60.02% contribution of irrigation system in the area. Apart from the above tubewells, canals, ponds are thought as other significant sources of irrigation which are contributed as 23.55%, 08.48% and 03.33% of irrigated area of the total area as irrigated. Remaining 04.60% area of whole

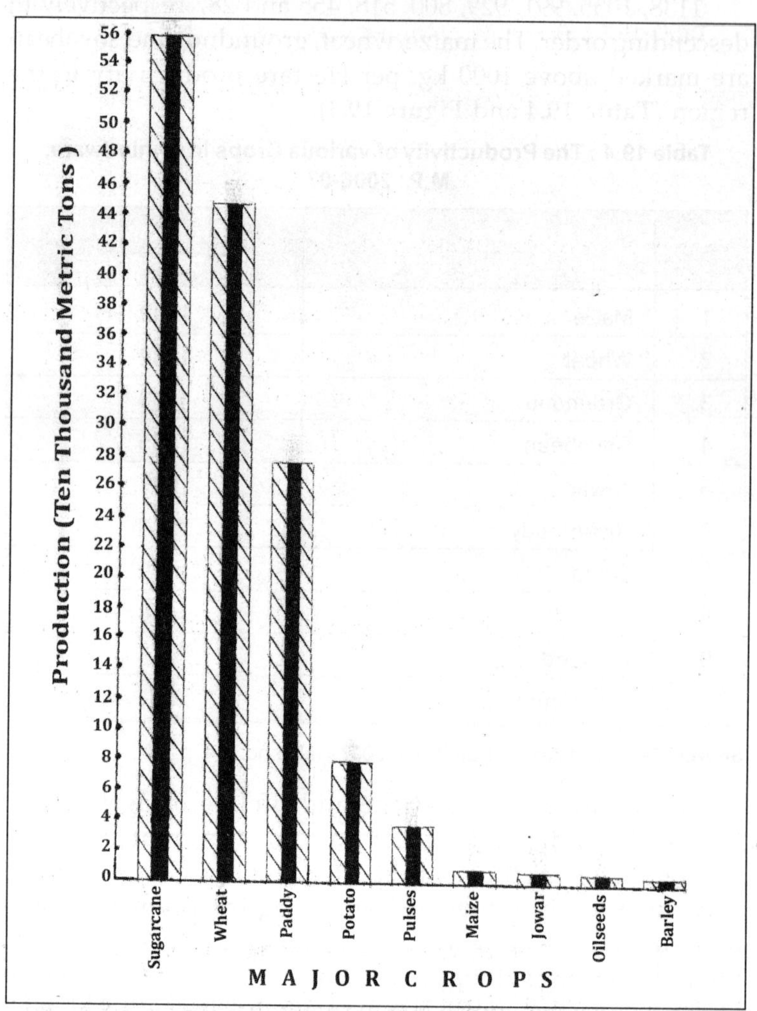

Fig. 19.4. Production of Major Crops in District Sultanpur: 2006-07

irrigated area irrigated by other some minor sources (**Table 19.5** and **Figure 19.5**). It is fact that only 26.54% area is irrigated in net area sown which covers 126805 hectares irrigated area of 477798 Hectares net area sown. Although the study region is well drained but irrigation potential is not sufficient in view of agricultural progress in the area.

Table 19.5 : Source-wise Irrigated Area in Chhindwara, M.P. 2006-07

Sl.No.	Sources of irrigation	Irrigated area	
		In Hectares	In Percentage
1.	Wells	76113	60.02
2.	Tubewells	29867	23.55
3.	Canals	10749	08.48
4.	Ponds/Tanks	4236	03.33
5.	Others	5842	04.60
	Grand Total	126805	100.00

Source: District Statistical Handbook, 2007, Table no. 3.6, pp. 35-36.

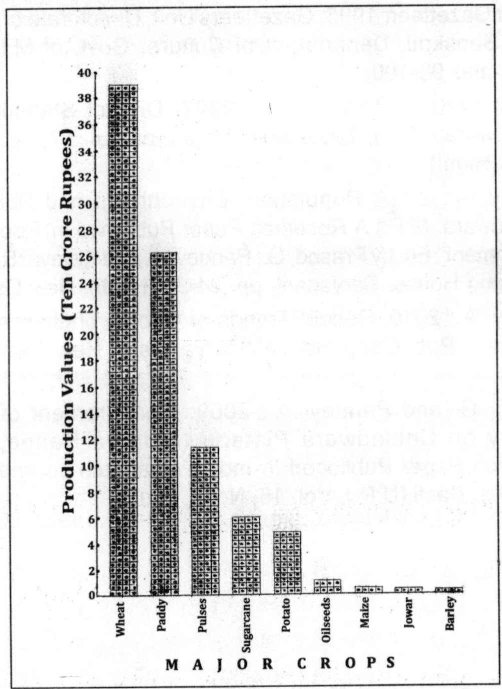

Fig. 19.5. Production Values of Major Crops in District Sultanpur, 2006-07

Conclusion

The trend of land use changes is founding like a stable stage since last half century. The impact of net area sown and forest area is much dominating to land use but leading consistantly. Maize is the most significant crop but soyabean and wheat is also important. The maintenance of productivity needed for sufficient production of agricultural products. Agro-diversity is the boon of nature in the region but the potential of irrigation system is highly and dominantly required in the study area.

REFERENCES

1. Census Abstract of Chhindwara District, 2001.
2. District Development Book; 2007; District Statistical Office, Chhindwara (M.P.), Table No. 1.1, pp. 16-17 (Hindi).
3. District Gazetteer; 1995: Gazetteers Unit, Directorate of Rajbhasha Evam Sanskriti, Department of Culture, Govt. of M.P., Bhopal, pp.1-2 and 95-100.
4. District Statistical Handbook; 2007: District Statistical Office, Chhindwara (M.P.), Table Nos. 3.1-3.2 and .4-3.7, pp. 24-29 and 32-36 (Hindi)
5. Pandey, A., 2007: Population, Environment and Public Health (Chhindwara, M.P.) A Research Paper Published in 'Population and Environment', Ed. by Prasad, G.; Pandey, A. and Kislaya, S., Discovery Publishing House, Daryaganj, pp. 24-26 (Hindi), New Delhi.
6. Pandey, A.; 2010: Recent Trends of Geomorphological Analysis, Discovery Publishing House, Darya Ganj, New Delhi-110 002 (Hindi).
7. Prasad, G. and Pandey, A.; 2009: Measurement of Drainage Density on Chhindwara Plateau (Satpura Range, M.P.). A Research Paper Published in Indian Research Journal of Social Sciences, Basti (U.P.), Vol. 16, No. 2, p. 123.

Index

U

V

W